THE BARE-FACED PSYCHOANALYST

THIRD EDITION

AN ILLUSTRATED MANUAL OF SELF HELP THERAPY
BY JOHN SOUTHGATE AND ROSEMARY RANDALL

Original illustrations by FRANCES TOMLINSON,
re-drawn by Angela Thwaites.

GALE CENTRE PUBLICATIONS LOUGHTON ESSEX.
ISBN: 1 870258 06 1

First Edition October 1976. Second revised edition May 1978
published by the Association of Karen Horney Psychoanalytic
Counsellors,
12 Nassington Road, London NW3

Third Edition September 1989
Published by Gale Centre Publications, Whitakers Way, Loughton, Essex.
Copyright: Gale Centre Publications.
ISBN: 1 870258 06 1

PREFACE TO THE THIRD EDITION

It is thirteen years since the first edition of this book appeared. It has been translated into several languages and to this day people find it useful as an introduction to self-help therapy. Its unique (and some might say bizarre) combination of Harvey Jackin's co-counselling with the work of 1930's psychoanalyst Karen Horney seems to have a lasting appeal. We thought of revising it in the light of today's conditions but decided that this would destroy its character, as one aspect of the personal politics and therapeutic endeavours of the period.

The authors, though still friends and colleagues, have gone their separate ways. Rosemary Randall lives in Cambridge, is a mother, and works as a writer and psychotherapist. Frances Tomlinson is a Lecturer at a Polytechnic and only occasionally finds time to do illustrations. (The drawings in this edition are based upon the original ones but are not drawn by Frances). John Southgate is involved full time in developing the Institute for Self-Analysis, an organisation which is pursuing ways of combining self-analytic work with the help of an advocate or companion which is in the tradition of Alice Miller and John Bowlby. This approach involves contacting the hurt or abused child within the adult. Anyone who is interested in the development should write to John Southgate, Institute for Self Analysis, 12 Nassington Road, London NW3 2UD.

We hope that the third edition will prove as useful as the first (1976) and the second (March 1978).

John Southgate, Rosemary Randall, Frances Tomlinson. August 1989.

CONTENTS

		Page
PREFACE		
INTRODUCTION		1
SECTION ONE	Basic methods Creating a relationship Working in a group	3
SECTION TWO	Using interventions and theory	97
SECTION THREE	Advanced counselling, tools and theories for working on the unconscious	205
APPENDICES	Coping with a crisis List of useful addresses	254 259
BIBLIOGRAPHY		261

INTRODUCTION

This book has been written by and for members of the Association of Karen Horney Psychoanalytic Counsellors. We intend it to be an aid for learning and teaching mutual self-analysis. We also hope that many people will be able to get themselves off the ground by working with friends so that they can later take part in courses having already taught themselves some basic methods. In this way we economise on what is at present a very scarce resource: teacher- counsellors.

This process will also help to achieve the basic goal of the Association- which is to initiate psychoanalytic self-help groups among ordinary people. Perhaps this is most succinctly expressed in a phrase that started as a joke - 'the barefoot psychoanalyst'. In China they created the 'barefoot doctor' who, after some basic training in medicine, went into the villages and towns to introduce health care. The idea behind the 'barefoot analyst' is similar.

We do need to make an important statement to those who use this book and who are not on one of our courses. Clearly we cannot take responsibility for people we are not in personal contact with. In general this will not be a problem. For most people who use this book the worst that could happen would be to get bored or frustrated. At best, some people may be able to become highly skilled even without training, if they have a flair for this work. However, if you are very depressed or find yourself in a state of acute anxiety, panic or hallucination you may well need some specialised help- which may be hard to obtain unless you are rich. You might still find the book a help especially if you have a group of supportive friends or others. The main necessity for any two-way process however is the ability to give attention to another person. If you are acutely anxious then you won't be able to do this until the anxiety reduces. You may also make demands for time and attention that others cannot give. And if you are getting into heavy emotional discharge you may alarm your partner and both find that you cannot continue. We don't want to give the impression that people cannot cope with such a situation because most of us can and do. But a reality is that if you are extremely distressed, you may need some temporary help from experienced people- and a book, however good, cannot be a substitute in such a situation.

This first edition of the book has developed out of the first six months of the teaching and learning that our members have done. Our own theory of knowledge means that continual change is inevitable and that this book is out of date, so to speak, as soon as it is printed. However, new knowledge does not come automatically- it requires deeds. The most important deed for us, is to get feedback on how the book succeeds or fails and to get the new knowledge that comes from creative counselling. So please let us know how you find this book- whether or not you are a member.

We recommend that if possible you work through this book in a group. You will then be able to meet to discuss the exercises and theory, explore the possibilities, give each other support and work with a number of people.

Write to us with your comments and criticisms. We will also try to answer any requests for advice or help. If your group works right through the book and wants to continue, contact us and we will try to arrange for a teacher-counsellor to visit you.

Section One

Basic methods
Creating a relationship
Working in a group

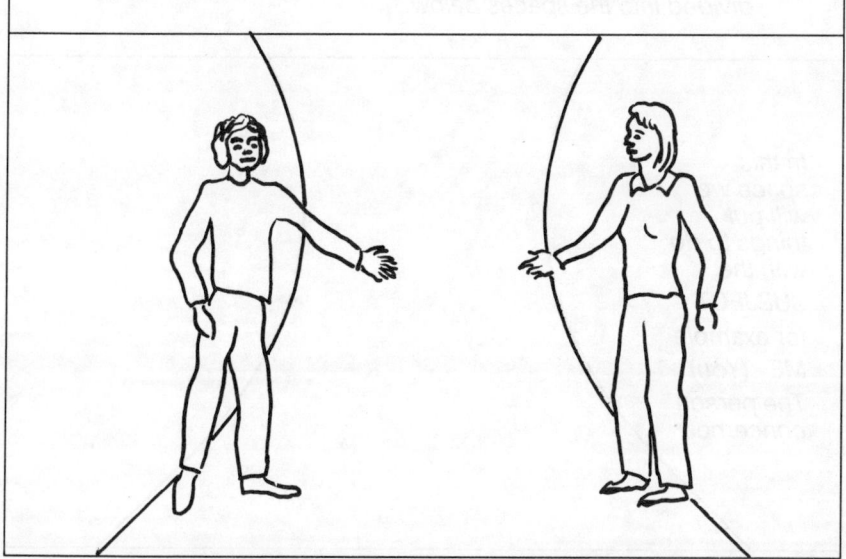

Karen Horney counselling is essentially a process of two people helping each other.

The kinds of things that they help each other about vary enormously, but typical examples are:

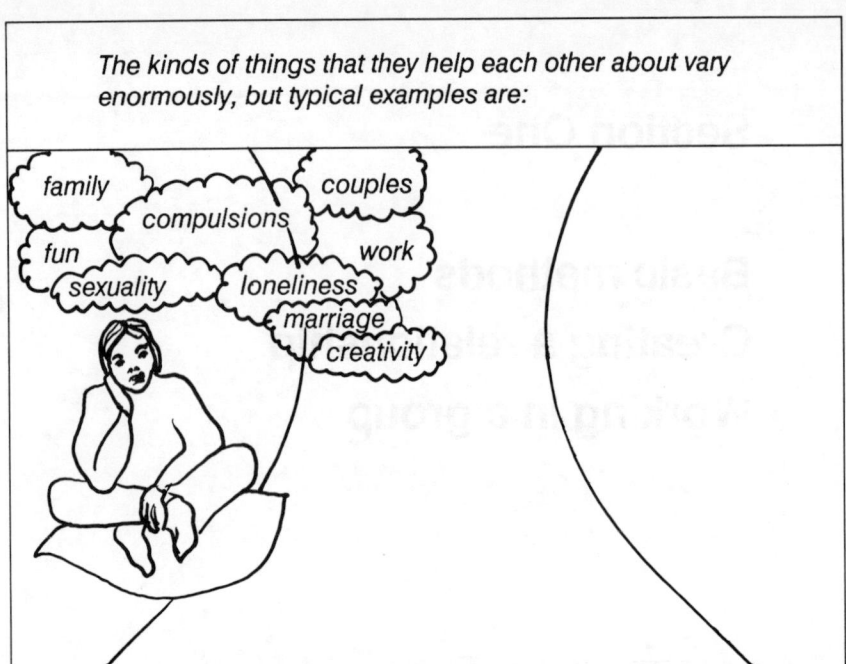

family, compulsions, couples, fun, work, sexuality, loneliness, marriage, creativity

The rest of the book is about how to start this mutual helping relationship. Before this, we want to explain why the page is divided into the spaces below:

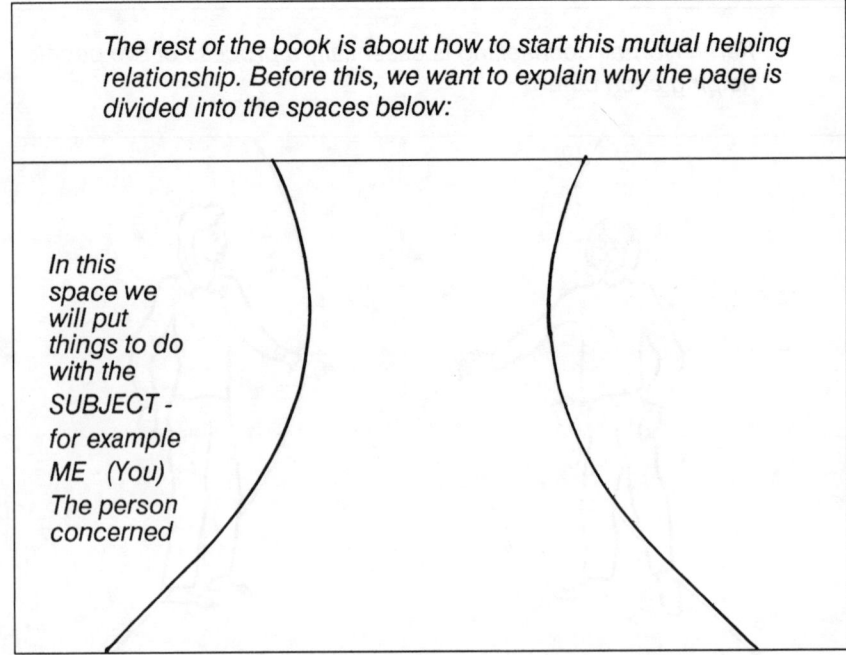

In this space we will put things to do with the SUBJECT - for example ME (You) The person concerned

and:

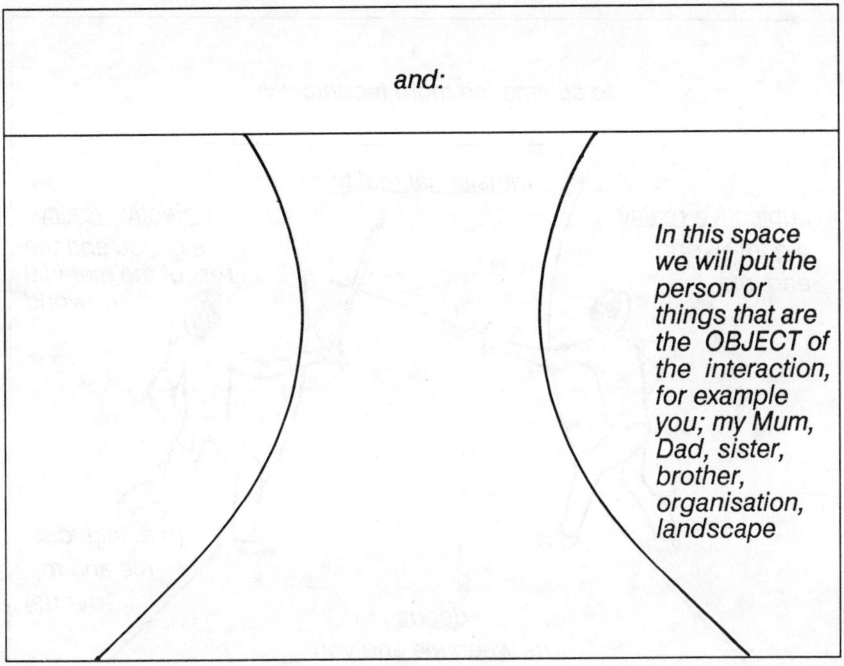

In this space we will put the person or things that are the OBJECT of the interaction, for example you; my Mum, Dad, sister, brother, organisation, landscape

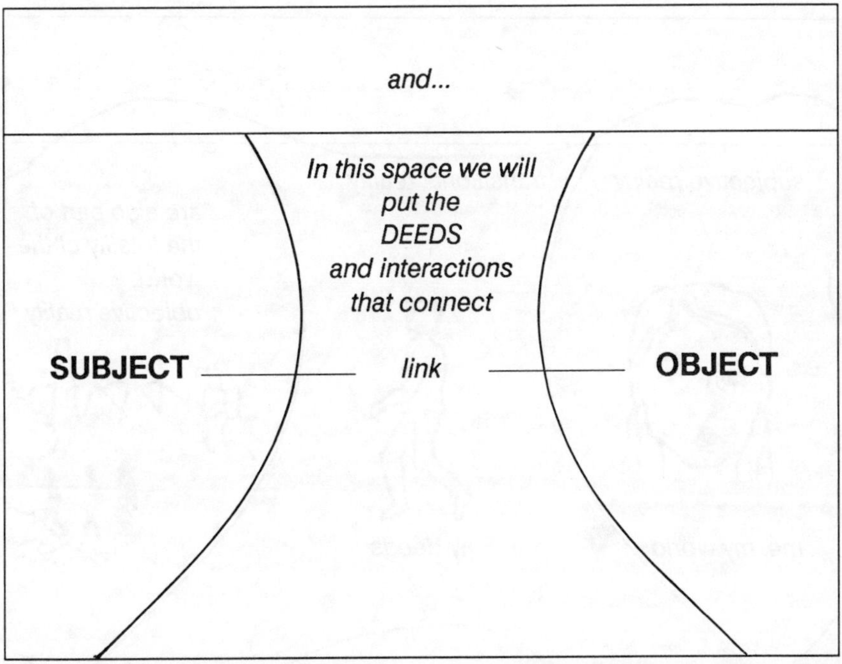

and...

In this space we will put the DEEDS and interactions that connect

SUBJECT —— *link* —— **OBJECT**

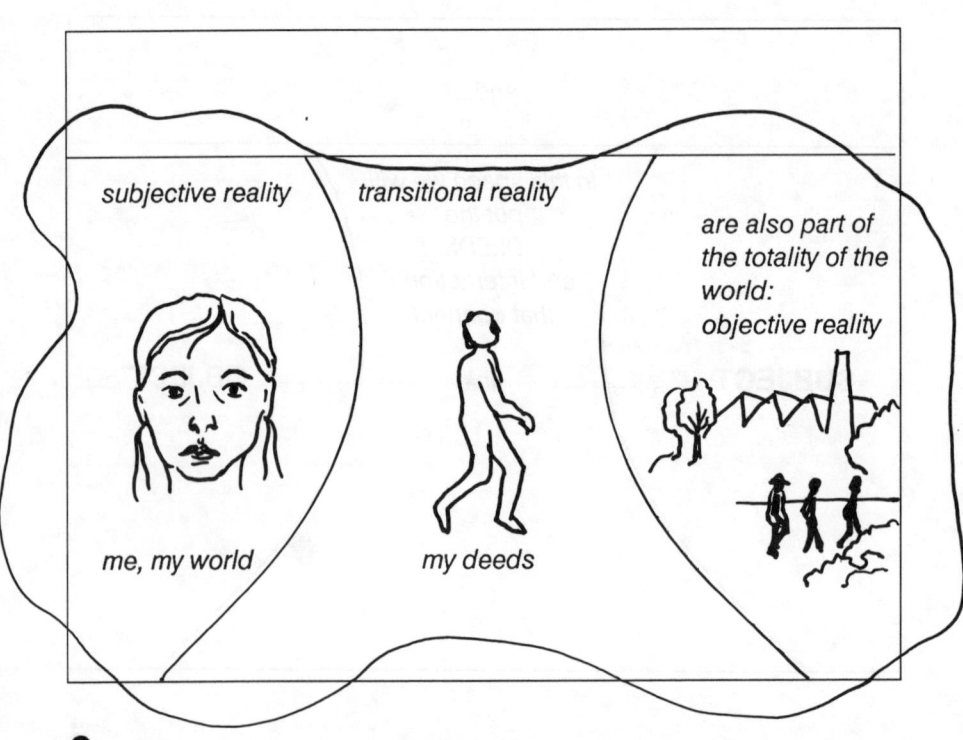

So: the rest of the book explains our methods and theory and has training exercises that pairs (and groups) can do.

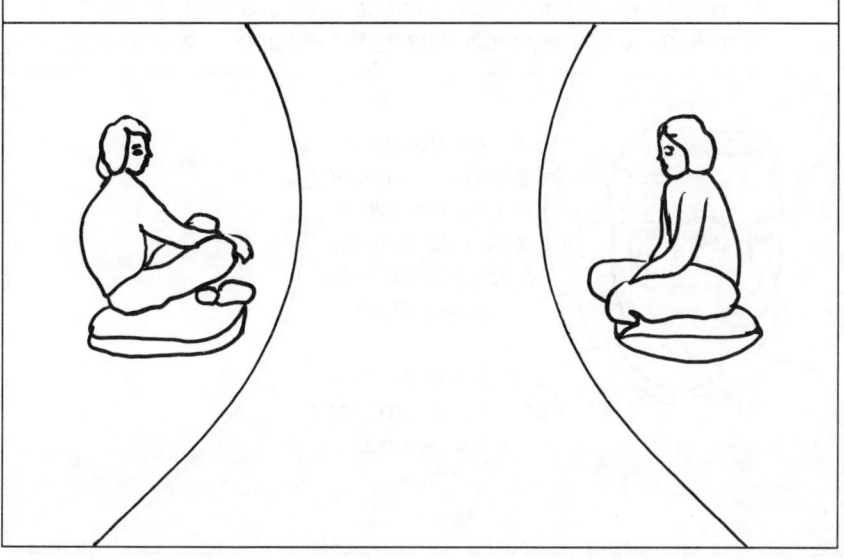

A preliminary word about theory: most of the theory in this book is based upon that of Karen Horney.
   She ---------

was born in 1885 and died in 1952.
Pupil of Freud

her deeds: taught and practised psychoanalysis in Berlin until 1932 when she left for the USA. She questioned some of Freud's basic assumptions and developed her own methods

The fruits of her work are found in the associations she founded and books like:
SELF ANALYSIS,
OUR INNER CONFLICTS,
NEUROSIS AND HUMAN GROWTH,
NEW WAYS IN PSYCHOANALYSIS,
FEMININE PSYCHOLOGY

7

The idea of co-counselling was invented by Harvey Jackins. He was the first person to develop simple and practical ways in which people could help each other by counselling. We have tried to develop his practice using the insights of psychoanalysis.

*his deeds:
invented co-counselling the method where 2 people mutually help each other by counselling*

set up organisations and classes to teach his method.

Many people assume that psychoanalysis and counselling are for people with nervous breakdowns who are mentally ill, or mad. But ....

I have benefited from counselling and I am in no sense "mad" or "neurotic". I have similar problems in life to you.

We say this is definitely NOT SO. Counselling is for all people, young, old, woman, man or child.

All persons can learn more about themselves and improve their life and relationships and "grow" regardless of whether they are "ill".

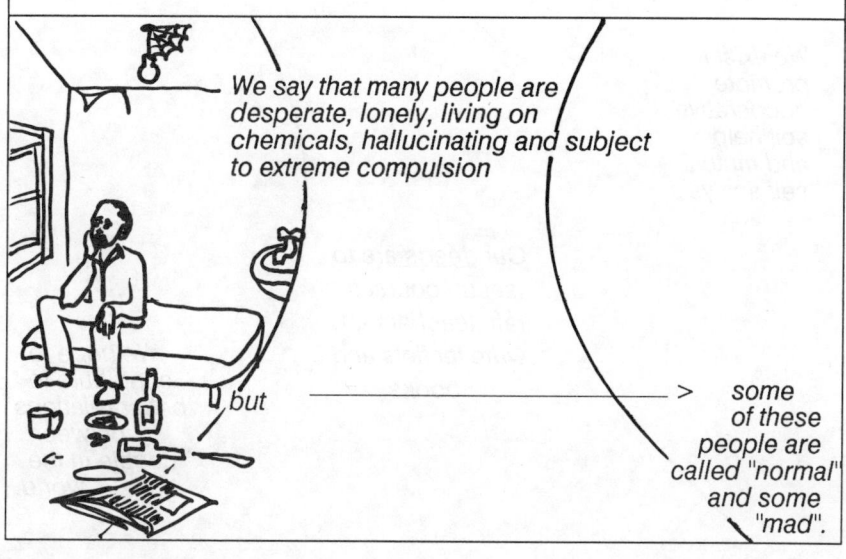

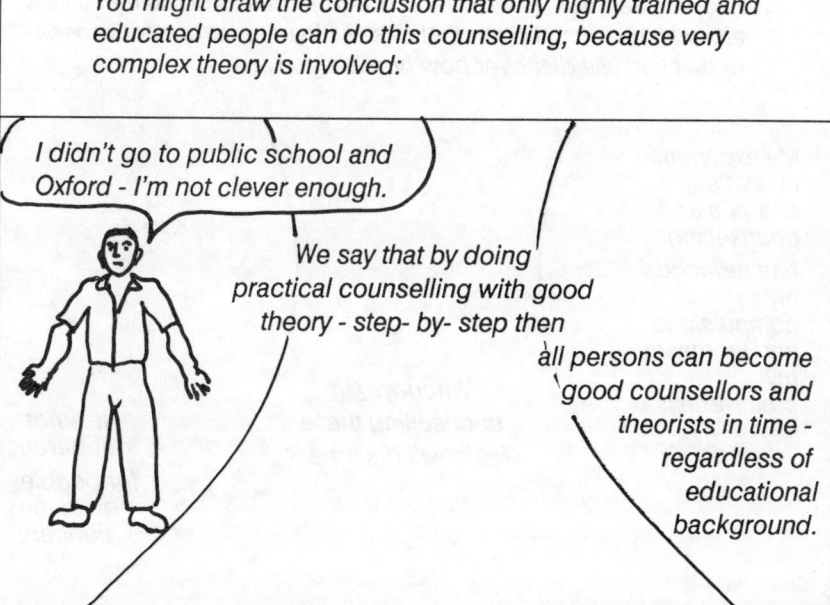

This starts to explain the goals and aims of the Association of Karen Horney Psychoanalytic Counselling. Essentially:

We exist to promote cooperative self help and mutual self analysis

Our <u>deeds</u> are to set up courses, train teachers and write leaflets and books

We hope to contribute to better relations between people in the world.

People often ask us whether it is dangerous to do self-analysis etc. with the assumption that this will lead to introspectiveness - or that you will discover how horrible you are:

My experience is that self analysis and counselling has reduced my compulsions and increased my creativeness.

When we <u>do</u> counselling these fears will disappear

It is not dangerous for people - quite the contrary.

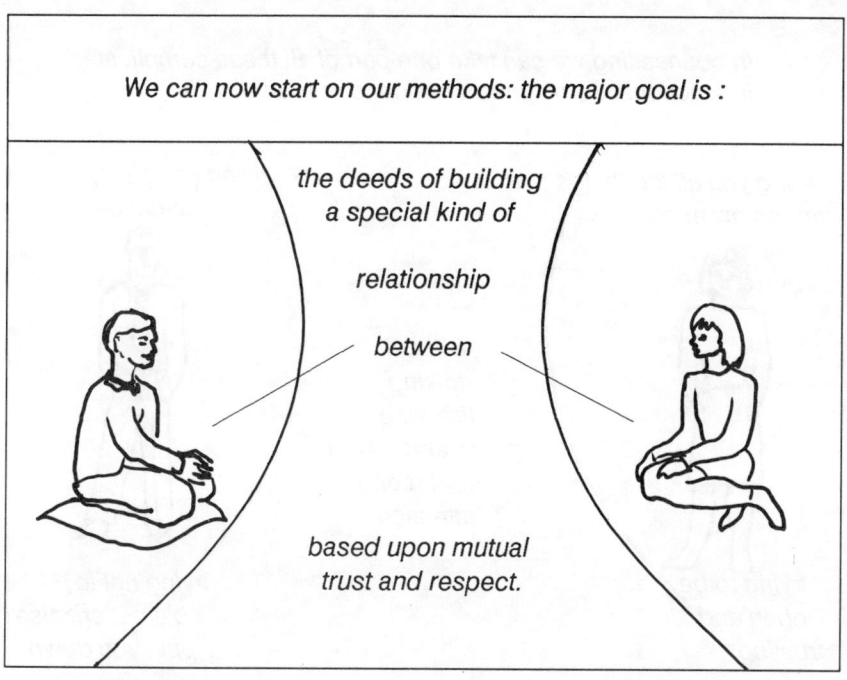

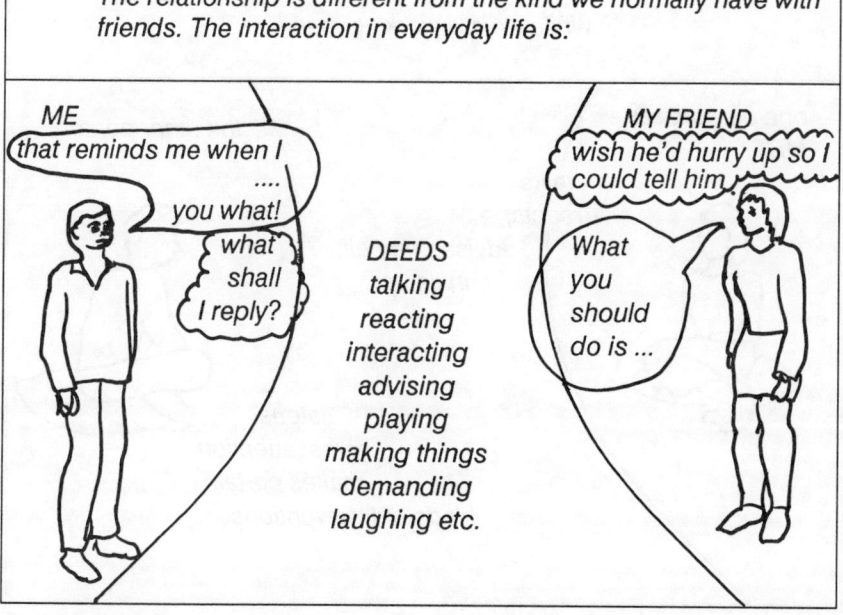

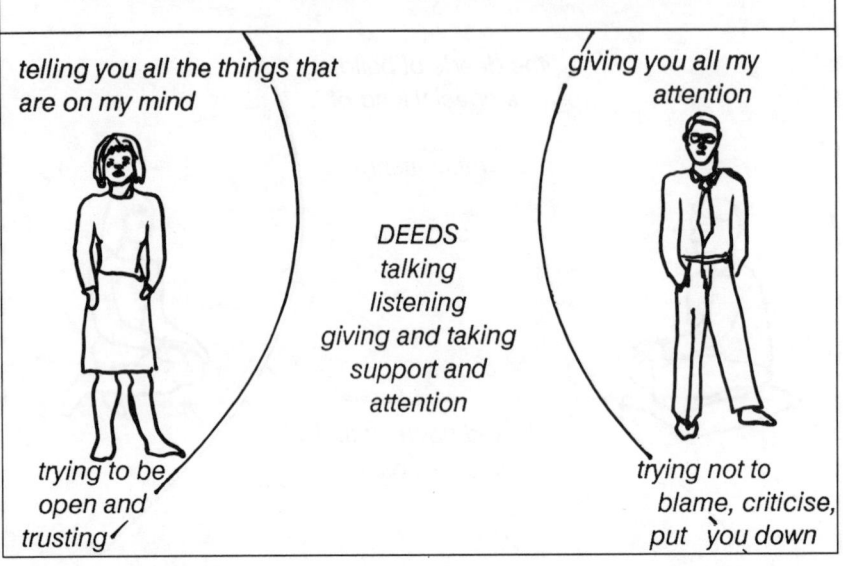

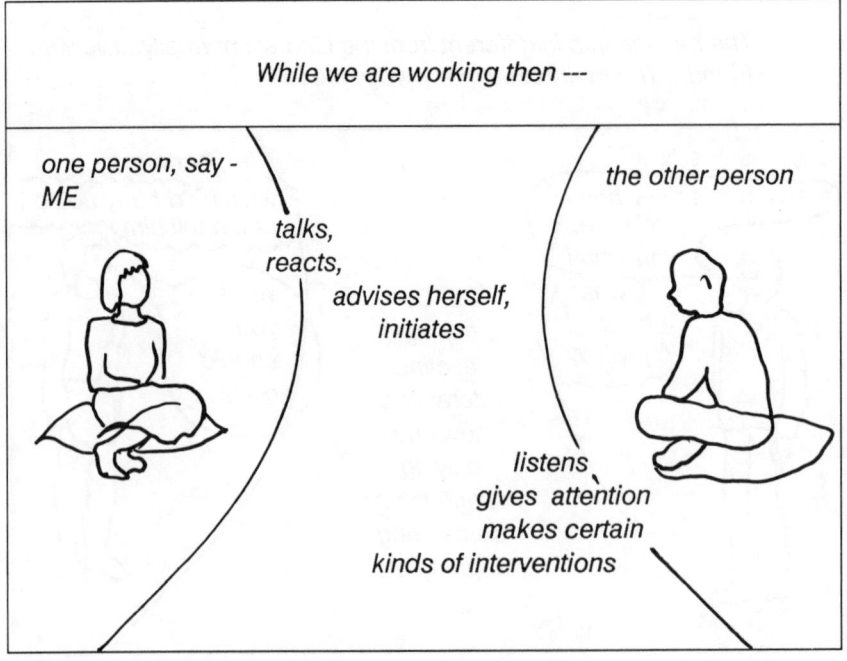

In order to explain the basic roles in the interaction we need to digress a moment. First we will explain the <u>opposite</u> of the counselling relationship.

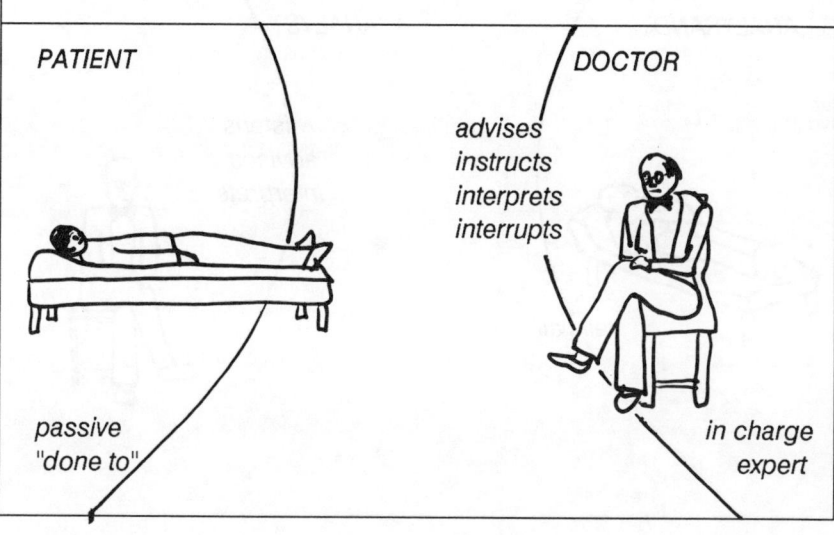

The above kind of relationship is one where power is <u>one sided</u> like:

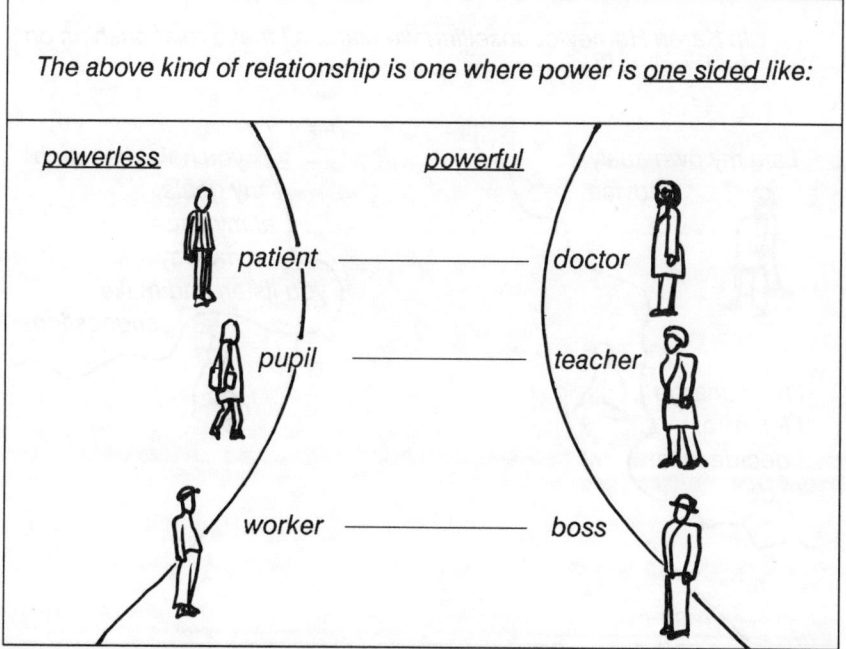

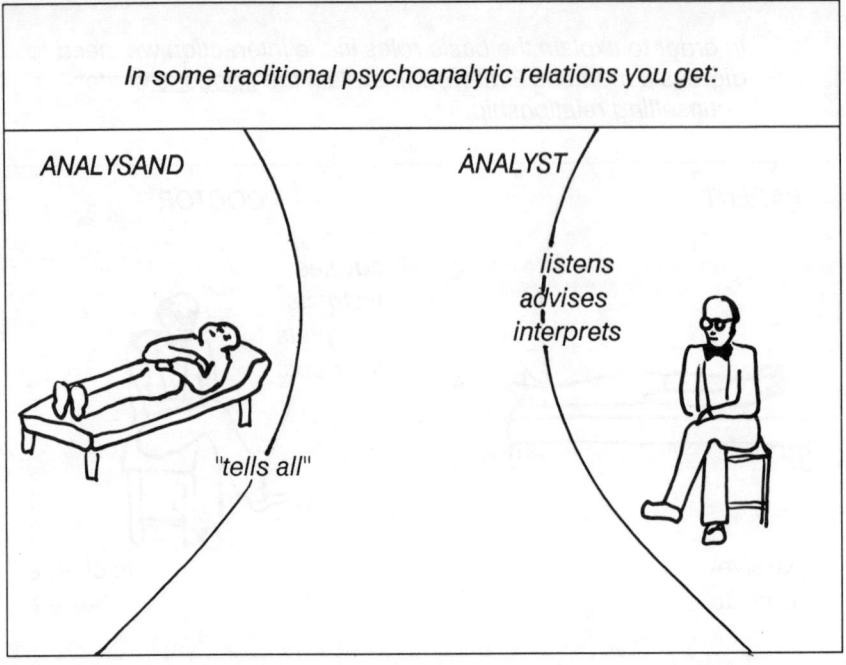

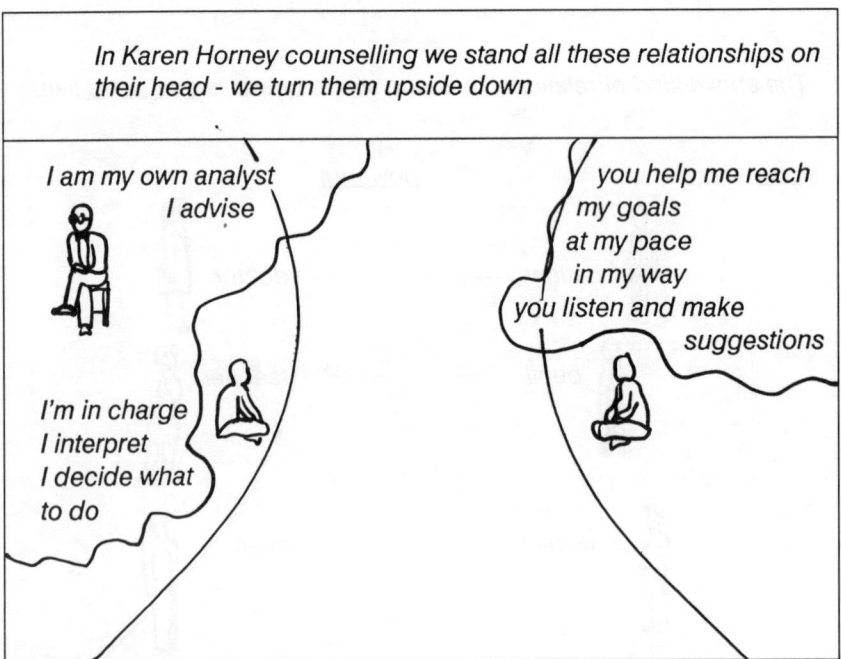

To constantly remind ourselves that we are not in the doctor - patient situation we have names for these roles -

I WORK on myself

you ASSIST me, the worker to reach _my_ goals

I am called the WORKER

you are called the ASSISTANT

So: to summarise:

WORKER
is "in charge"
makes the decision
decides what pace to work at
decides what to do and how to do it
is totally responsible for "progress" and method
can accept or _reject_ suggestions

ASSISTANT
listens
gives attention
gives support
goes along with what the worker wants
makes suggestions of things to say or do

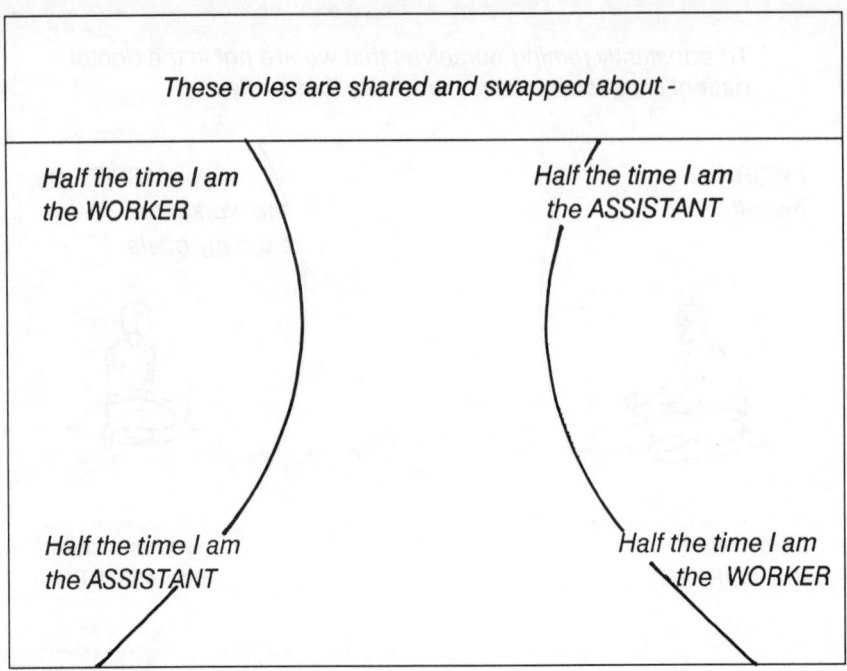

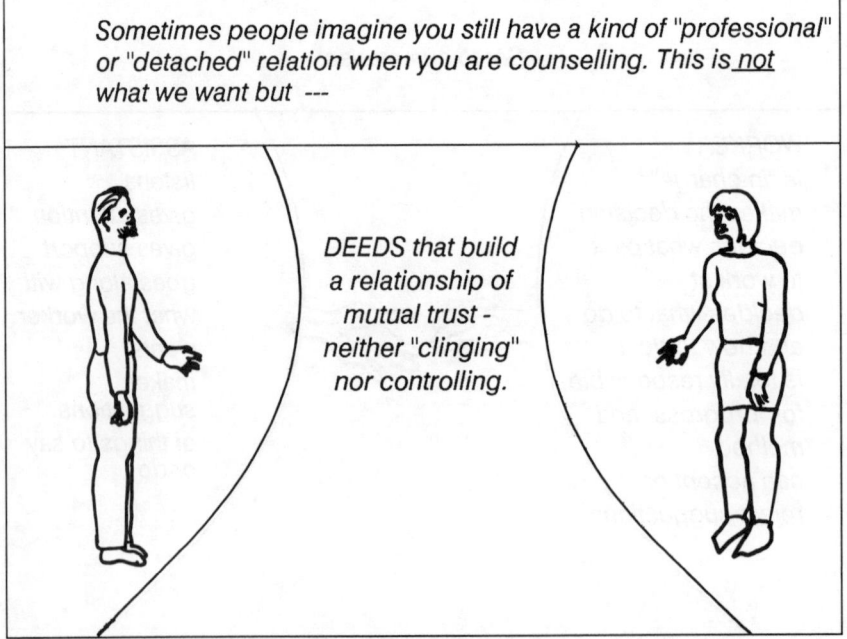

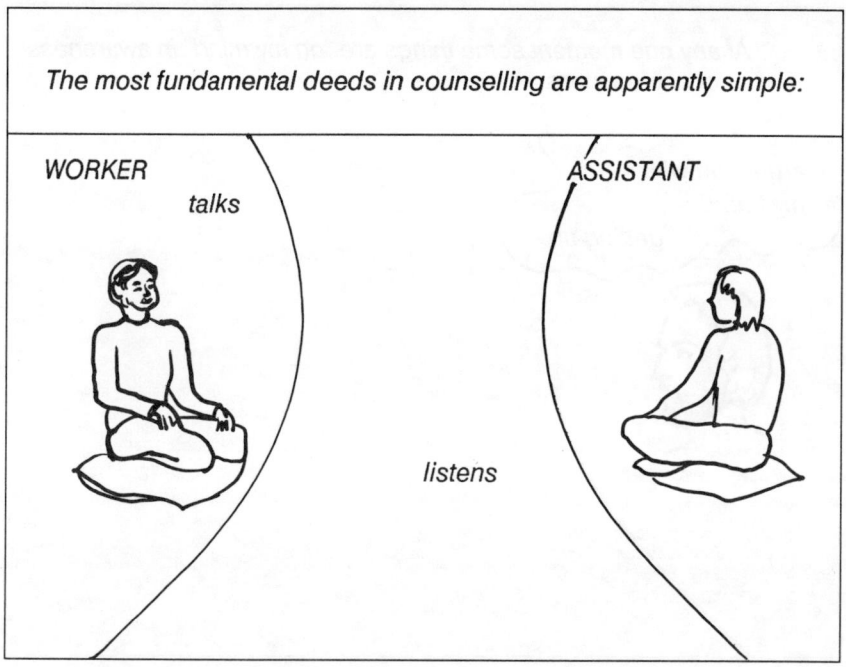

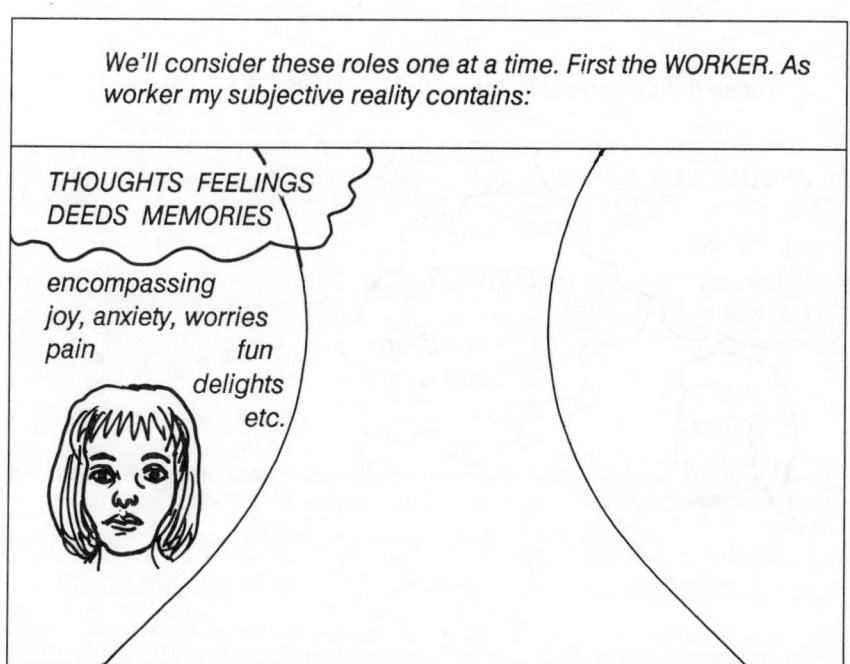

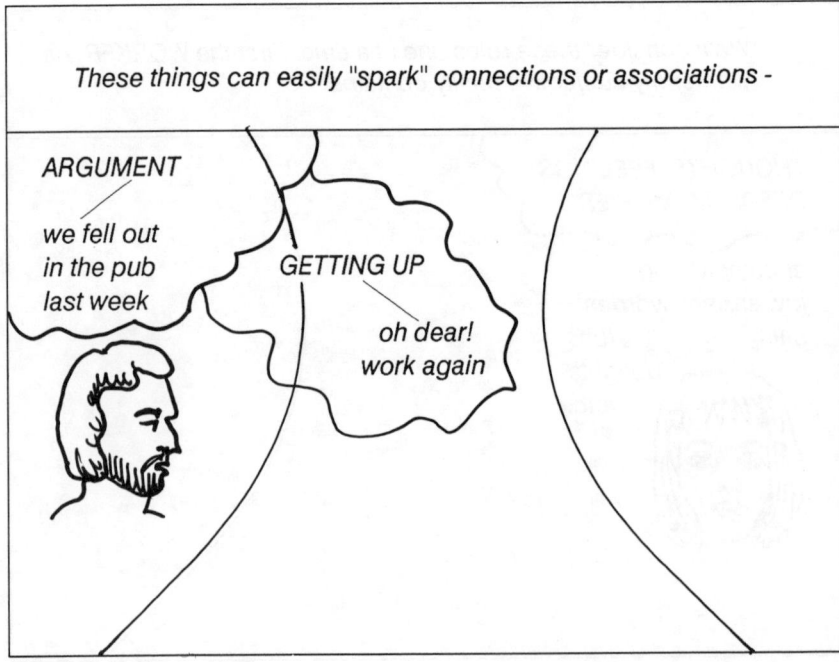

My deeds as the worker commence with:

sharing what's on the "top of my head" by talking:

felt bleary eyed this morning ---
I had a big row with Fred in the pub and ---

As worker, you talk to your assistant, but you can do this in a way that is different from most everyday conversations:

DEEDS

I can say just what comes to mind

I don't have to be sensible or coherent

I can pause or ramble

I can go from one thing to another illogically

I can be "silly", sensible emotional, or anything

Funnily enough - I am also "talking to myself" - and my assistant is here to give me attention and support. It is important to appreciate that:

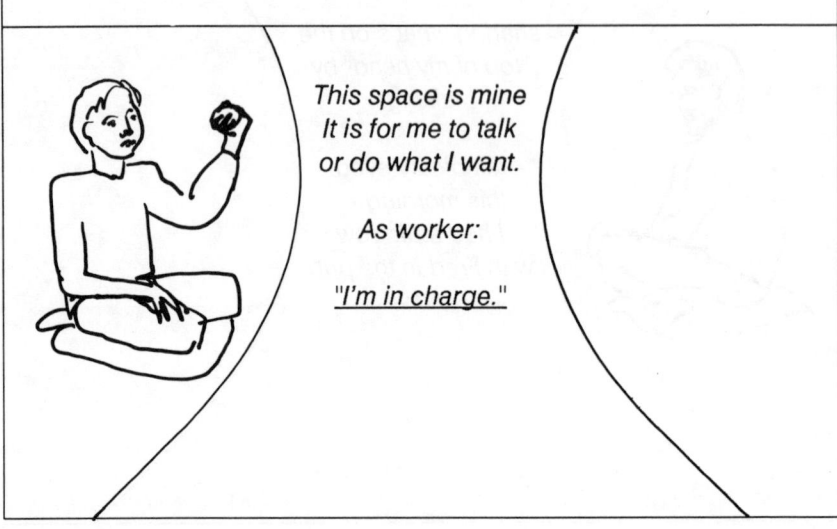

This space is mine
It is for me to talk
or do what I want.

As worker:

"*I'm in charge.*"

As I talk, more connections and associations will appear:

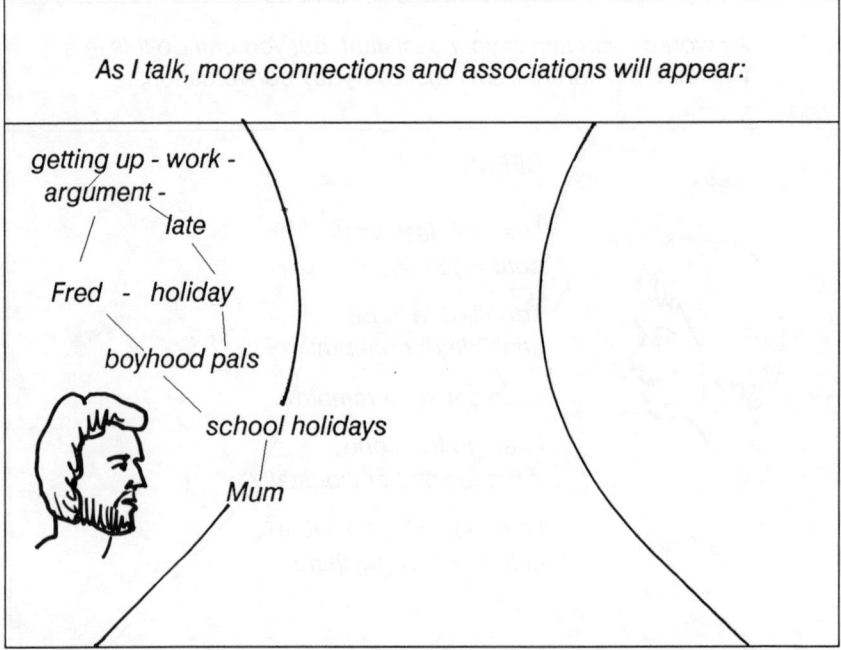

getting up - work -
argument -
late

Fred - holiday

boyhood pals

school holidays

Mum

I may "jump" from now to the past, from recent events to remote plans for the future, from feelings to thoughts.

The deeds of talking and exploring my thoughts and feelings, memories and deeds <u>link</u>

"top of my head"

memories

associations

The <u>goal</u> of the worker is to:

Explore the feelings, thoughts and images that express parts of my life; in a spontaneous free wheeling way "as it comes"

my deeds are to talk or to do things in the company of -

my assistant

21

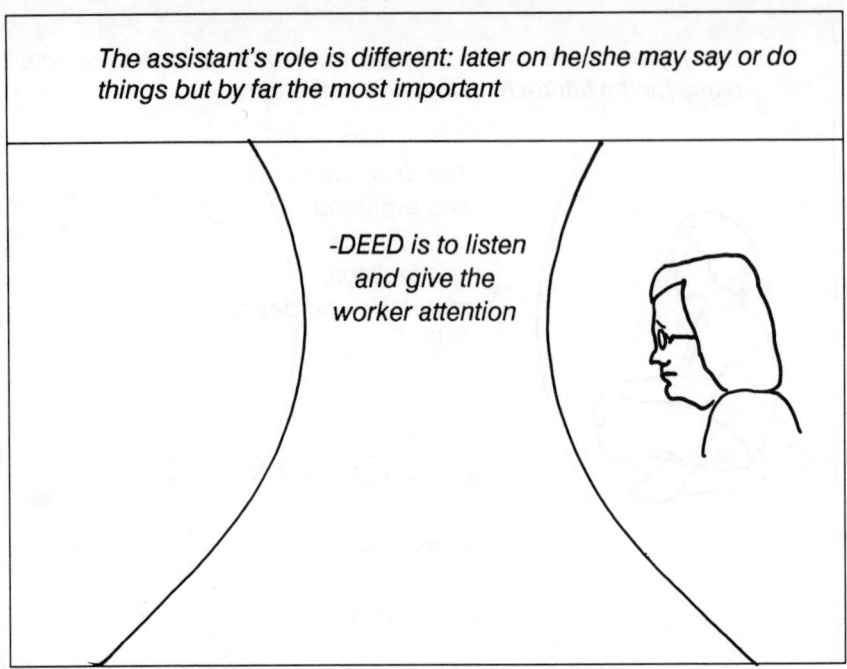

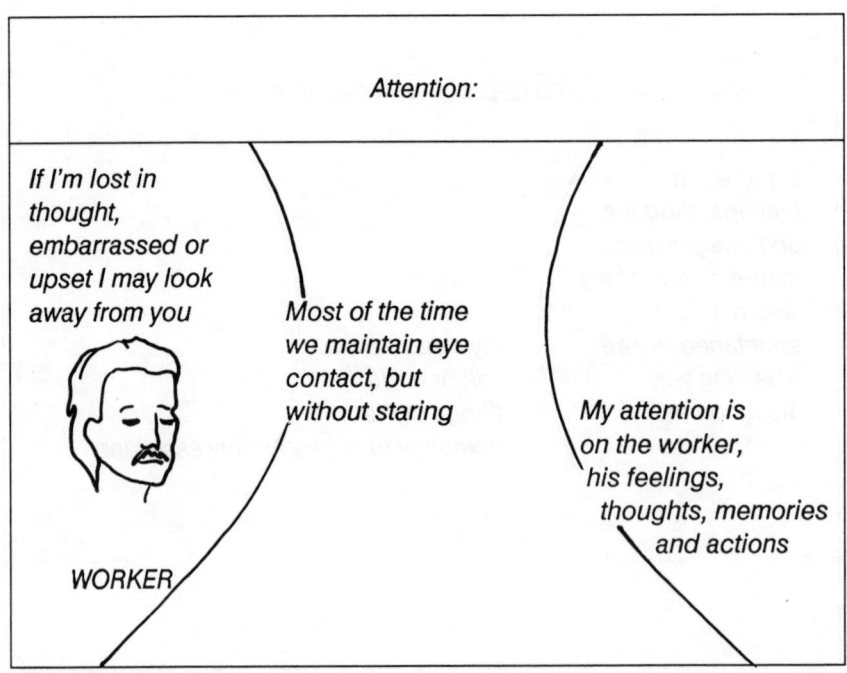

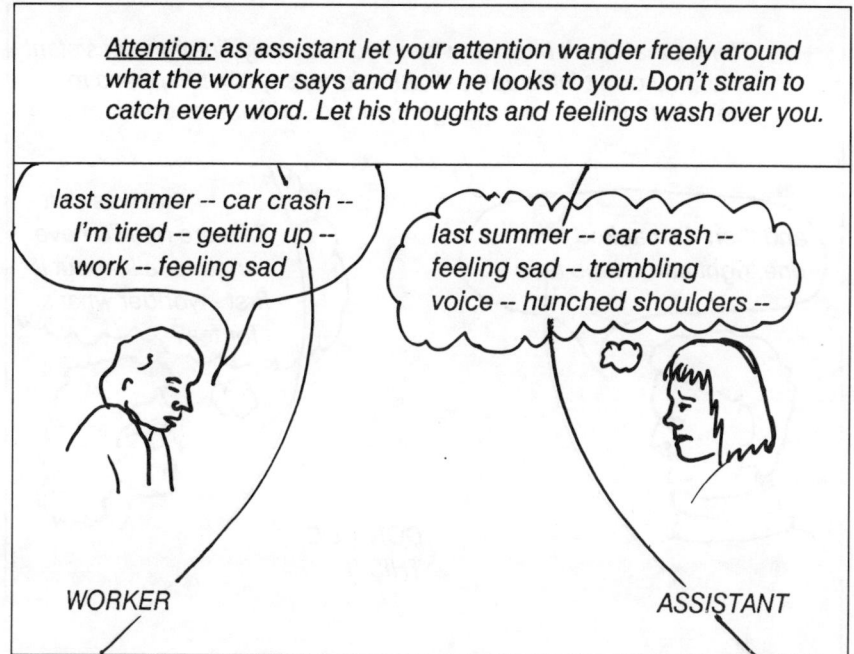

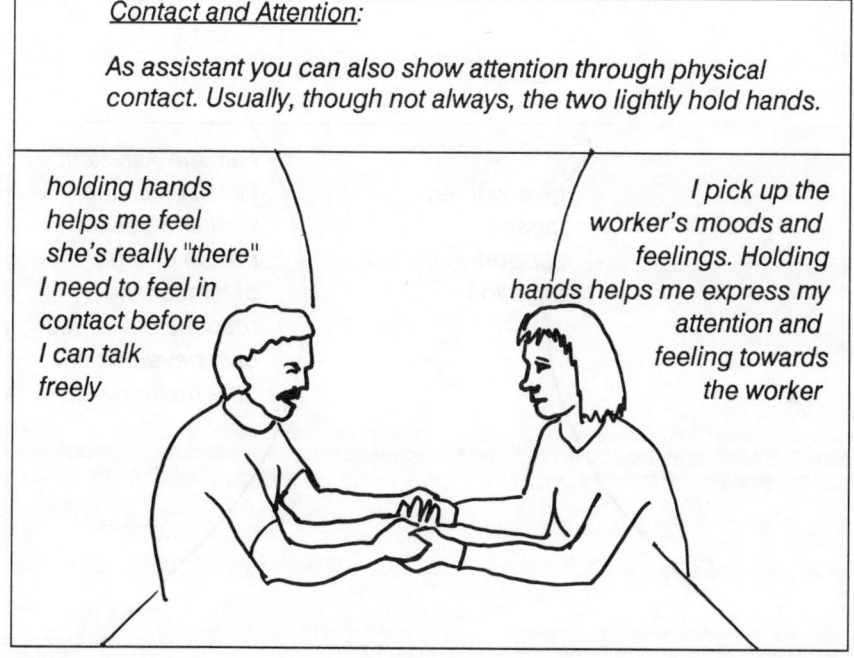

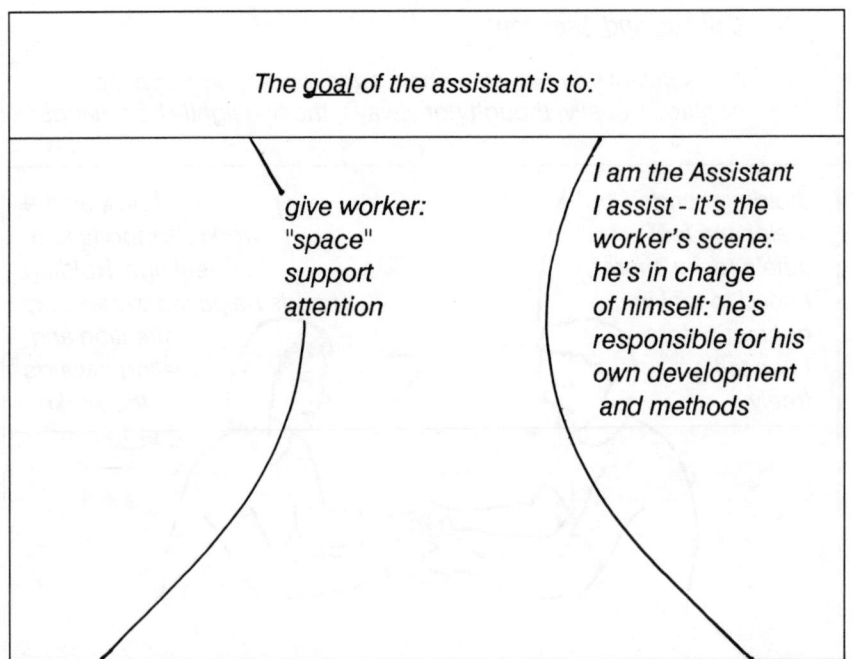

We can now put in both sides of the relationship

WORKER

talks spontaneously associates and connects: is "in charge"

ASSISTANT

listens
gives
support and
attention

"free floating" expression of feelings, thoughts and deeds

"free floating" attention

We propose that you do some deeds together - some exercises to practise counselling.

WORKER

You need to sit comfortably on a cushion or chair and lightly hold your partner's hands.

ASSISTANT

Get into a comfortable position you can stay in for some time. Hold your partner's hands and look at him.

25

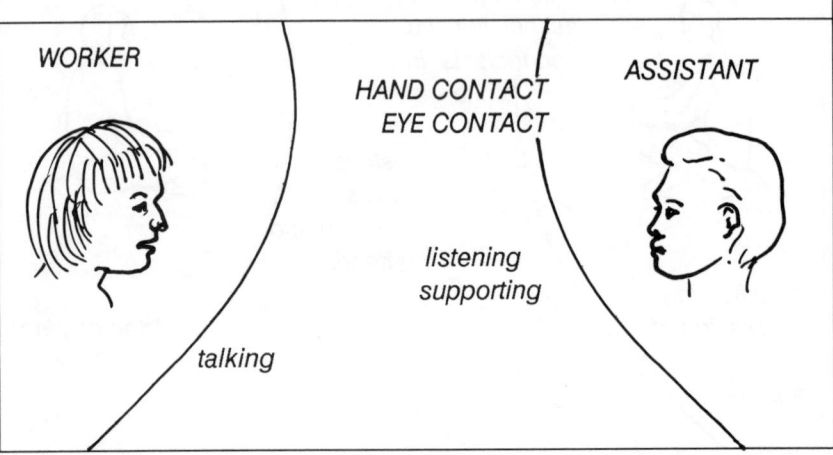

AN EXERCISE FOR TWO PEOPLE
(a) For 5 minutes one of you talks as worker, and the other listens as assistant

(b) Then change roles, the worker becomes assistant and the assistant the worker again for 5 minutes.

WORKER — HAND CONTACT / EYE CONTACT — ASSISTANT

talking

listening
supporting

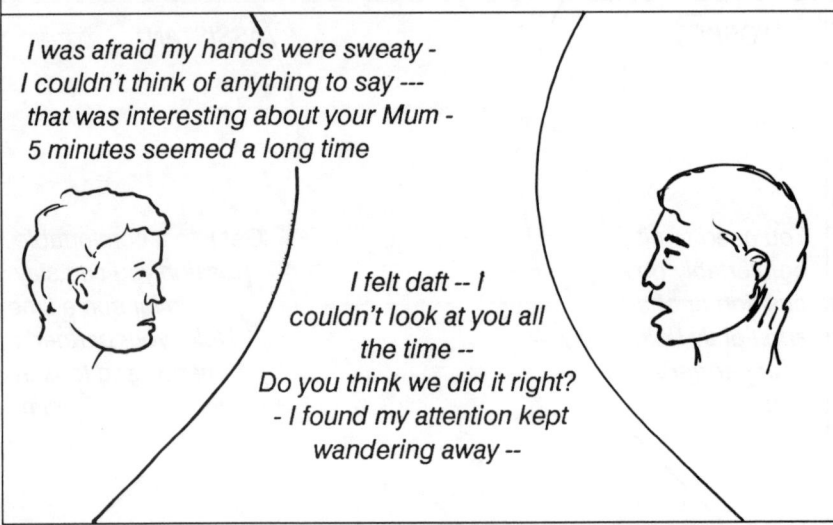

(c) Spend about 5 minutes discussing how you felt. Now you can interact in the normal way, sharing and exchanging information about how you felt in each role

I was afraid my hands were sweaty -
I couldn't think of anything to say ---
that was interesting about your Mum -
5 minutes seemed a long time

I felt daft -- I
couldn't look at you all
the time --
Do you think we did it right?
- I found my attention kept
wandering away --

When you are the worker you can talk about anything you like. Start with the things that are uppermost in you mind. We usually call this 'talking off the top of your head'. Follow whatever comes into your mind. Remember you don't have to be logical or coherent.

Here is an example of someone talking for five minutes 'off the top of the head'. Remember it's only an example - what you have to say may be totally different.

WORKER "Well... it was a real rush to get here. I thought I wasn't going to make it in time and you might have given up and gone to the pub instead. I waited half an hour for a bus at Kings Cross and then when one did come there were two more behind it and I got irritated with the conductor - said why couldn't they run the bloody buses on time - and he got annoyed back and said it wasn't his fault. And I felt bad because I know it wasn't his fault personally and everyone says things like that to them. But I was really worried I wasn't going to get here. Like when I was a kid if I missed the bus home from school I had to wait twenty minutes for the next one and I knew that if that happened, by the time I got home mum would have left for work - I always used to run up the road in case she hadn't - but she always had and I had to let myself in and there'd be a note on the table and my tea. I used to hate that. One time that happened and I came in and she was still there - hadn't gone to work - and she was sort of upset - crying and that - and it turned out she'd lost the job and my dad might be cross and they needed the money and stuff - but really I was glad because it meant it wouldn't matter if I missed the bus home. She'd still be there. I don't remember what happened in the end. I think she must have got another job.

I still feel out of breath actually. I was sort of half-running from the bus-stop. It's daft really because I knew you wouldn't have gone to the pub, but I was really afraid you might have. I guess I'll try breathing slowly - might relax me a bit (Pause). I went to the pub at lunch time - that's sort of on my mind because I made a resolution I wouldn't any more because it makes me sleepy in the afternoon. (Pause). I had a nice conversation with Sally though. (Pause). There's a hundred things I should have done at work today and didn't. (Pause). And I forgot my brother's birthday. And I was supposed to make a dentist's appointment for Mike. And I forgot to let the cat out. And... and... and.. all these things I should have done and didn't. I suddenly got this picture of us all - rows of kids - in school assembly - that prayer - can't remember how it goes - 'Oh Lord, forgive us for the things which we have left undone' - something like that... 'and forgive us for the things we have done that we ought not to have done'... that's not right, but something like that. I used to pray to God that the factory where my mum worked would burn down. And then I'd have to do another prayer to ask him to make sure that all the people got out alive. And then I thought he might punish me by making it burn down with my mum inside and I'd have to do another prayer to say I was sorry I didn't mean any of it. I don't think I really ever forgave her for having to go out to work. I really should have made Mike's dentist appointment. His teeth'll all fall out and it'll be my fault. Being a good mum. If I'm not a good mum my kids'll feel about me like I did about my mum - never forgive me. It's daft. Like I know it's not my fault and I know it wasn't my mum's fault - I talked to her about it recently and she was telling me about how guilty she used to feel - they had all this stuff on the radio about latchkey kids and delinquents. She used to read all the things in the women's mags - you know. But it's like the bus conductor - I knew it wasn't his fault and I still blamed him.

I feel kind of sad now. I've got that heavy feeling in my stomach. And a bit anxious. My hands feel sweaty. I think I'll stop now. That's my five minutes."

You may like to repeat this exercise trying it for slightly longer periods of time.

For the time being if you are the Assistant refrain from making any interventions. It's important to learn how to give someone else space and also how to take it for yourself. You'll quite often find that if you allow the Worker to go on talking without making an intervention he will reach the insight you thought of for himself. Insights that you arrive at yourself are usually more useful than those someone else has suggested. This is one of the things you might discuss in the group if you have one, or with your partner.

Making interventions is covered in Section 2 of this book.

Some information on working in a group is on p. 89.

The next set of exercises derive in part from the theories of D.W.Winnicott which can be found in his book *Playing and Reality*. We will return to his ideas about mothers and babies at various points in this book. One of his ideas is that underlying the counselling relationship is a process of relating that derives from babyhood when the mother reflects the baby as one of the first means of communication. In fact he argues that this process underlies all forms of human relating but is particularly important in counselling.

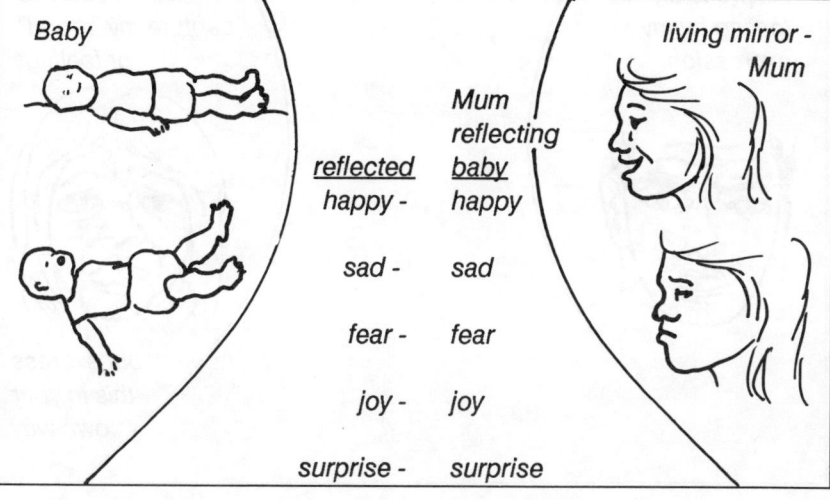

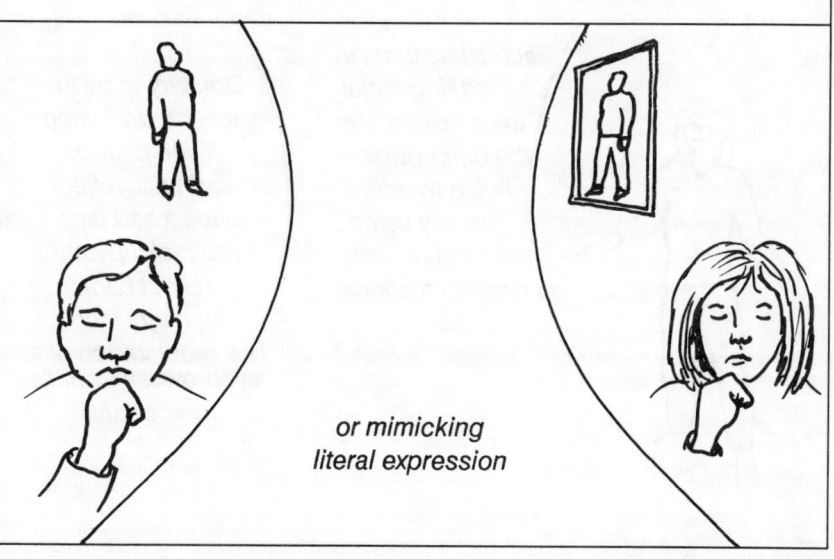

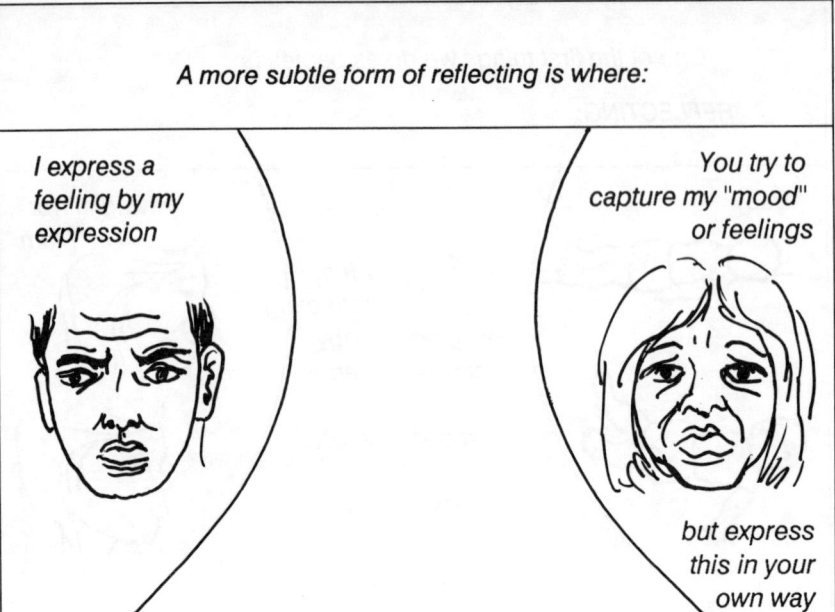

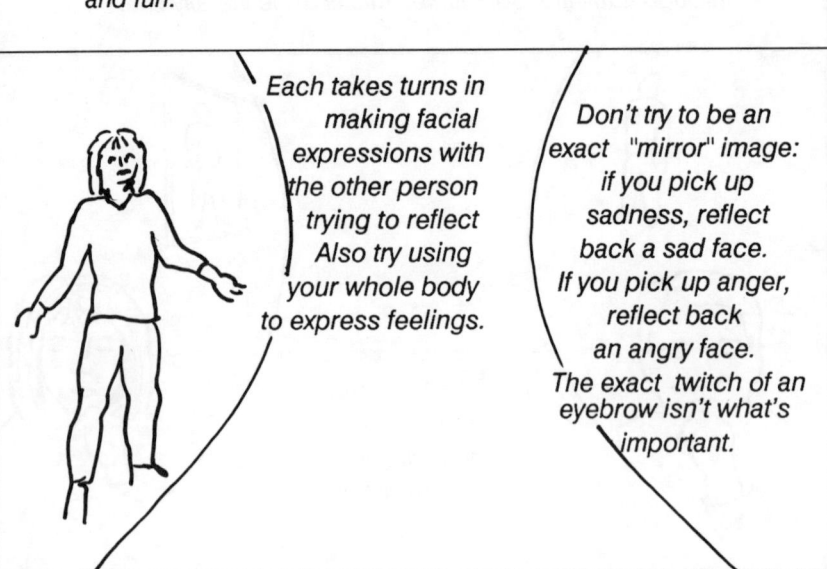

If you are working as a group

try the above in pairs - also you can "pass" an expression around the group and see how it changes as you go around.

A listening exercise that incorporates some part of reflecting.

WORKER
talks for 5 minutes as before.

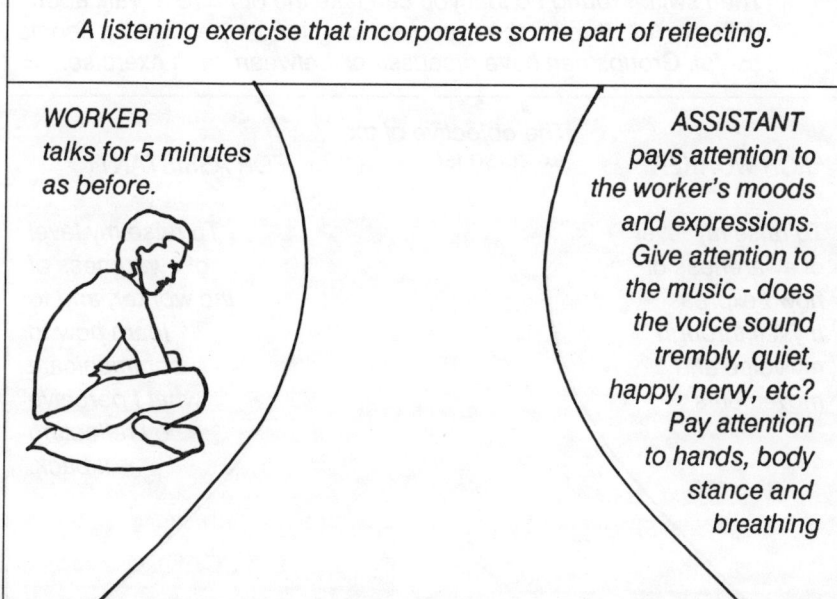

ASSISTANT
pays attention to the worker's moods and expressions. Give attention to the music - does the voice sound trembly, quiet, happy, nervy, etc? Pay attention to hands, body stance and breathing

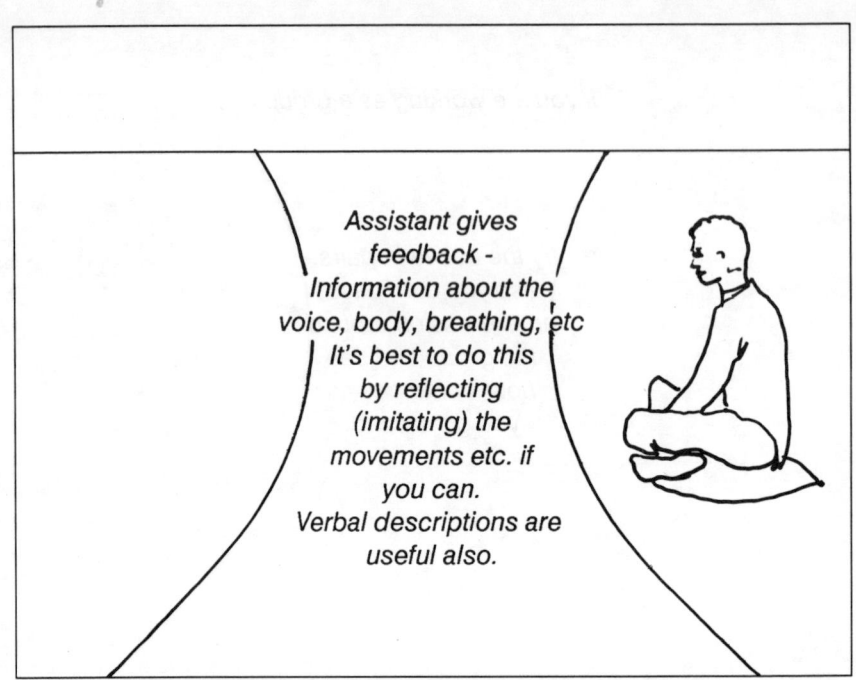

Assistant gives feedback - Information about the voice, body, breathing, etc. It's best to do this by reflecting (imitating) the movements etc. if you can. Verbal descriptions are useful also.

Then switch round so that you can take the other role. Talk about how you felt. Repeat the exercise using longer periods if it seems useful. Groups can have discussions between each exercise.

The objective of the exercise is:

FOR WORKER

To raise my level of awareness of how I express myself through my voice and movements

FOR ASSISTANT

To raise my level of awareness of the worker, and to learn how to communicate what I perceive by reflecting it back.

SCANNING

People often ask when they start counselling - "What should I talk about?" In broad terms, the answer is anything at all that is important to you, but in practice, particularly at the beginning, it is often useful to focus on particular topics or areas and explore them in both your present and past experience. One way of doing this is *scanning*. The object of the exercise is to become more aware of your past history by looking at how different events affected you and at what feelings and experiences have been significant or insignificant for you. You may find unexpected connections between actions and experiences that are widely separated in time. The exercise is very simple. Choose a topic or theme like the ones suggested below and simply scan your memory around it. You can take a particular period of time if you like such as 'this week' or 'this year' or 'since I got married' or (and this is usually the most interesting way to do it) you can scan over your whole life, from your earliest childhood memories to the present day.

When you are doing longer counselling sessions you may sometimes find it useful to use scanning to help look at a particular issue that has come up - where else, when else did you feel like that? What are the connections?

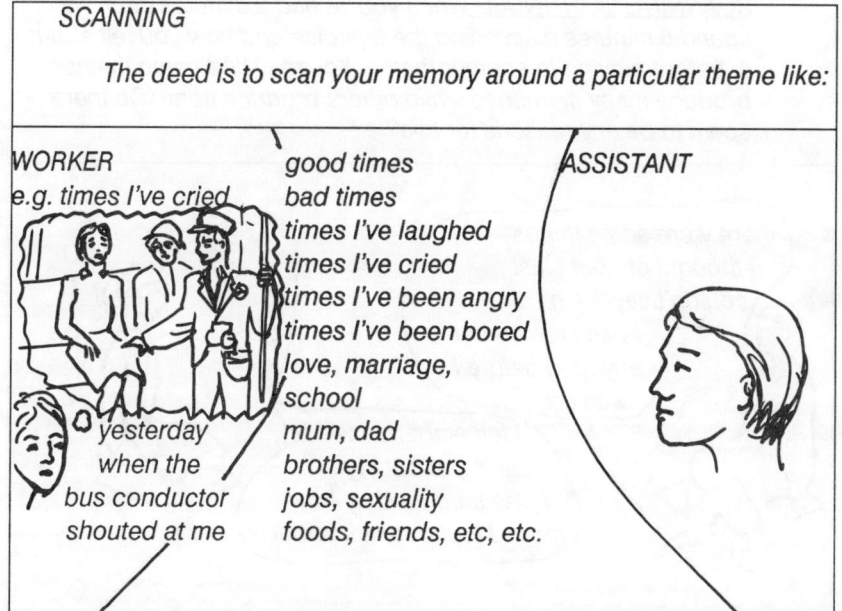

SCANNING

The deed is to scan your memory around a particular theme like:

WORKER
e.g. times I've cried
yesterday
when the
bus conductor
shouted at me

good times
bad times
times I've laughed
times I've cried
times I've been angry
times I've been bored
love, marriage,
school
mum, dad
brothers, sisters
jobs, sexuality
foods, friends, etc, etc.

ASSISTANT

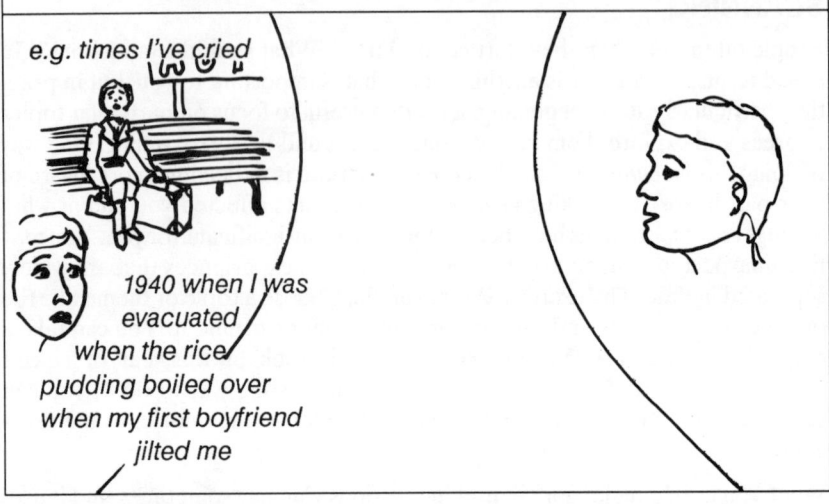

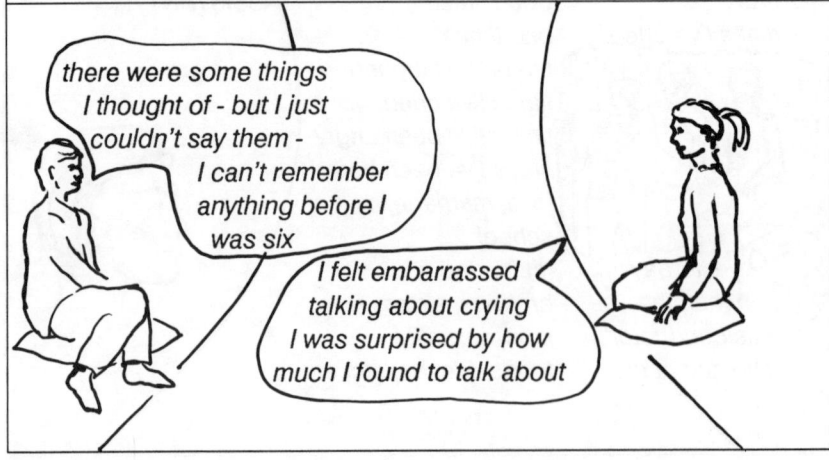

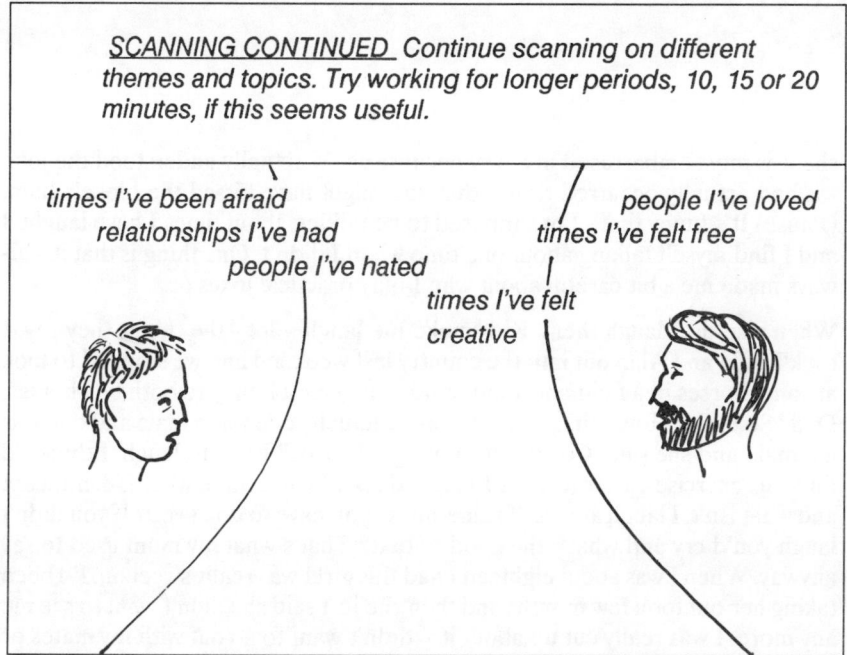

SCANNING CONTINUED Continue scanning on different themes and topics. Try working for longer periods, 10, 15 or 20 minutes, if this seems useful.

times I've been afraid
relationships I've had
people I've hated
times I've felt creative

people I've loved
times I've felt free

AN EXAMPLE OF SCANNING ON 'TIMES I HAVE LAUGHED'

WORKER "Well... I laugh all the time really so I don't know where to begin. Story of my life. I've always liked practical jokes and anything vulgar. One thing I've never forgotten was a family party we had when I was about twelve. There were a lot of aunts and uncles there and everyone was getting fairly boozed except for one rather elderly unmarried aunt of my mother - Aunt Christine her name was. One of the uncles suggested we play that game where you blindfold someone and then hand them objects to guess what they are. When it came to my aunt Christine's turn they blindfolded her and they did a few fairly innocent ones like you say 'this is Nelson's eye' and you stick the person's finger in an orange - you know the kind of thing. Well then they said 'We want you to kiss the Pope's hand.' She was a catholic you see. Anyway she was too embarrassed to say she thought it was sacrilegious and one of them who had fairly hairy arms rolled up his sleeves and placed his elbows together - like that. And the other one led her forward and when she'd kissed them whipped off the blindfold and there was another bloke just pulling up his trousers. I remember her slowly starting to blush - this kind of crimson colour starting round her neck and slowly spreading up round her face. No-one laughed. No-one said anything for what seemed like an eternity and then she just walked quietly out of the room. I think she was most embarrased in a way because she'd actually understood the joke - it had actually occurred to her that she might have kissed the bloke's bum. (Pause) It's funny that - I'm supposed to be talking about times I have laughed and I find myself talking about one time when I didn't. One thing is that it's always made me a bit careful about who I play practical jokes on.

When else do I laugh then? Kids make me laugh a lot - the things they say. I took Linda and Alan out into the country last weekend and we stopped to look at some horses in a field and Linda said 'You can tell they're both boy horses, Dad.' So I said 'How's that then?' because actually one was a male and one was a female and she said 'Cos they've both got beards.' I had to laugh. I think I'd find this exercise easier to do if I laughed less. I can't think what is significant and what isn't. I laugh at myself sometimes - you have to don't you? If you didn't laugh you'd cry and what's the good of that? That's what my mum used to say anyway. When I was about eighteen I had this girl I was really sweet on. I'd been taking her out for a few months and then she just said she didn't want to see me any more. I was really cut up about it - didn't want to go out with my mates or nothing. I just sat at home and moped. And then I thought - well just look at you - a great bloke like you, sitting here like a tragedy queen, mooning over that silly bitch. Why don't you get up and do something you silly bugger? So I went out and got pissed up with me mates and forgot all about her."

etc. etc.

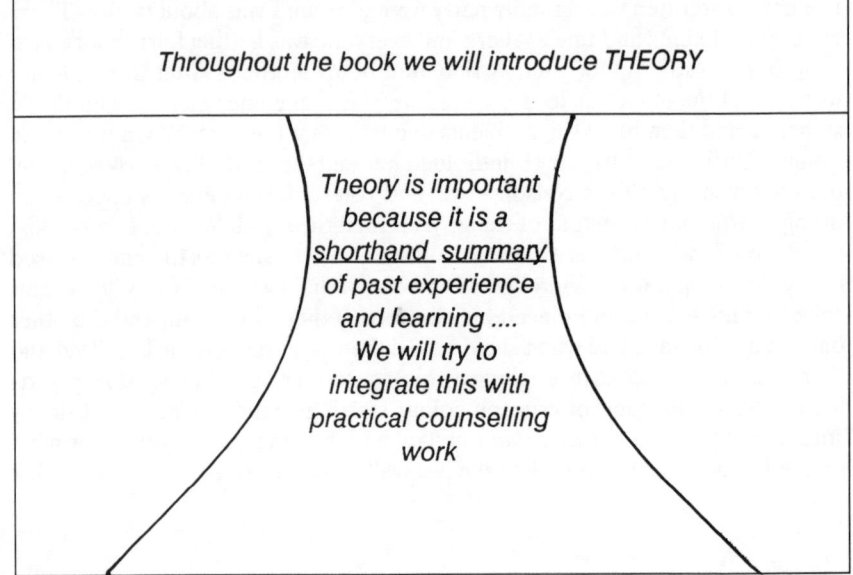

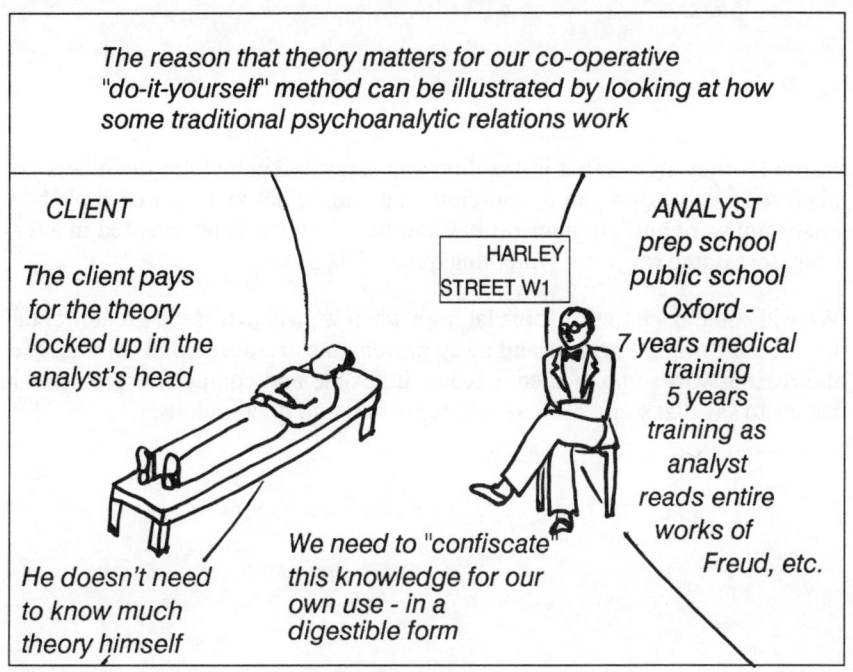

TOWARDS-AGAINST-AWAY INTRODUCTORY STATEMENT

Towards, Against and Away are three of the most basic concepts from Karen Horney's theory. You will notice that they all involve movement. Karen Horney argues that in very broad terms all human activity can be categorised in terms of movements towards, against and away from other people, things, ideas, feelings etc. Sometimes these movements will be flexible and spontaneous. Sometimes they will be inflexible and rigid. Sometimes they will change from one to another. How we develop our abilities to move towards, against and away will depend on our actions and experiences from birth to the present time.

In an ideal world people would be able to move spontaneously towards, against or away from each other as the situation demanded. When the best response would be to get angry we would do so. When it would be good to show affection we would be able to. When we need solitude we could withdraw. Life is very rarely like this. If you look at your life you will probably find that for you one direction is much easier than the others. You might, for example, have no difficulty in showing warmth and affection but be terrified of getting angry.

Karen Horney argues that if one direction is predominant then the others are likely to be repressed and unconscious. You might not know for example how angry you were until, to your dismay and horror, it suddenly erupted in a terrible, screaming row over something quite trivial.

We will come back to this topic later on when we will discuss in greater detail how these towards, against and away movements are developed through life, the reasons why some of them become inflexible and compulsive and what it means to say that some of them are repressed and unconscious.

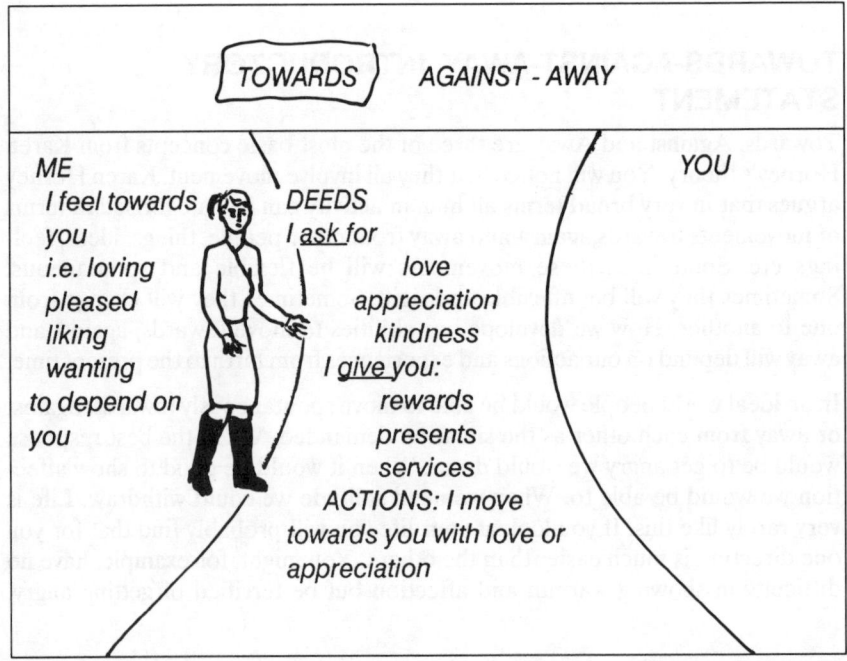

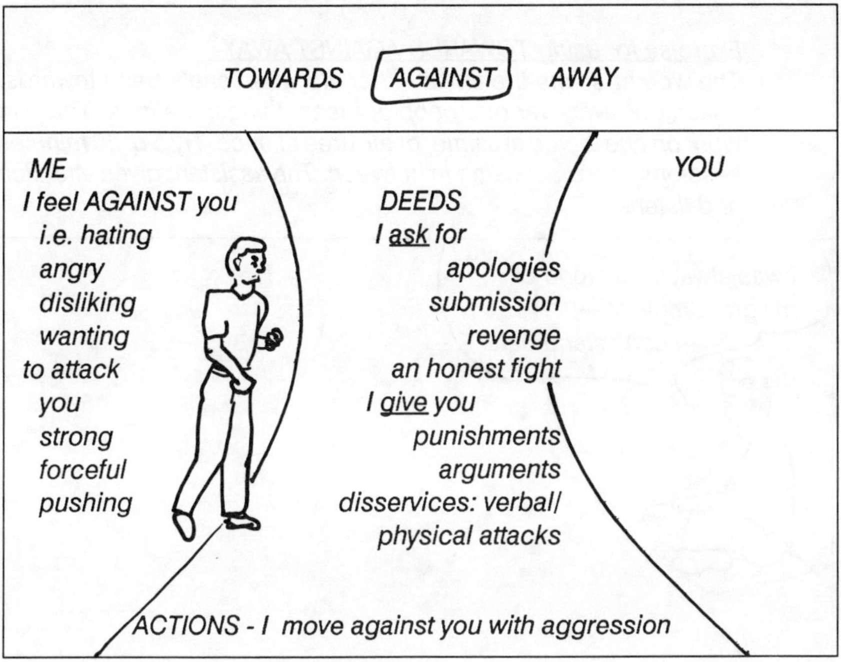

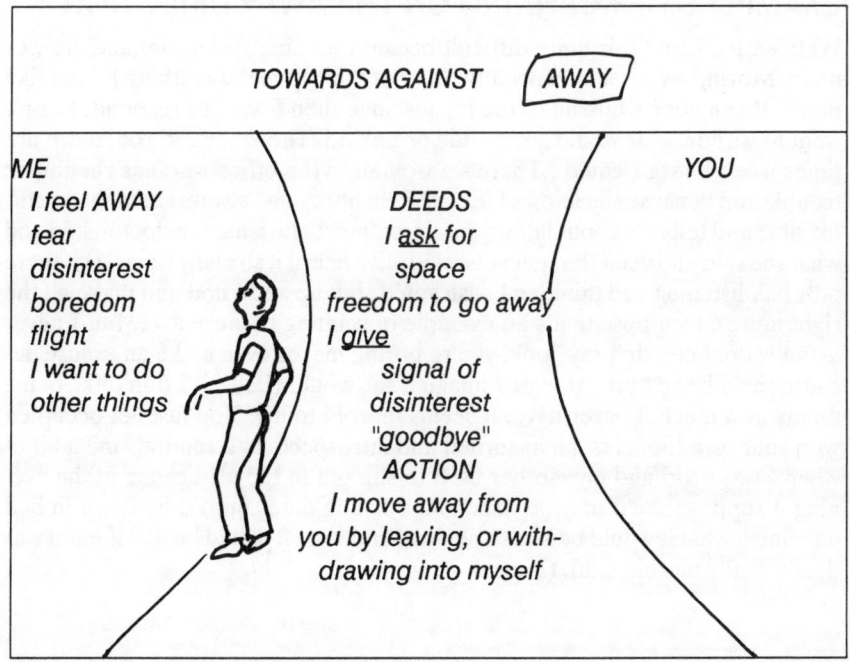

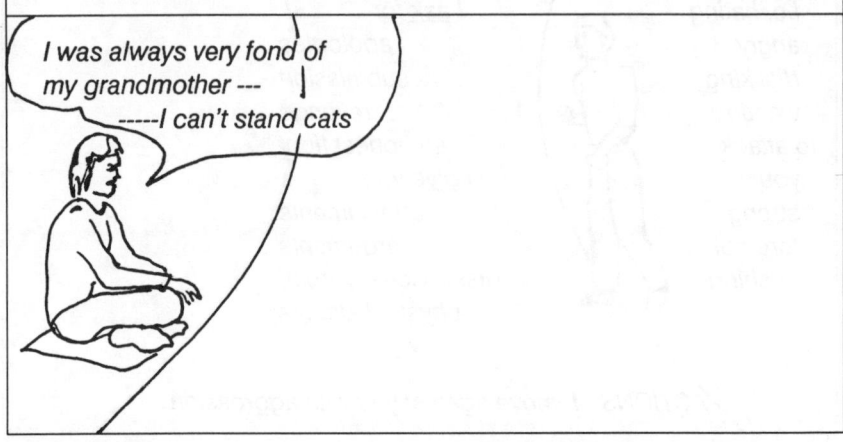

Exercise for using TOWARDS AGAINST AWAY
The worker scans the times in her life when she's been towards, against or away various people, ideas, things, feelings. You can work on one theme at a time, or all three at once. Try 5 or 10 minutes sessions with discussion in between. The assistant gives attention and listens.

I was always very fond of my grandmother ---
-----I can't stand cats

EXAMPLES OF SCANNING ON THE AWAY DIRECTION

WORKER "I find this quite difficult because nothing springs immediately to mind. Moving away seems a negative kind of thing to me, something I don't like much. If someone's talking to me for instance then I want to respond, I don't want to withdraw. It would seem rude or unkind. Though, mind you, there are times when I wish I could . There's a woman in the office who has rheumatic trouble and because she knows I used to be a nurse, she always grabs me at coffee time and tells me about her hospital treatment and what the doctor said and what she said and what the specialist said. I've heard it so many times. I sit there only half listening and thinking I wish you'd shut up and I nod and make all the right noises. I suppose that's an example of wanting to move away but I never actually do. I couldn't say 'look, you're boring me' or even make an excuse because she'd be so hurt. At least I imagine she would (Pause). I don't like being on my own much. I never have. It seems morbid to me. You just get occupied with your own thoughts, all in-turned and introspective. It reminds me a bit of when I was a kid and my mother used to slip out to the off-licence in the evening. I suppose she'd only be gone about five minutes but I'd lie there in bed imagining what it would be like to be dead and what it would be like if mum was dead - really morbid stuff. (Pause).

Mind you, there are times now when I want to be away - I like going for long walks on my own in the country - getting away from the kids for a day and just walking and walking - that's glorious. Then there's things I'm not interested in. I suppose you could say that's a kind of 'away' direction. I'm not interested in politics for instance. If people start talking about that, I just switch off. (Pause) What else? I really can't think of much. My main direction's 'towards' I think. I could think of loads of things to say on that (Pause). One time I was really 'away' actually was when I first went to school. I was really scared of the other kids and I hardly talked to them. I remember standing in the playground staring at the shapes the wire-netting made, trying to pretend that I didn't care. Then I'd wander round the playground from group to group, never actually stopping to ask if I could join in - just keeping on walking so no-one would realise I didn't have anyone to play with. I had this imaginary friend I used to talk to... I was really lonely when I was a kid. And then when I lived in the nurses' home - I was lonely then. I was really homesick at first. Everyone seemed to know each other except me. I suppose one of the things about being 'away' in my life is that it's mostly been something unpleasant, something I've not chosen..."

CREATIVE DEEDS AND PLAY

In the following section we introduce one of the three fundamental processes in life. This is:

1) Deeds that create new knowledge about myself, others and the world - creative deeds.

(The other two fundamental processes, which we develop later are:

2) Deeds that lead to mystifying and idealising myself, others and the world - compulsive deeds.

3) The deeds in (1) and (2) affect and mould the instinctive, biological drives we call orgasmic processes - that is our bodily and erotic needs.)

In this section we illustrate how we learn to do many basic things that we take for granted - for example, how we learn we are alive, a person, how we respond, how to get information from the environment, how to walk, talk and make things happen. The things normally thought of as 'creative' like art, music or dancing are a more complex development of the same process. Creativity is a crucial matter for counselling because we not only want to reduce the compulsions that make life miserable but also to make our lives more creative in both personal relations and elsewhere.

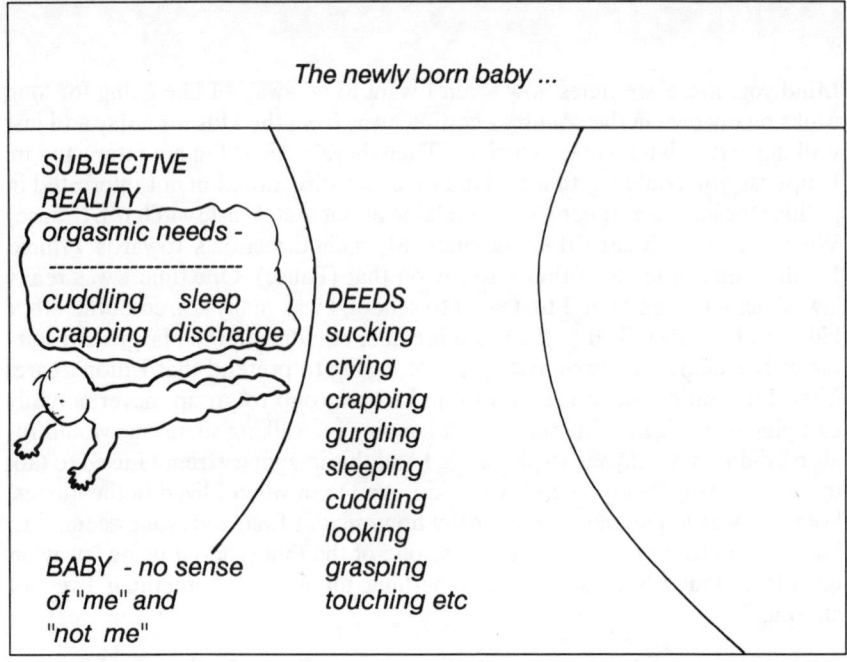

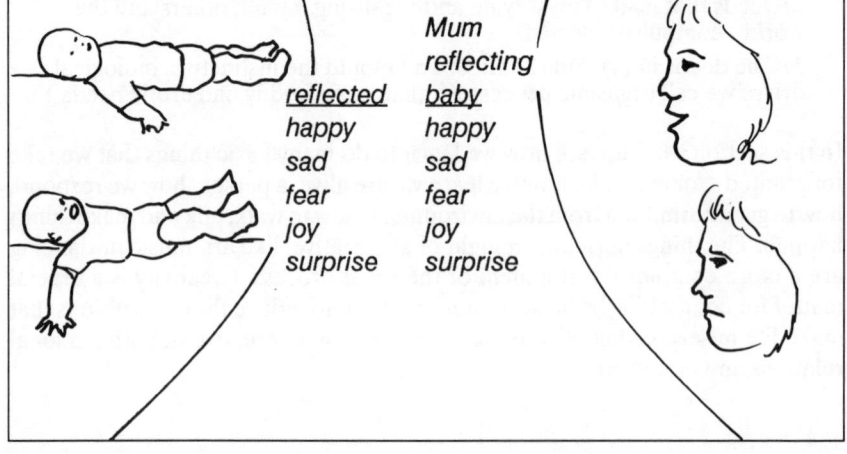

Often the mother will also initiate expressions. She will smile, for example, to get the baby to smile. This process of mutual reflection is the first form of playing that the baby experiences.

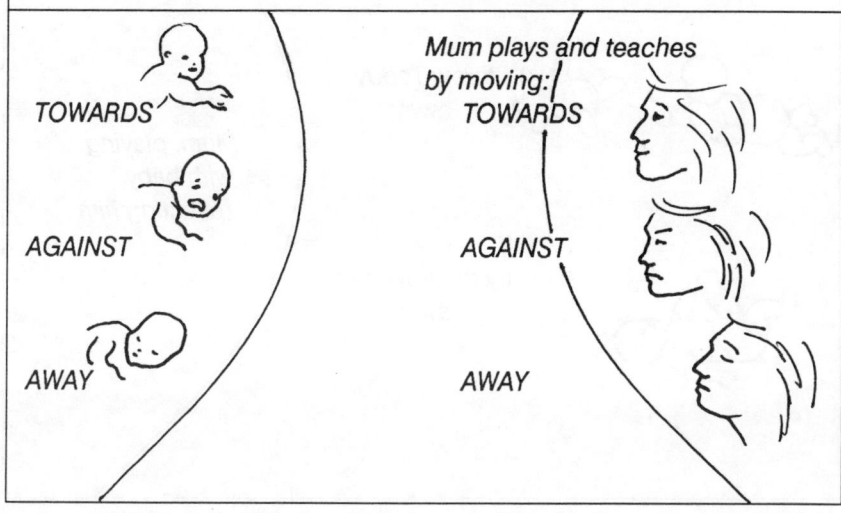

The mother also initiates play by offering the baby objects to hold and investigate. The baby starts to learn about the world.

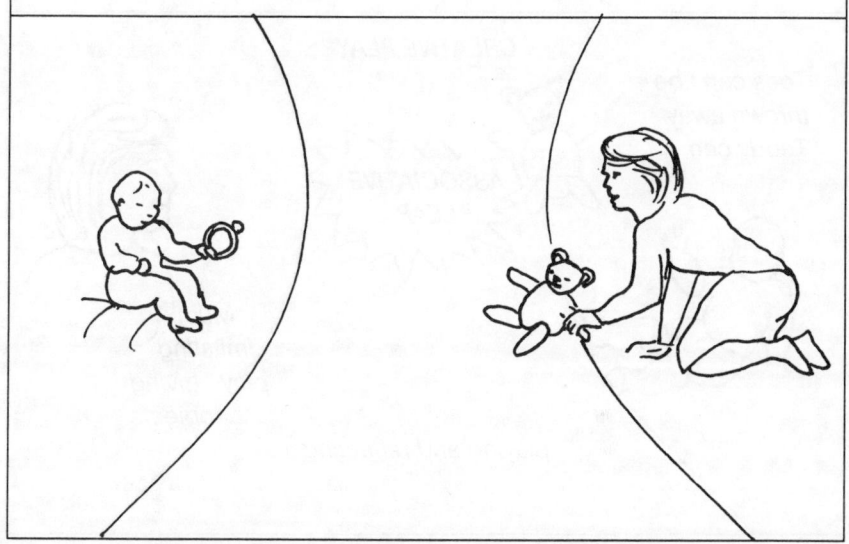

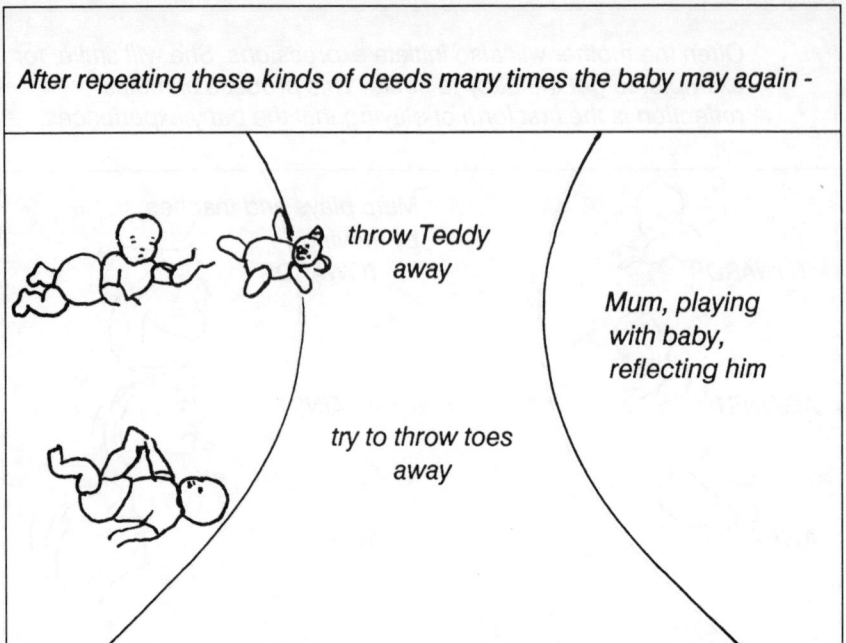

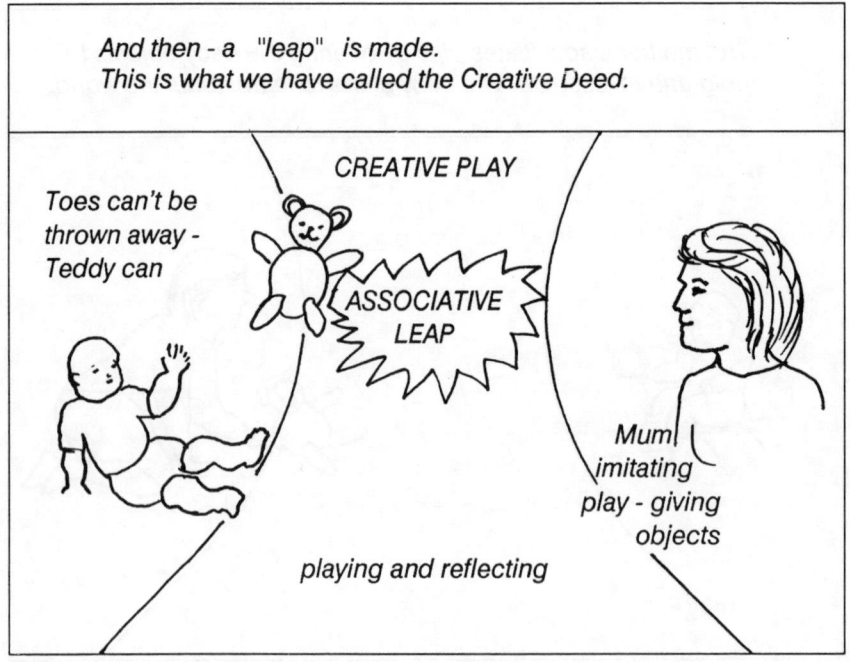

The baby now has new knowledge of self-identity, the knowledge that 'me' and the world are in some sense separate. This is a qualitative change. The deeds of the investigating himself and objects are repeated many times until there is a change from quantity to quality. (See p 128 for an explanation of 'quantity and quality').

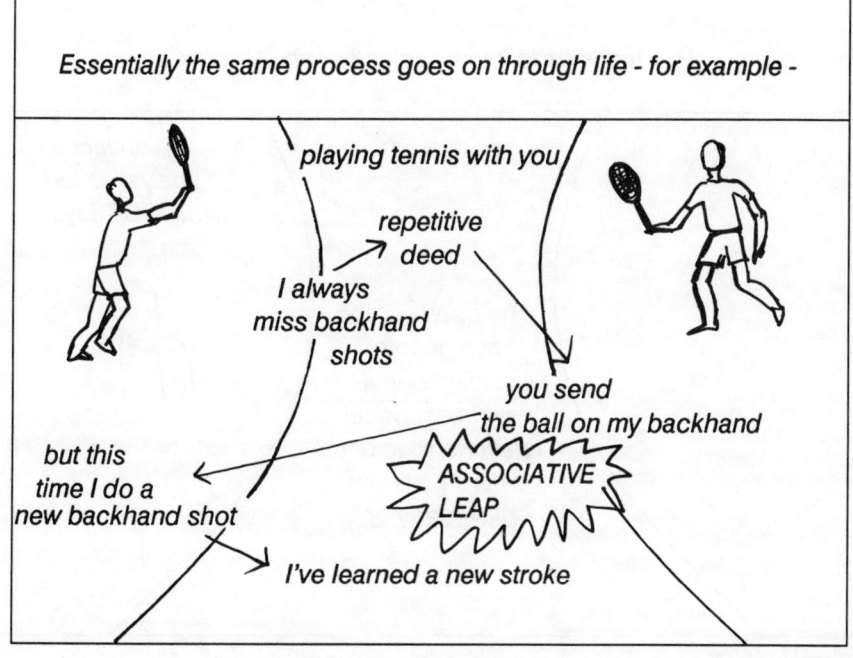

One of our goals in counselling is to develop each other's creative deeds, so at the start of counselling we often

PLAY TOGETHER

This helps us to know each other and to relax:

In fact an analyst called WINNICOT says:

"The deeds of the two people engaged in a psychoanalytical relationship is one where 2 people <u>play together.</u>"

SOME EXERCISES FOR PLAYING TOGETHER

These exercises are all useful ones to do at the beginning of a counselling session and should help you to 'warm up'.

1) Reflection

This is described earlier in the book, so we won't go into it again here.

2) Mutual fantasy One of you starts a fantasy. It can be about anything you like, but it is usually fun if you include both of you in it. After a few sentences the other person takes over and continues the fantasy. You continue to swop about like this till the fantasy seems finished. The only rule is that you must take over whatever the other person has started though you can then add whatever inventions you like.

3) Shared drawing Take a large piece of paper. One of you starts the picture - draw anything you like, it could just be a line or a squiggle, you don't have to be good at drawing. The other person then continues it. Then you have another turn and so on. You can either treat the drawing as primarily one person's, with the other person responding to them, or you can both be responsible for initiating.

4) Conversation without words Have a conversation without using any words. You can use signs, expressions, noises, anything you like apart from words.

5) Body drums One of you starts up a rhythm on your own body or your partner's. The other person joins in with another rhythm. See how many different sounds and rhythms you can get from your two bodies.

You can probably invent more exercises along the same lines. The criteria is that the games should be fun, they should be interactional, they shouldn't be competitive, they should be co- operative.

You will probably find that they are all useful for looking at transference.

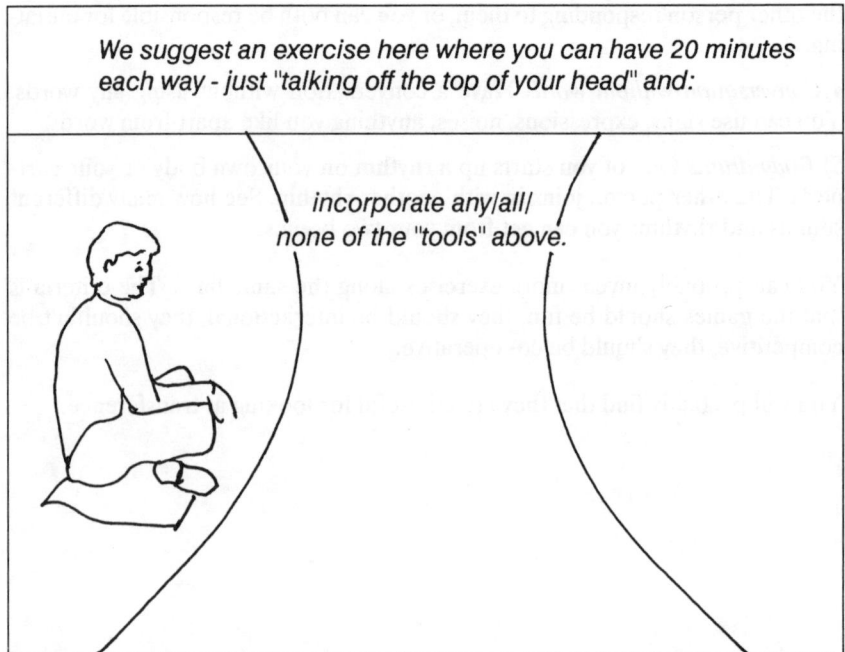

COMPULSIVE DEEDS AND COMPULSIVE TRENDS

So far we have only dealt with creative play and creative deeds. Of course not all play and not all deeds are creative. Babies are not always accurately reflected and played with. New knowledge is not always produced. Some deeds are compulsive and develop as a response to pain, fear or anxiety. By a compulsive deed we mean an action that is performed in response to a certain situation or stimulus whether or not it is appropriate.

In this section we are again going to use a number of examples taken from the relationship between a baby and his mother. This does not mean that we are suggesting that a mother should always be able to play creatively with her child or that it is in any way her fault if she does not. And we are certainly not suggesting that even if this were possible this would be a way of producing happier individuals or a saner society. It is the society and its conflicts and contradictions that produce the kind of individuals we are and not the other way round. We choose the example of mother and baby because these conflicts and contradictions affect us right from the moment of birth and the way we learn through them affects all our subsequent development.

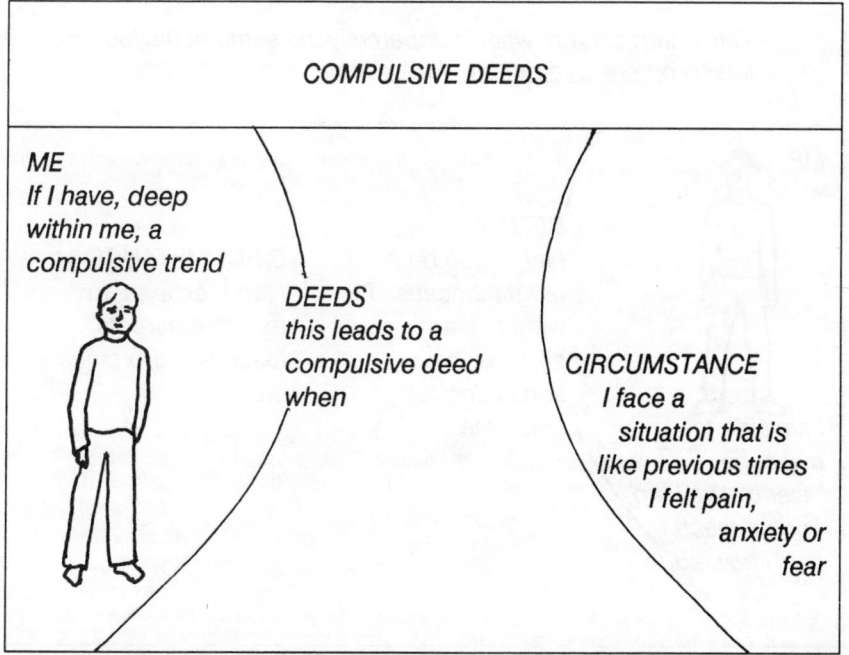

49

for example:

ME

DEED
to placate
be obsequious
be polite
to reassure
be subservient

CIRCUMSTANCE
I face "authority figures"
e.g. parents
teachers
policemen
bosses
judges
kings
ministers

A compulsive trend of "dependency" is deep within me

This contrasts with what is apparently the same behaviour but based on <u>creative deeds -</u> for example:

ME

DEED
I let myself be taught because I want to learn and they have something to teach me.

CIRCUMSTANCE
I face "experts" for example parents, teachers, sportscoach etc.

I am able to make the "associative leap" and so reach new knowledge

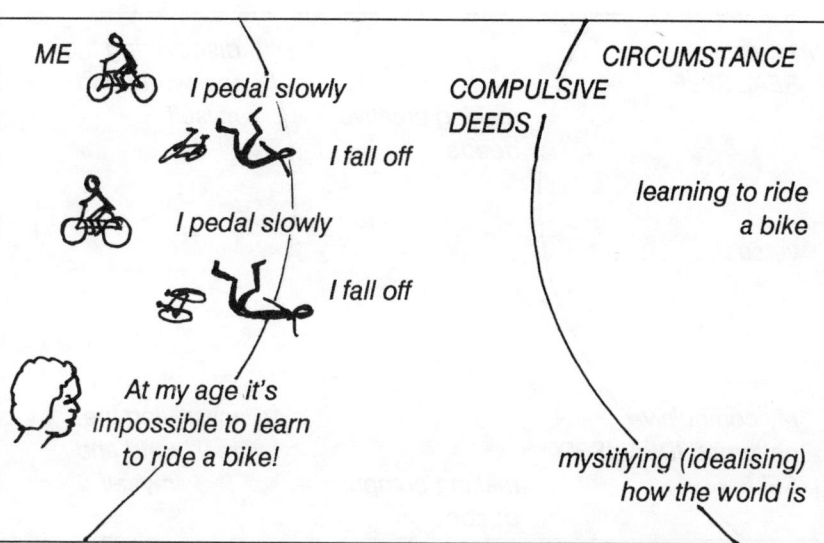
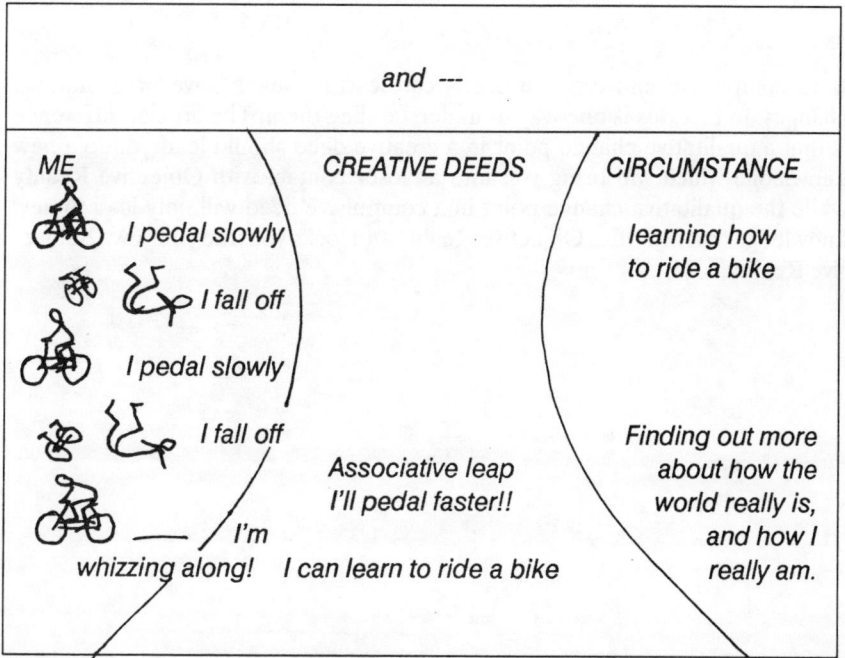

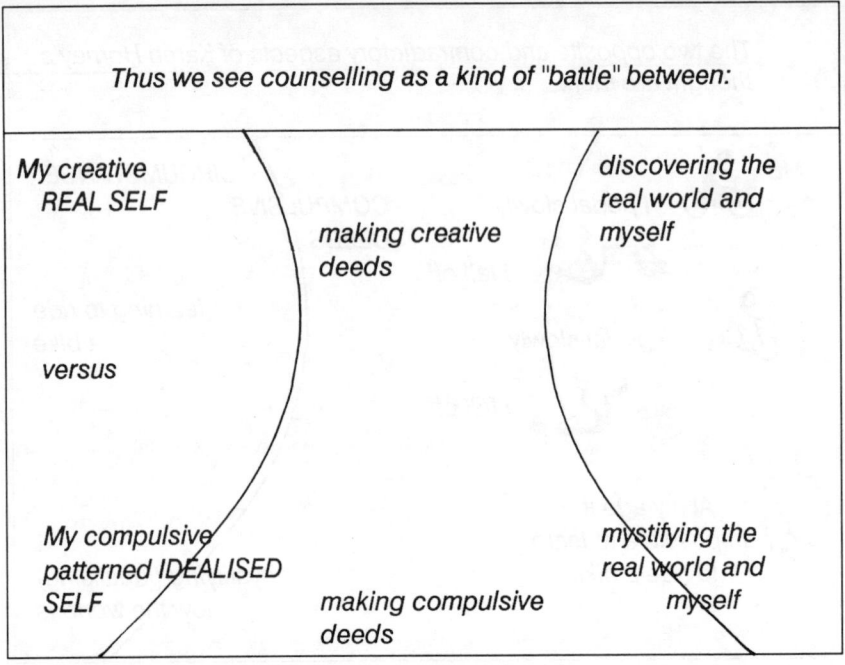

Both compulsive and creative deeds can lead to quantitative or qualitative changes. In fact this is one way of understanding them. The crucial difference is that a qualitative change point in a creative deed should lead you to a new knowledge which will bring you into a closer contact with Objective Reality while the qualitative change point in a compulsive deed will only lead to new knowledge that mystifies Objective Reality and locks you into your own Subjective Reality.

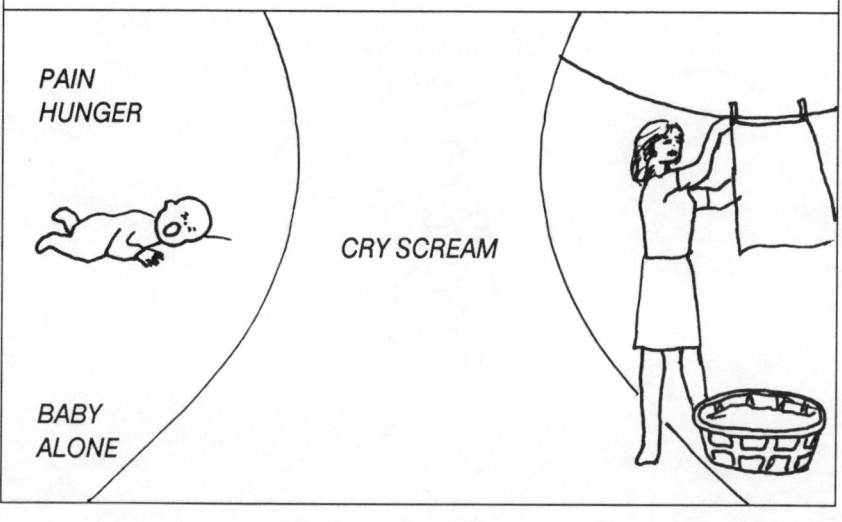

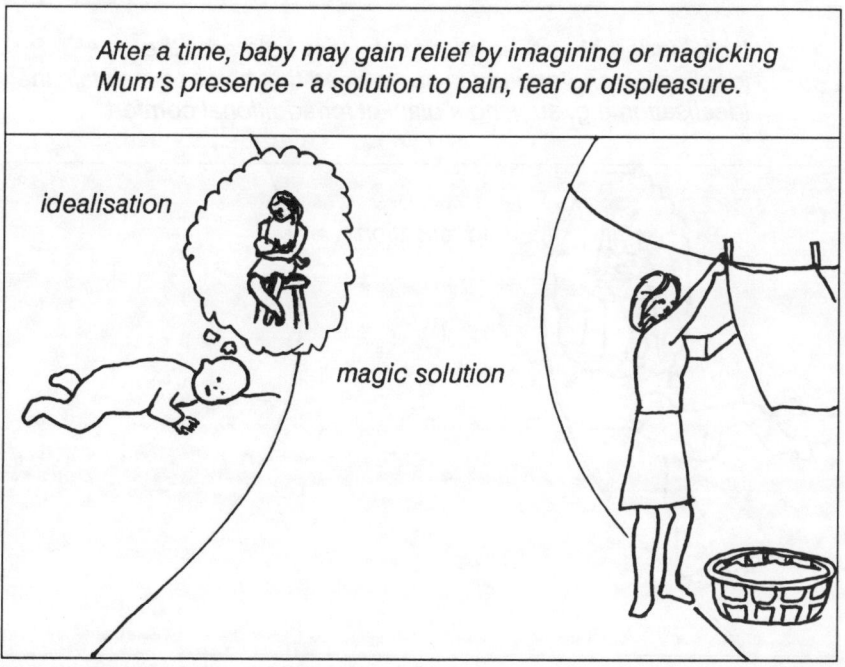

If Mum returns, then the magic solution (called an <u>idealisation</u>) will fade away

idealisation fades

If prolonged absences occur baby may hold onto the idealisation and engage in some deed that helps to maintain the idealisation e.g. sucking a blanket for additional comfort

idealisation

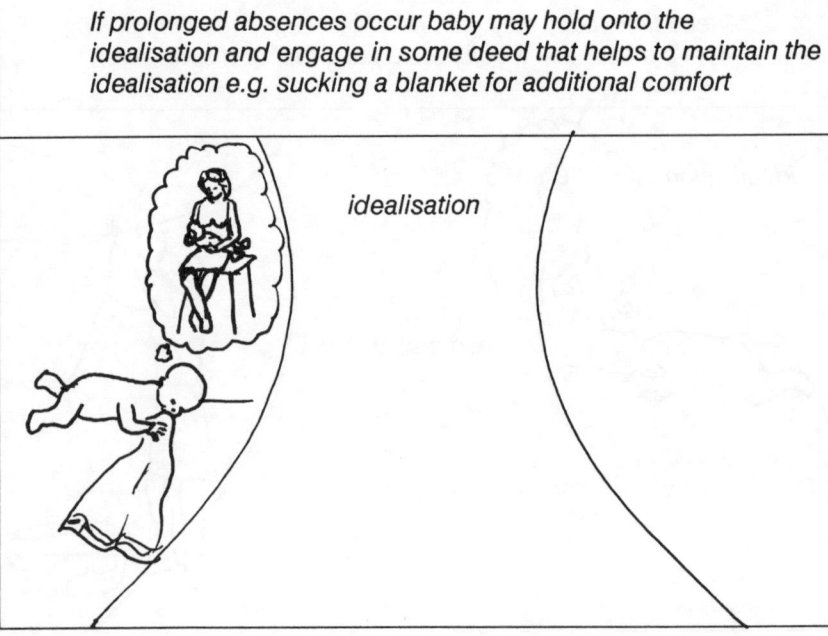

Eventually maybe both the idealisation and the deed no longer allay anxiety and baby's solution becomes one of "cutting off from the world", a kind of being "dead".

Mum may now have difficulty in getting any reaction from baby and if he can't play, he can't learn.

"Magicked" or idealised solutions are built by the same process through life. If, for example, as a young teenager, every attempt to assert myself leads me into unpleasant conflict -

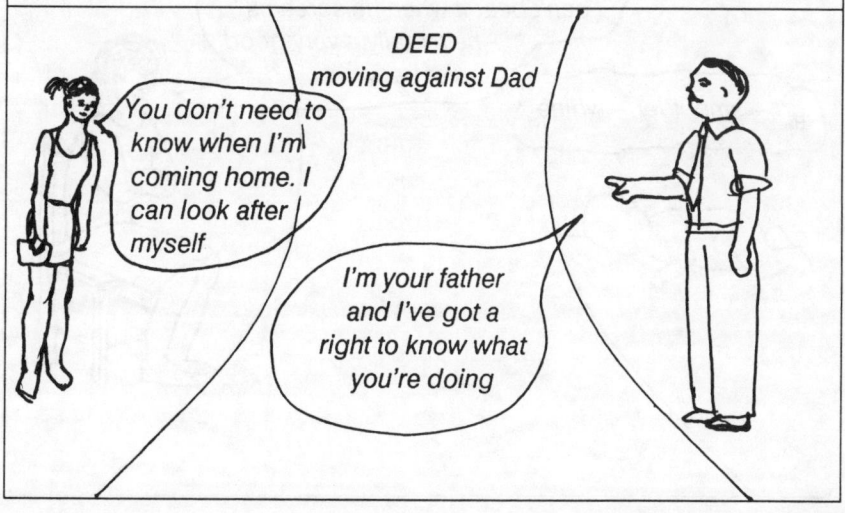

DEED
moving against Dad

You don't need to know when I'm coming home. I can look after myself

I'm your father and I've got a right to know what you're doing

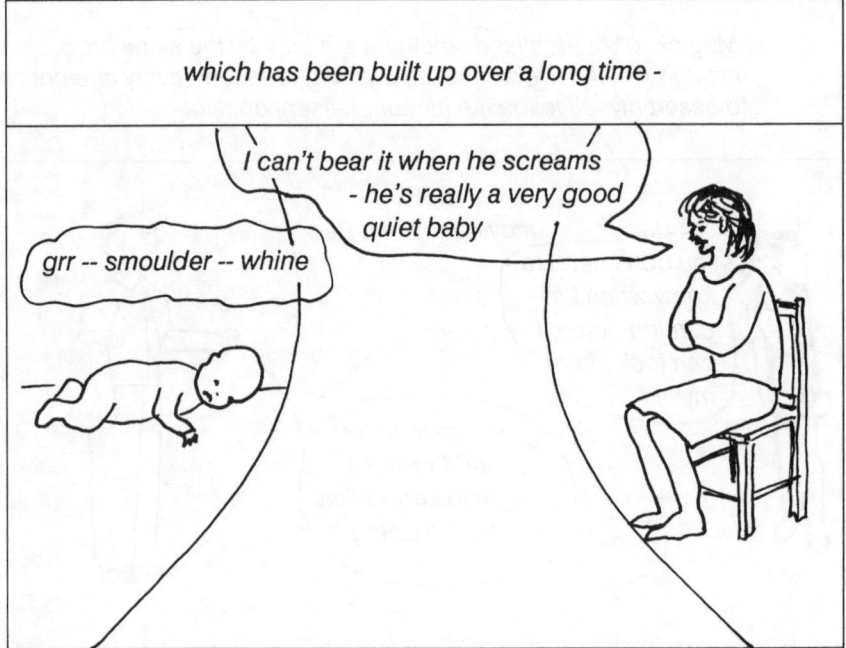

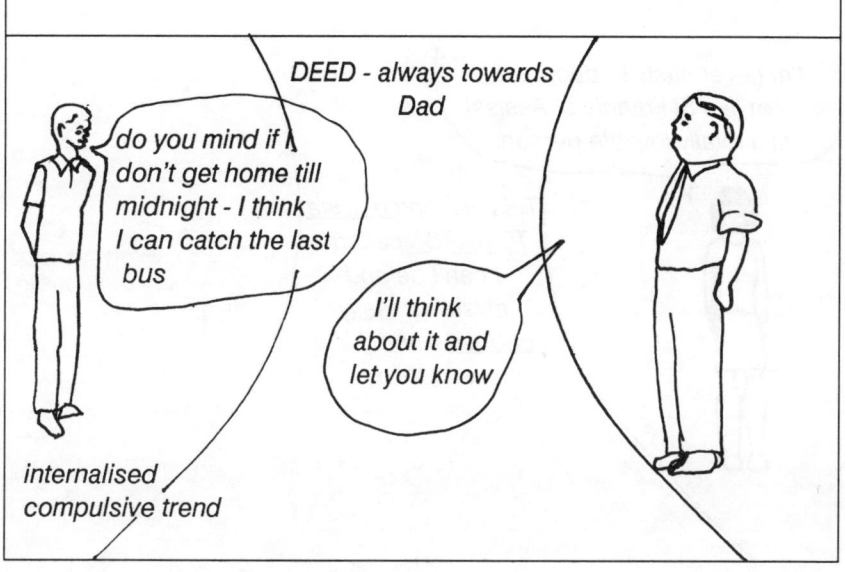
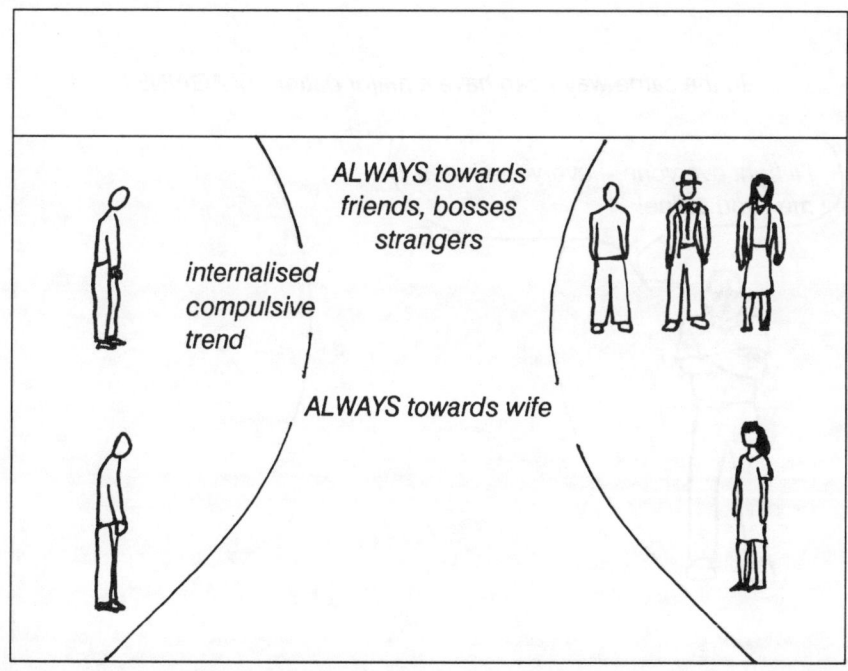

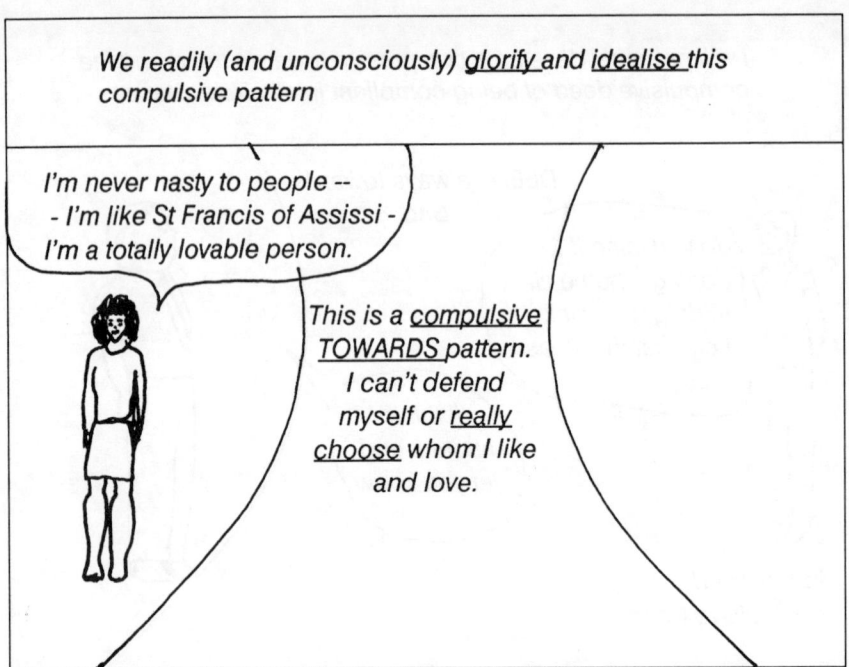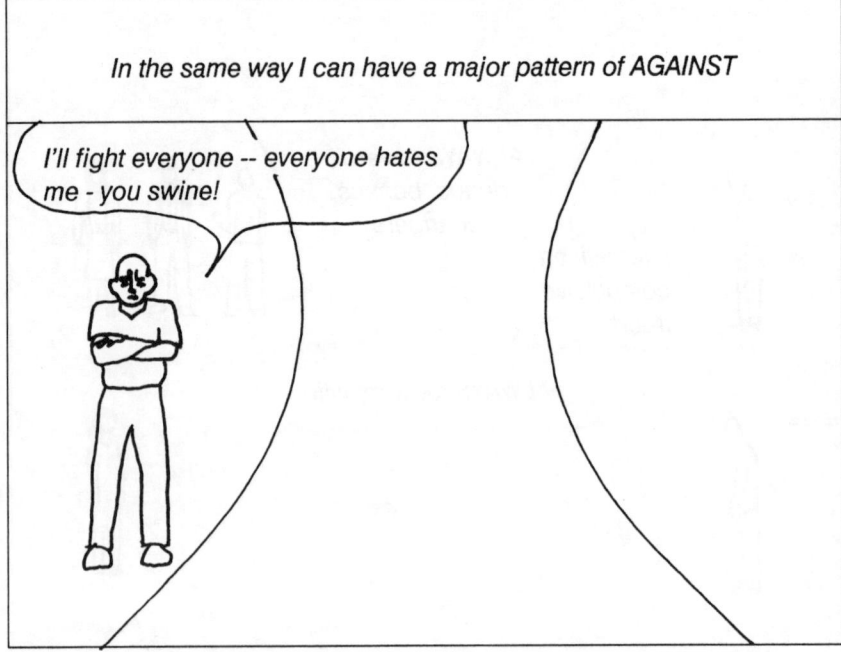

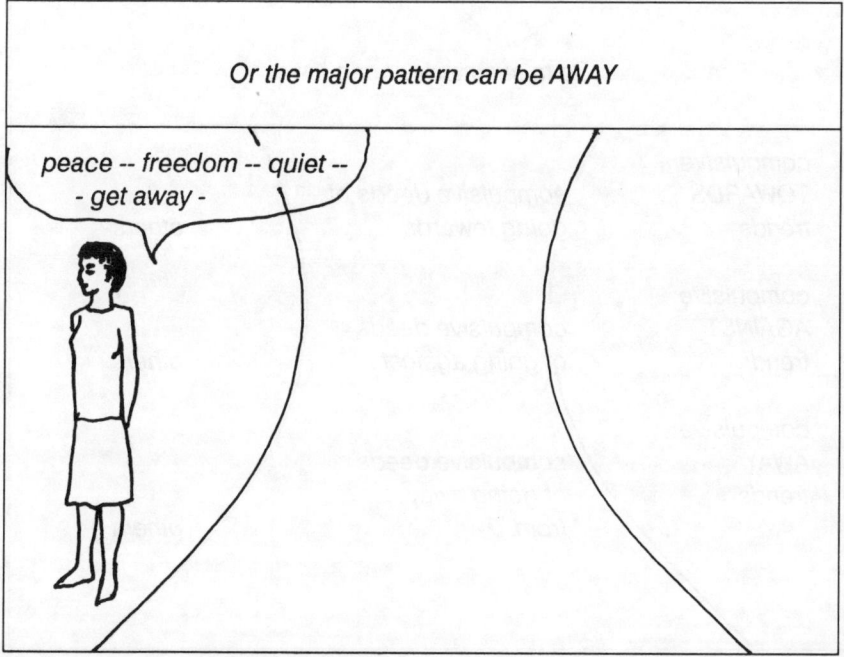

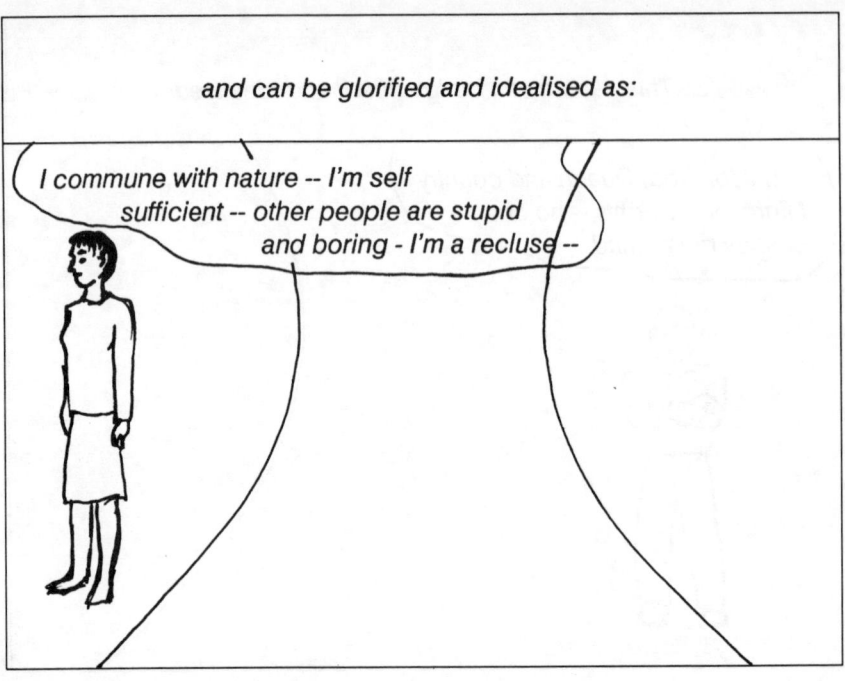

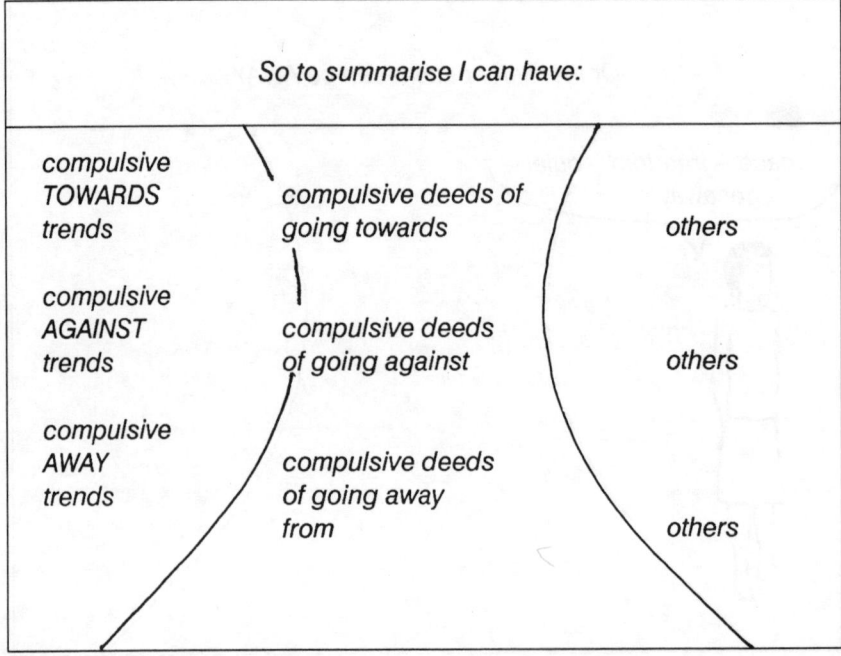

Karen Horney summarises these as:

Trends	Compulsive Deeds	World
compulsive TOWARDS	the never ending search for love	others
compulsive AGAINST	the never ending search for glory and control	others
compulsive AWAY	the never ending search for peace	others

All building the Idealised Self

Remember that each of the above has its Creative Opposite

CREATIVE TREND	DISCRIMINATING DEED	WORLD
creative TOWARDS	chosen love	others
creative AGAINST	principled fighting for what you think right	others
creative AWAY	getting space and time for your own creative activity	others

If one compulsive trend dominates, you will almost certainly find that others continue to exist unconsciously and may suddenly and seemingly inexplicably erupt. The previously compliant teenager may for example suddenly find himself in a phase of indiscriminately rebelling against everyone and everything

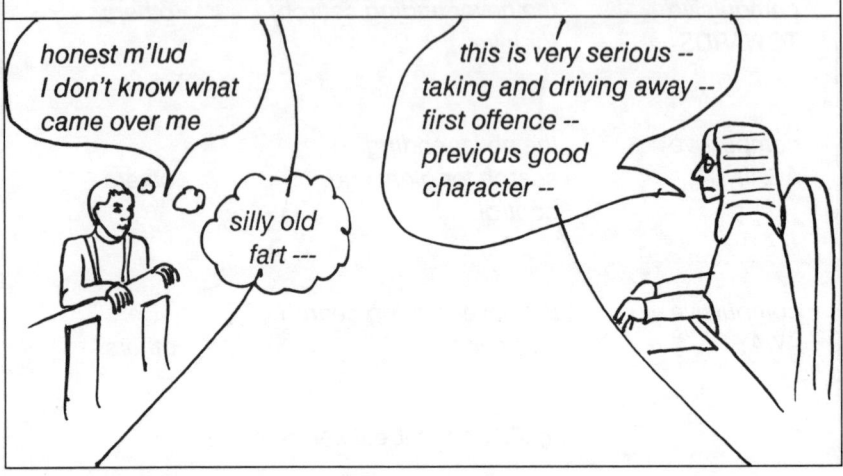

Exercise for two people
First do 20 minutes each way with discussion for 20 minutes. We suggest you repeat this session at least once

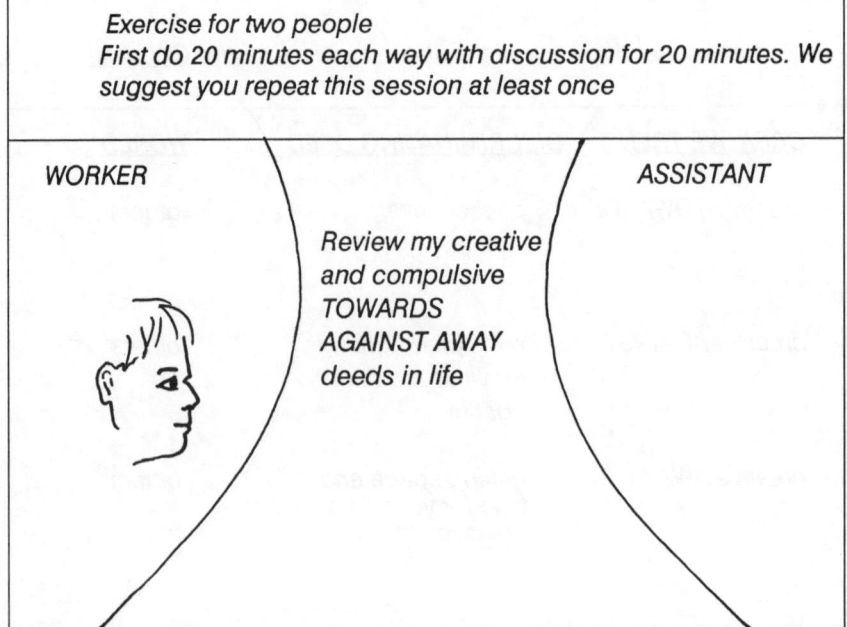

EXAMPLE OF SCANNING ON COMPULSIVE AND CREATIVE TOWARDS - AGAINST - AWAY TRENDS

WORKER "The thing that puzzles me about all this is that when you're a kid you don't really have much choice - you love your mum and dad because if you don't love them who are you going to love? And you need to be loved and looked after - so that means that everything you feel as a kid is bound to be compulsive, and that doesn't feel right. I don't feel that I was compulsive as a kid. I think I was much more spontaneous then. It's when I grew up that I got compulsive. (Pause)

One of the things I find hardest in this counselling lark is talking about me, about what I actually feel. I always want to have a discussion - to talk about whether I think the ideas are correct - rather than stick to my life, my experience. I've always been a bit like that. As a kid I always wanted to know how things worked. I asked endless questions - why? why? why? Where does this come from? How do you know that? My grandad called me the philosopher. I hated girl's talk. I thought girls were soppy - always kissing each other. I hated being kissed or touched in any way. It made me cringe. It was as much the words that went with that kind of thing. Sometimes my mum would try to take me on her knee and she'd put her face in my hair and pull me close to her and say 'Give your mum a hug then - show me how much you love me.' And I'd go all stiff. I'd clench my fists and tighten my body. My dad didn't like her doing it either. He used to tell her to leave me alone - said she'd turn me into a nancy-boy. I didn't know what it meant but I didn't like the sound of it. I wanted to be like him. He was a big strong man, very broad in the chest - bricklayer, used to carrying heavy weights. Didn't say a lot. My mum used to say he looked like Clark Gable - the strong, silent type. She used to say that when she had to apologise for him being morose at family gatherings.

I'm a bit like him in some ways - I was as a child too, though I was always a bit afraid of him. I suppose you could say I was a bit 'away' as far as expressing feelings was concerned. Yet I think it was a creative thing in a way - it was to avoid getting suffocated by my mother and my sisters. There were always so many women in the house. I was the only boy. It's almost like I had to struggle to be male or they'd have turned me into another girl. Now, I don't know so much though. I have this idea that it would be better if I expressed my feelings more, but deep down I don't really want to. Pat always likes me to say to her 'I love you' and stuff like that. I do love her but I don't like saying it. It doesn't seem necessary to me, but it's quite important to her. (Pause) I think she's compulsive about that. (Pause) I think I'm quite spontaneous in my feelings towards my kids. Far more spontaneous than my parents were towards me. I wish I could express things more - but that's about all. When I'm angry with them I tell them. When I want to be on my own I tell them to piss off. Sometimes I get angry with them about trivial things though. Linda'll do something daft like spill her cornflakes on the table and it's the last straw and I'll shout at her. I think that's a bit compulsive. I feel bad about it because it's easier to shout at kids - they're so powerless... can't hit back. It comes back to what I was saying at the beginning - kids *don't* have much choice..."

etc, etc.

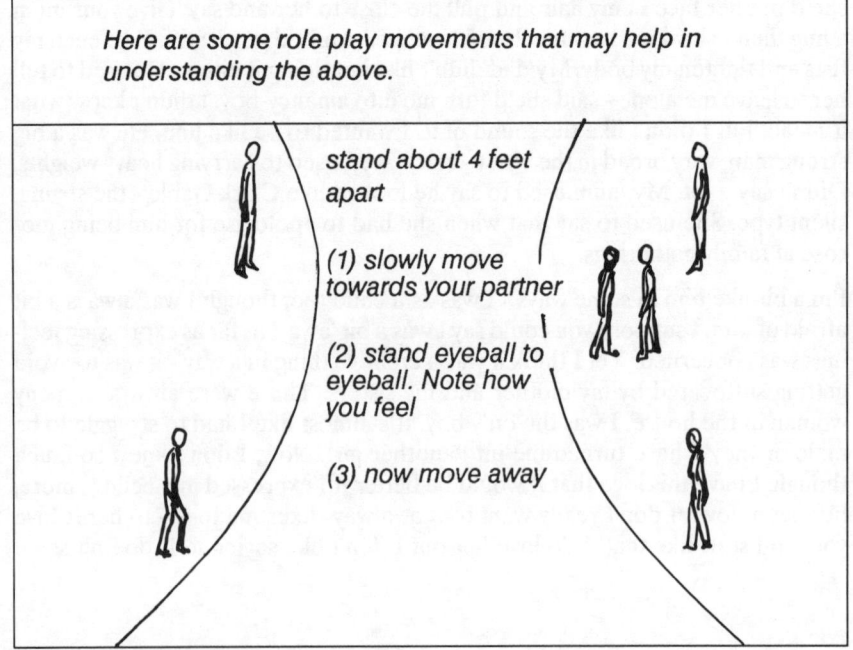

Here are some role play movements that may help in understanding the above.

stand about 4 feet apart

(1) slowly move towards your partner

(2) stand eyeball to eyeball. Note how you feel

(3) now move away

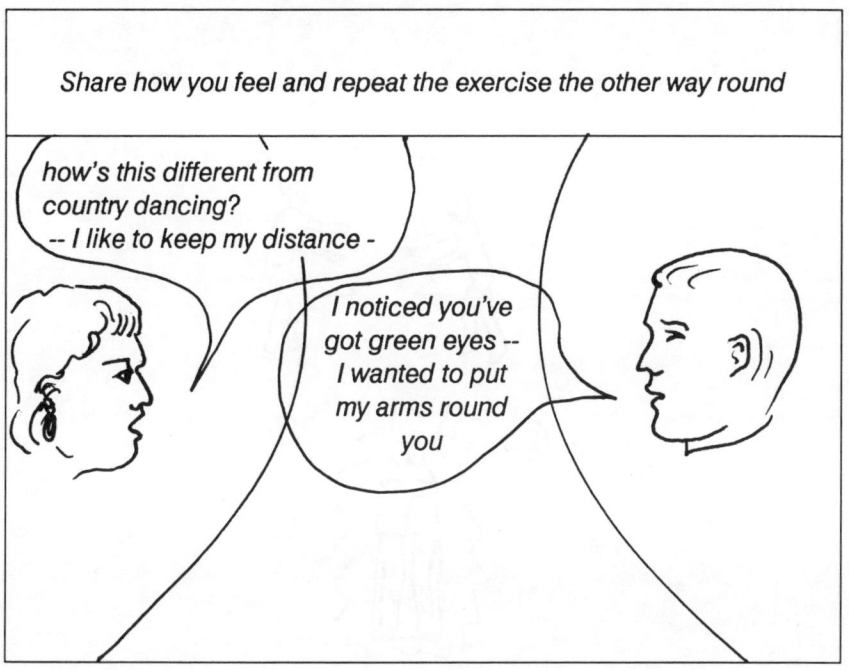

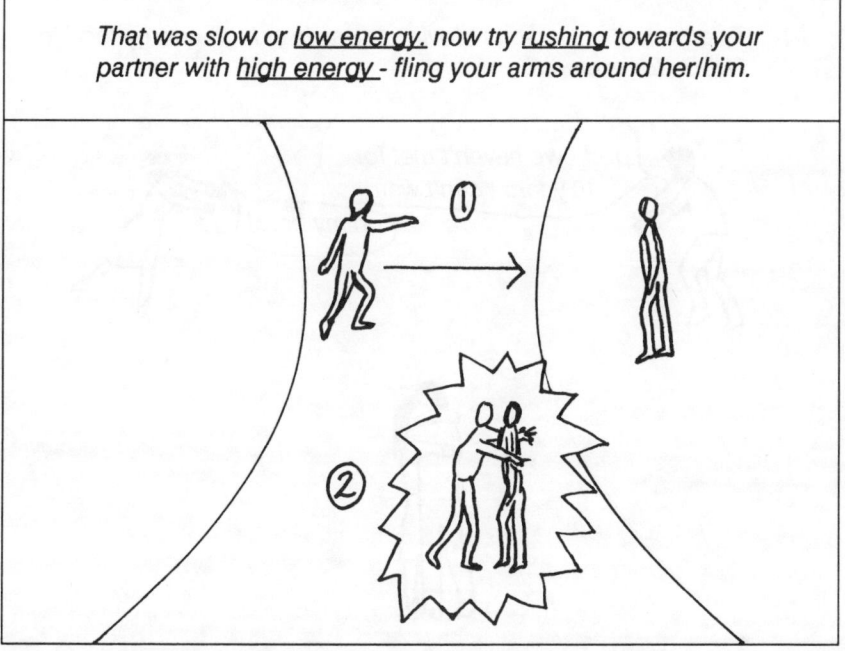

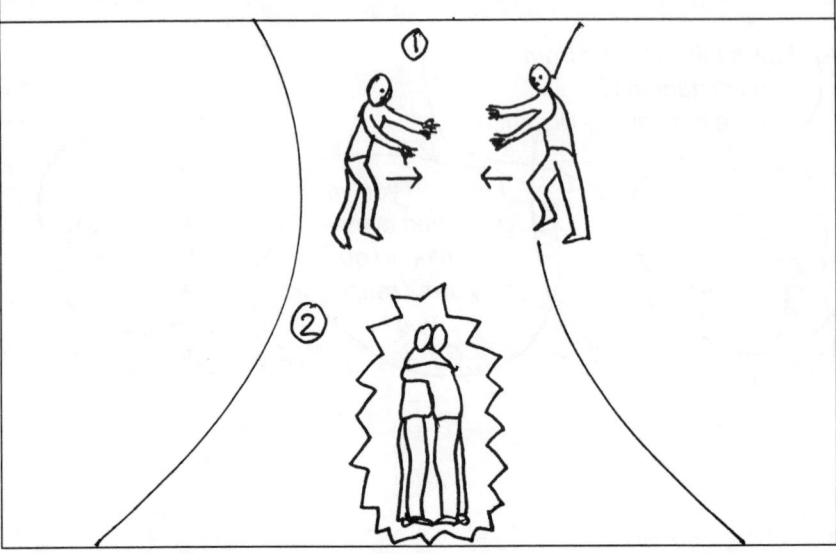

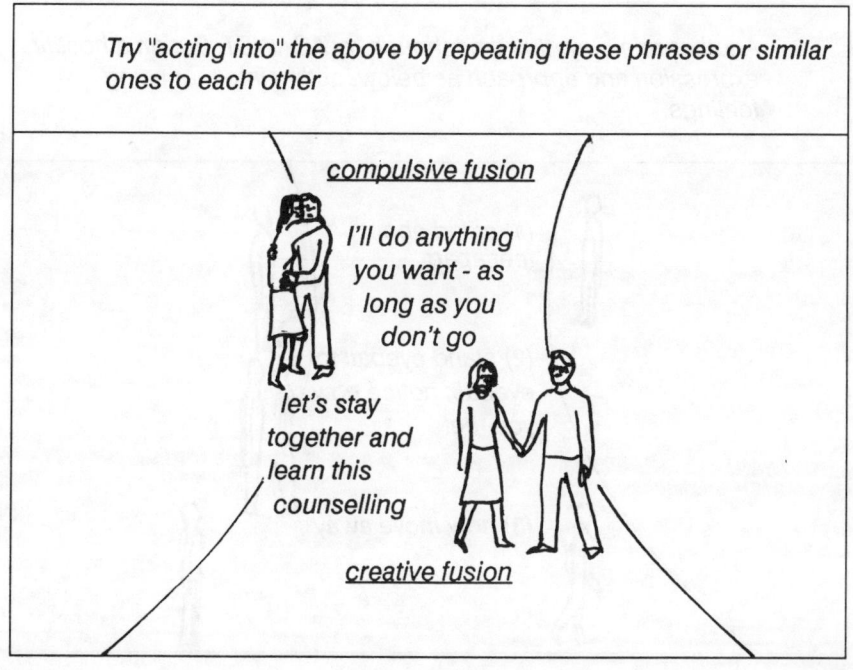

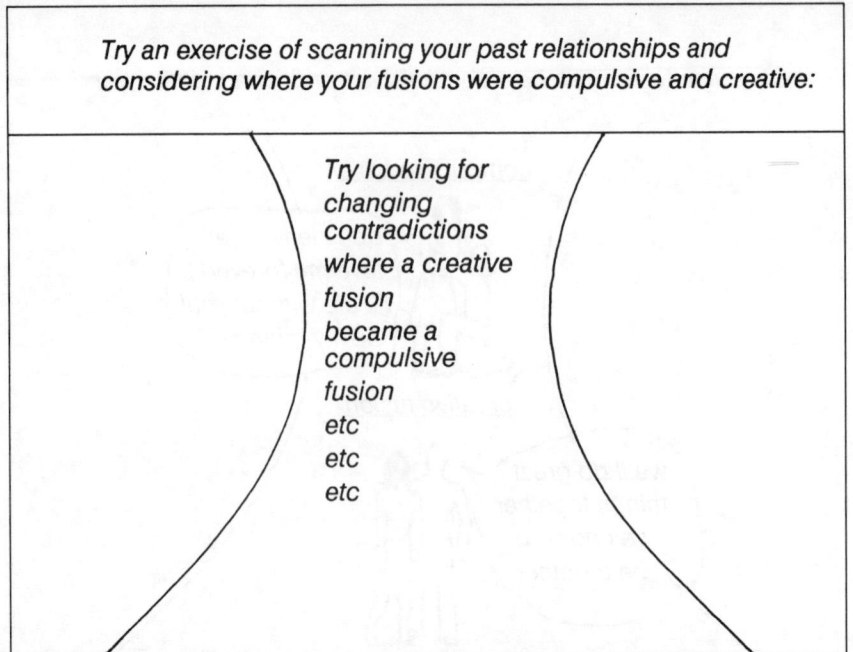

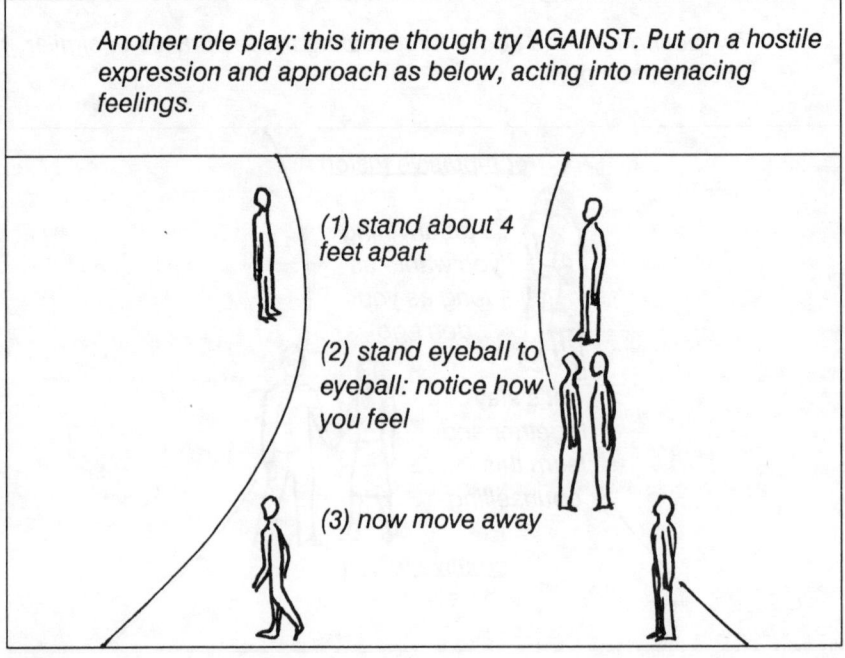

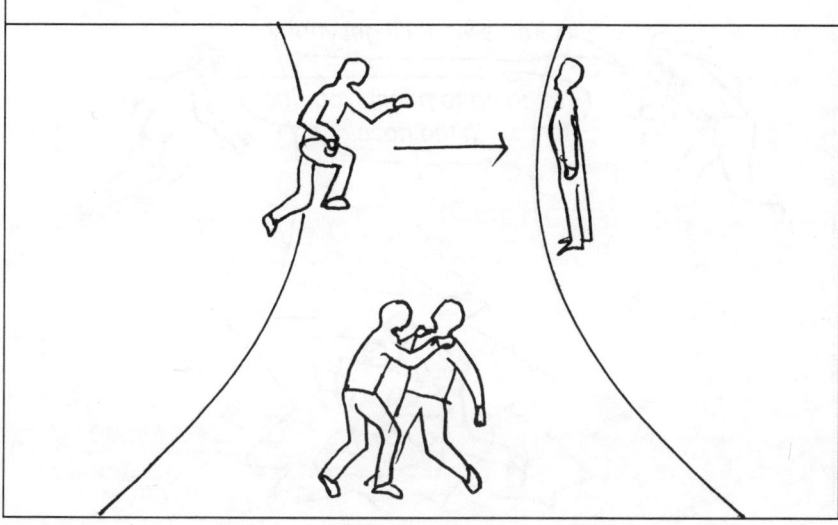

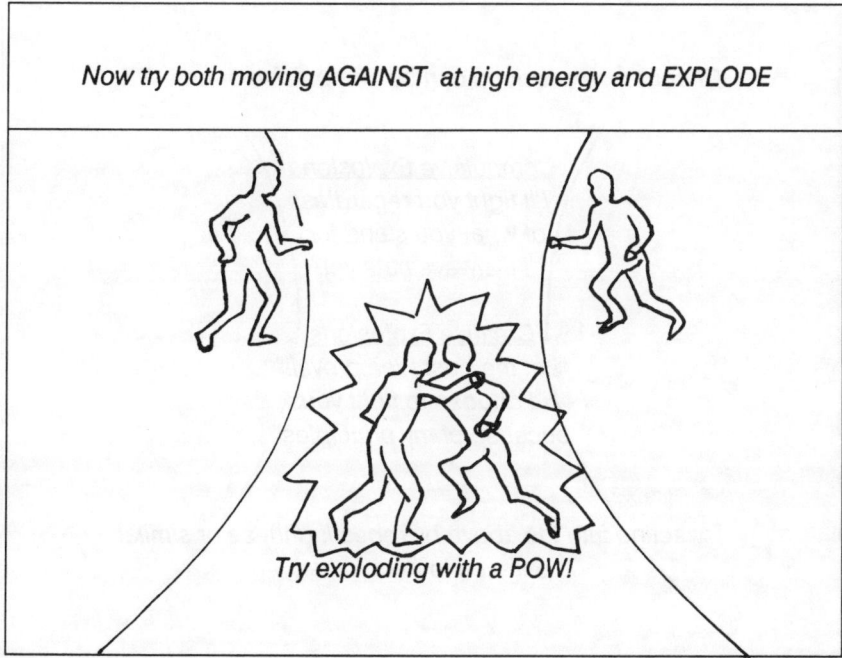

Two bodies or persons moving at high energy AGAINST tend to EXPLODE

Of course, explosions can be compulsive or creative

<u>Compulsive Explosions</u>
"I'll fight you regardless of what you stand for"
"I'll always hate you"

<u>Creative Explosions</u>
"Let the best idea prevail"
"I choose to fight you because of my principles"

Try acting into the above by repeating these or similar phrases to each other.

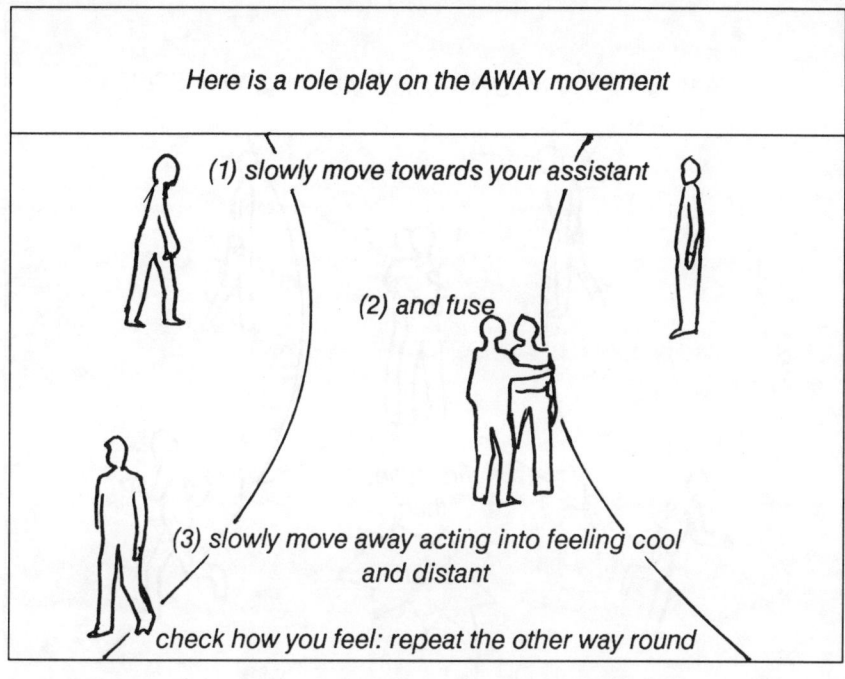
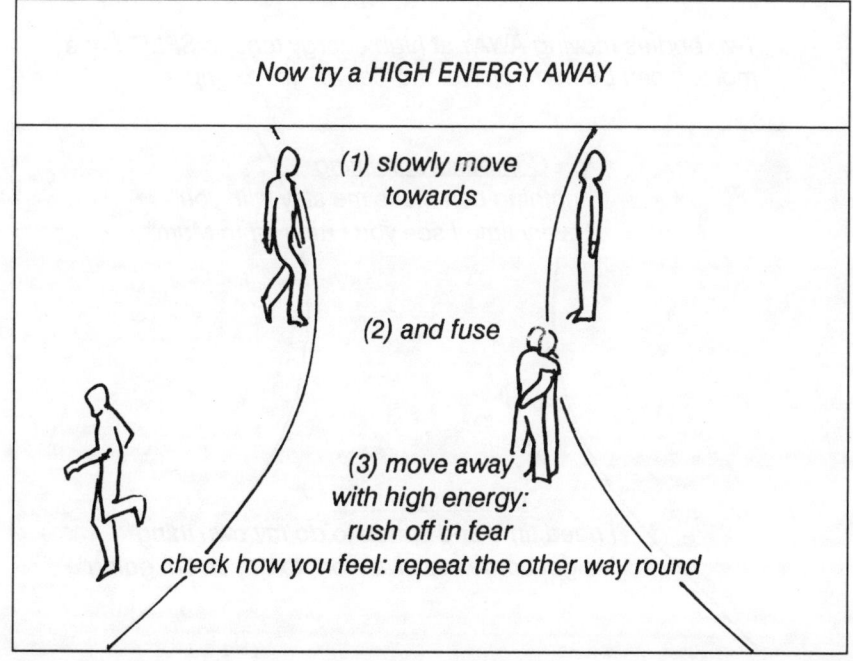

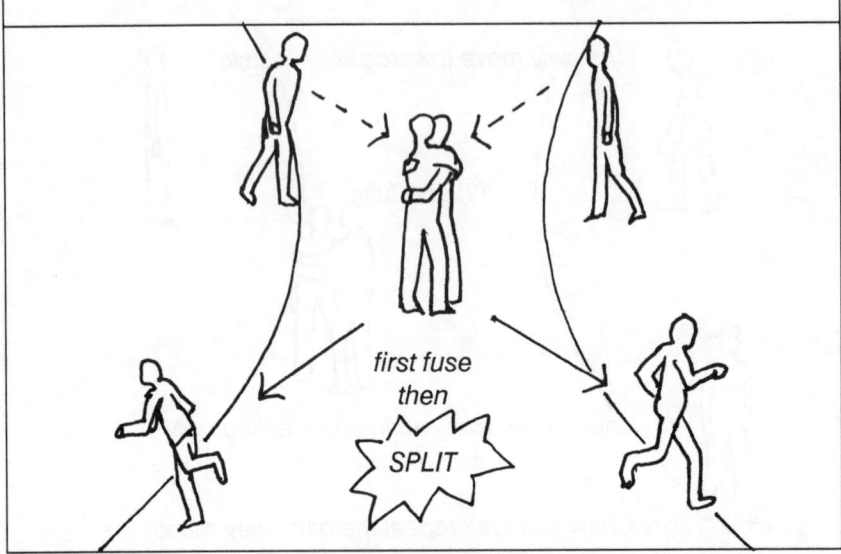

Now try both moving AWAY at high energy and SPLIT

first fuse then SPLIT

Two bodies moving AWAY at high energy tend to SPLIT once more. It can be compulsive or creative - for example

<u>Compulsive Splitting</u>
"nothing can make me stay with you"
"every time I see you I rush off to Mum"

<u>Creative Splitting</u>
"I need time and space to do my own thing"
"I've got some creative work to do, so I'm going"

We can now summarise these basic movements, which we use for all kinds of different reasons.

high energy TOWARDS	tendency to fusion	high energy TOWARDS
high energy AGAINST	tendency to EXPLOSION	tendency AGAINST
high energy AWAY	tendency to SPLITTING	high energy AWAY

Exercise: try (at least once) session of 20 minutes each way and:

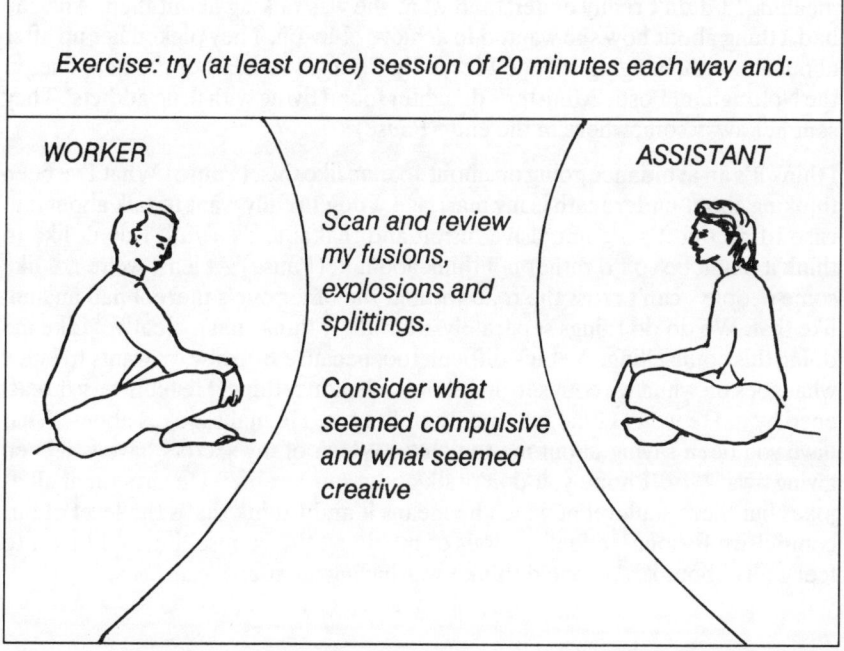

WORKER

ASSISTANT

Scan and review my fusions, explosions and splittings.

Consider what seemed compulsive and what seemed creative

EXAMPLE OF SCANNING ON COMPULSIVE AND CREATIVE FUSIONS, EXPLOSIONS AND SPLITS

WORKER "It makes me think of physics lessons at school - learning about splitting the atom. My friend Joanna who was so clever she understood everything first time around. I guess you could say that relationship was a creative fusion. We were very different people. Her dad was a methodist minister and they lived in a horrible, cold, dark house next to the church. They were quite poor because she had a lot of brothers and sisters and I don't think he earned much, but they were middle class people - educated - cared that their kids got educated. She used to like coming to my house she said because there was always a fire and the telly on and no-one asked her if she'd done her homework or what she'd learnt at school and my dad used to give us a sip of his beer sometimes. It was funny because I think I liked the things she hated in her own house - the rooms full of books and the solemn atmosphere, and she genuinely liked some of the things I was ashamed of in my house - like my mother putting out the lace tablecloth and the best tea things whenever anyone came to tea. We shared a lot, Joanna and I. We'd spent hours just talking - boyfriends, sex - she taught me how to masturbate - politics, religion, everything. And then she ran away from home. It was when we were 16. It was quite a scandal locally. She got very quiet over a few months - wouldn't talk in the old way, didn't want to come out. She sat in her room reading these books her father had - Nietszche and Kierkegaard. I've never forgotten the names though I've never read the books. She'd keep talking about - what was the meaning of life? How did you know it had a meaning? I didn't really understand what she was talking about then. And she had a thing about how she wanted to achieve oblivion. They picked her up after about a month, hanging around Piccadilly Circus. I remember the headlines in the Nottingham Post - 'Minister's daughter found living with drug addicts'. They sent her away somewhere in the end. (Pause)

I think it's an avoidance going on about Joanna like this. (Pause) What I've been thinking about underneath is my marriage. I don't really want to talk about it in case I find out it's a compulsive fusion and that sounds awful. I don't like to think it might be so I'd rather not think about it. (Pause) At least we're not like some people - can't cross the road without the other one's there. I had an aunt like that. We do do things separately after all - I think that's creative. Like me doing this counselling. Yet it's difficult too, because Bob always wants to know what goes on when we counsel - it's almost a jealousy thing. He feels very threatened by it. He won't come out openly and say so. He makes jokes about 'What have you been saying about me tonight?' 'Which of my secrets have you been giving away?' or 'I hope you don't talk about our sex life.' He says them all as jokes but there's a level at which he means it and I think that's the level of our compulsive fusion. He feels jealous of me doing the counselling and I start to feel guilty about it. Anyone'd think I was having an affair. " *etc., etc..*

Finally, most of the time we are not simply in "one movement" towards, against or away but changing all the time circling about us ...

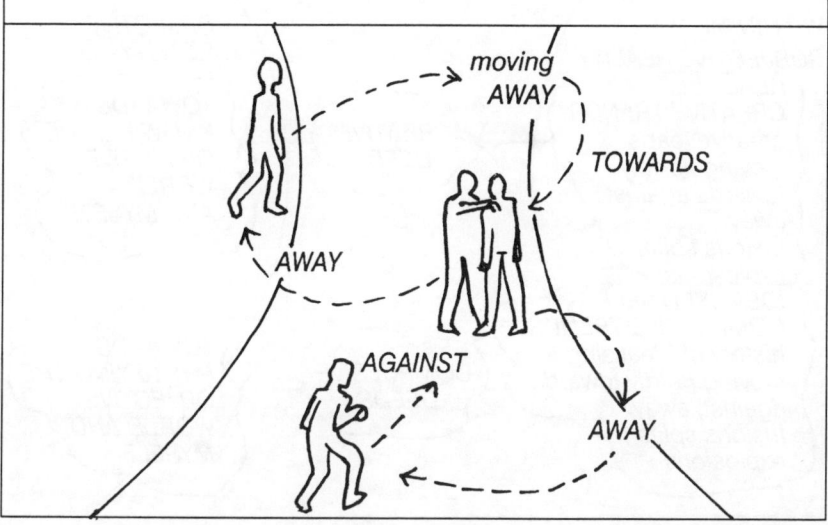

You can role play the above by walking round each other. This is usually fun done in a group

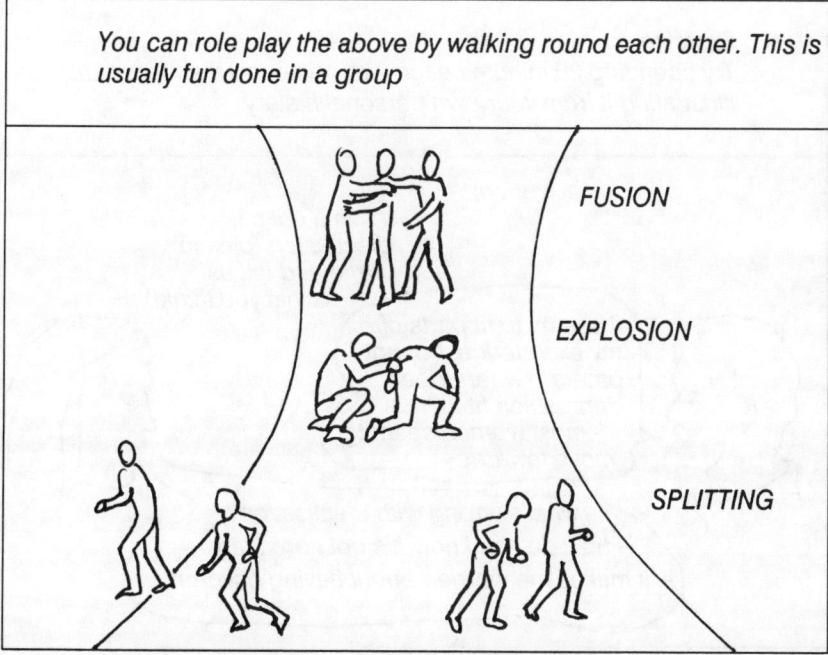

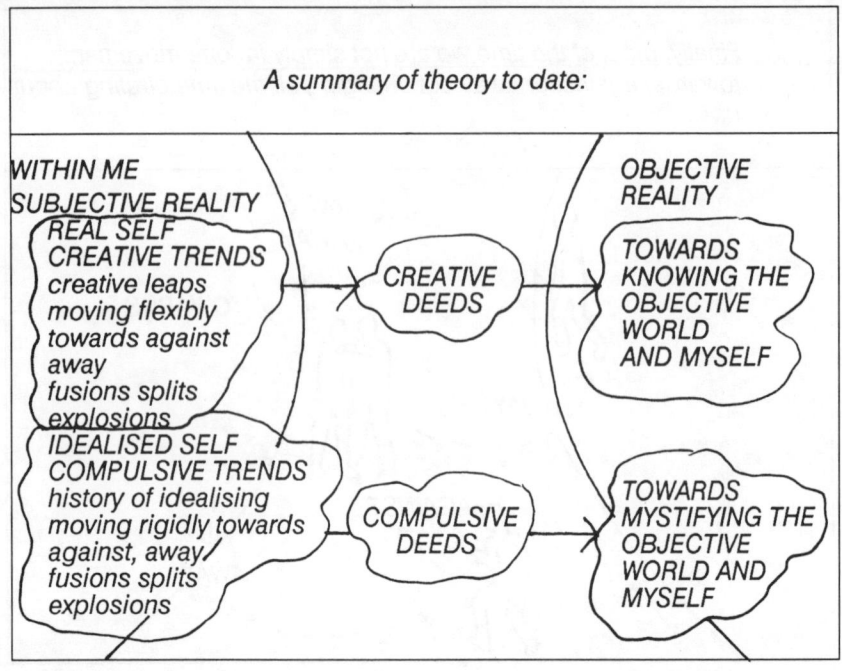

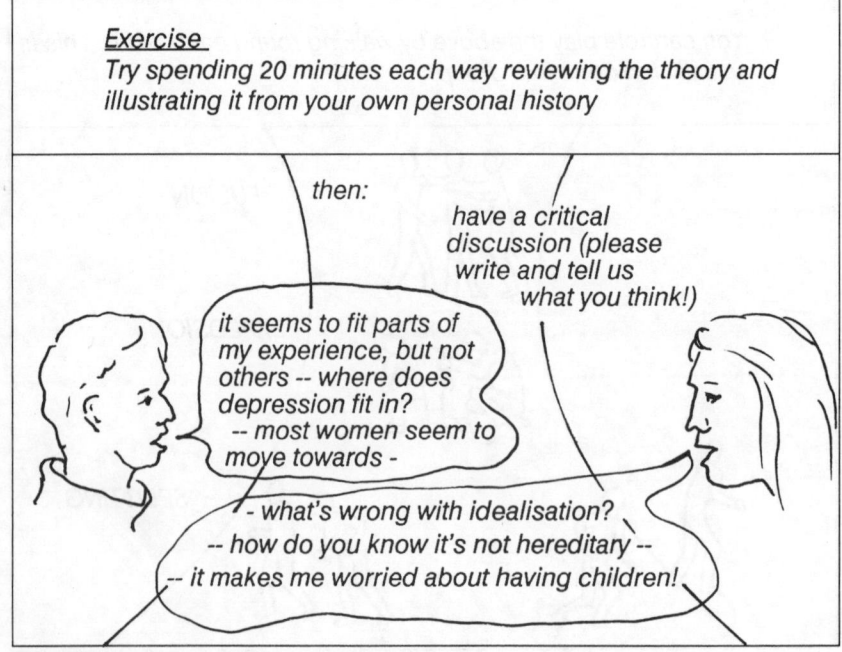

THE UNCONSCIOUS

For teaching purposes we have put off one of the most basic questions until the end of this section. This is the question of the unconscious.

There are a number of different definitions of what the unconscious is - for example, "It's just memory', 'It's things I've repressed', 'It's things I'd rather not know about', etc. For the moment we are going to put the question of definition to one side and try to look at how the unconscious develops. Once more, therefore, we return to mother and baby.

One term we use probably requires a few words of explanation. That is 'orgasmic drives'. By this we don't mean the genital orgasm that is experienced by the adult in sexual relations. We mean the process of tension leading to discharge and rest which can apply to a number of experiences, not just to sexuality.

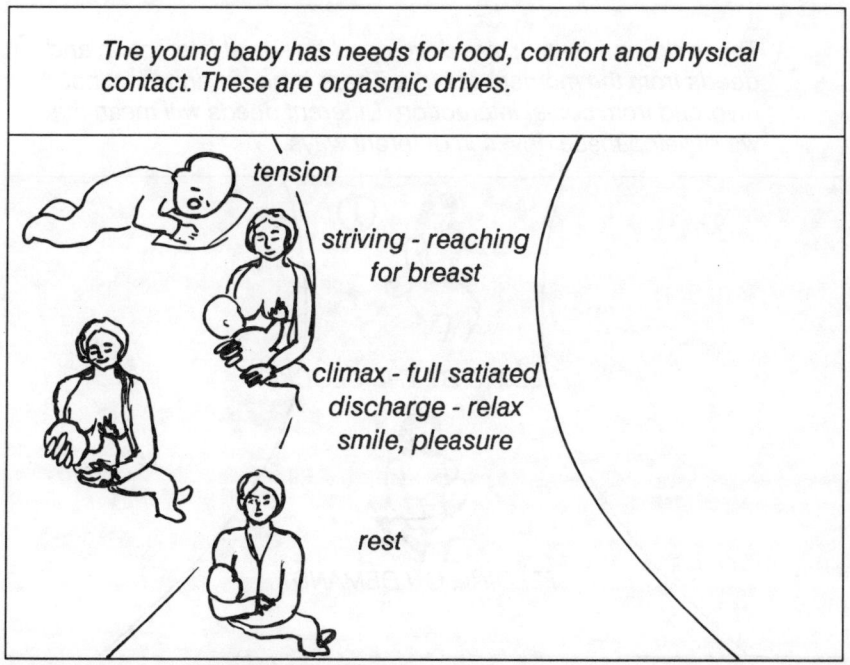

Not only is food essential, but physical handling also. Experimental work has shown that animals deprived of physical contact die even if fed. Their spines shrivel up.

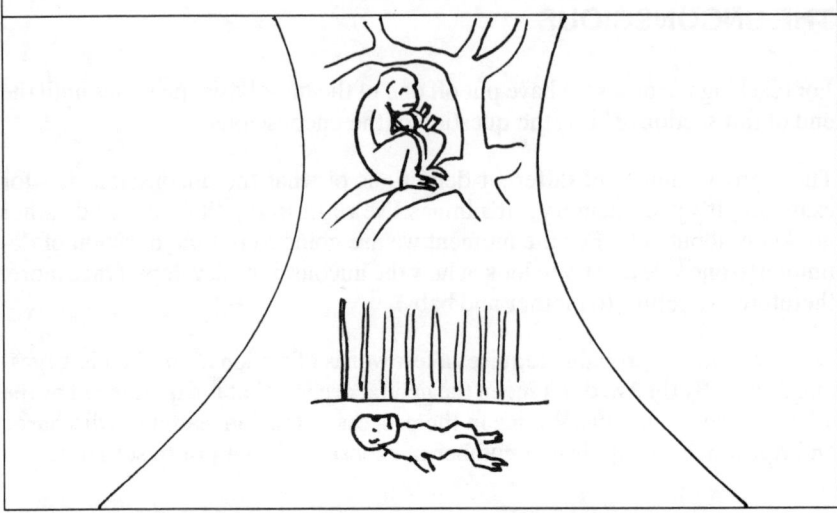

These drives within us are developed by social interaction and deeds from the moment of birth. There is no separate instinct divorced from social interaction. Different deeds will mean that we develop these drives in different ways.

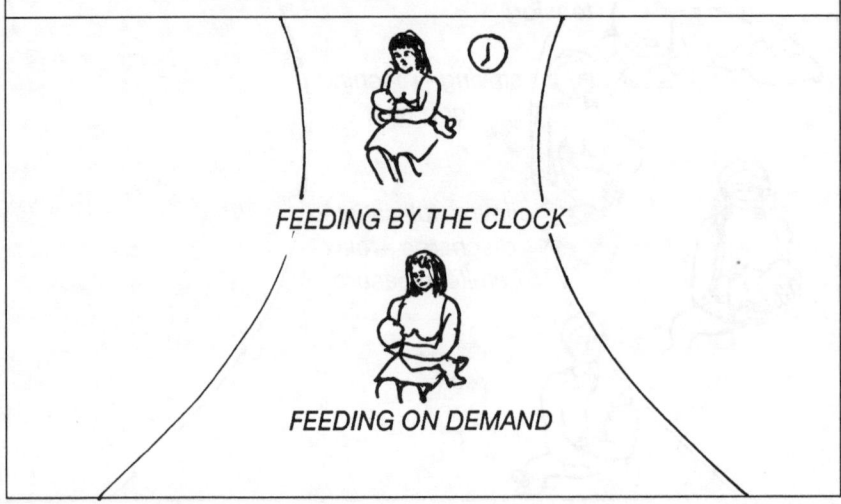

FEEDING BY THE CLOCK

FEEDING ON DEMAND

Through experience and action baby is in a continuous process of change and development - the change of quantity and quality we will refer to in section 2. Without the deeds we die - "instincts" and all.

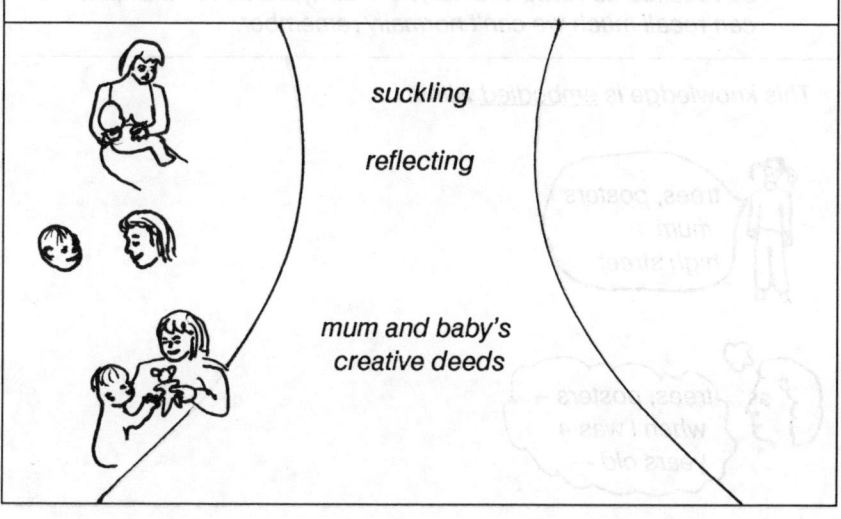

suckling

reflecting

mum and baby's creative deeds

At any moment baby is experiencing immediate impressions. This is also true of us through life though as we develop we learn new ways of organising the impressions we receive.

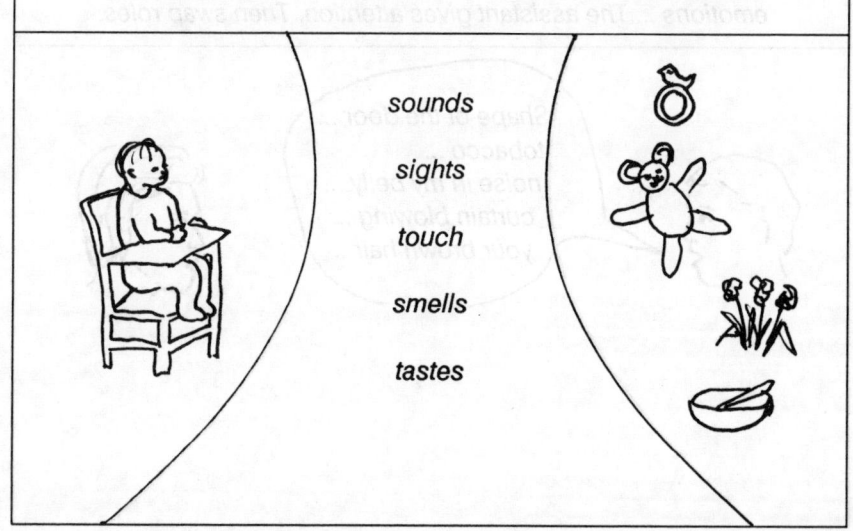

sounds

sights

touch

smells

tastes

Nothing we experience is ever "lost". Very early experience is embodied physically in the way muscular and bodily structure develops. Later experience (from the time speech develops) can be recalled as verbal memory. Under hypnosis for example, we can recall much we can't normally remember.

This knowledge is <u>embodied</u> within us.

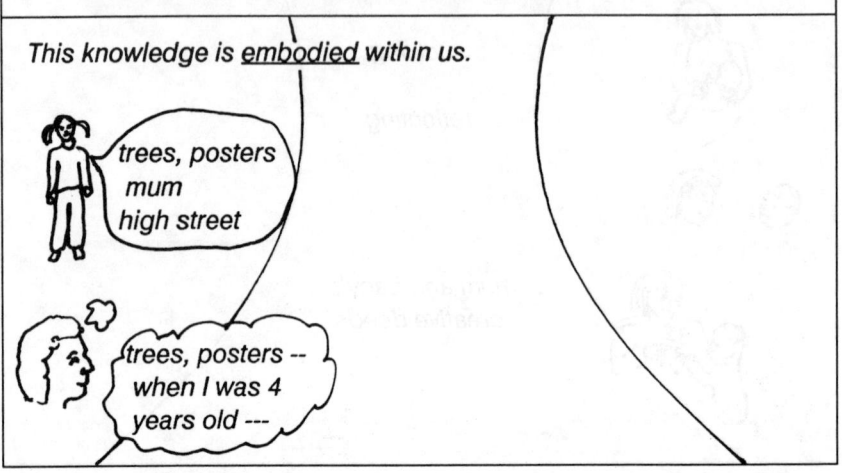

Try this exercise:
The worker tries to say each immediate impression he is experiencing "here and now" - smells, sights, body sensations, emotions ....The assistant gives attention. Then swap roles.

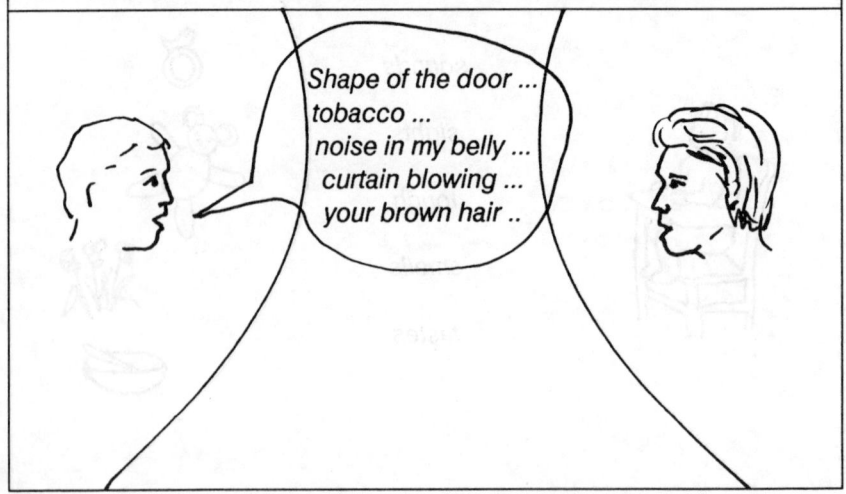

Our most deeply unconscious processes are literally embodied in us. These are sometimes referred to as reflexes. Examples would be the functioning of our organs and central nervous system, which we are normally unaware of and do not need to think about e.g. usually breathe, digest, etc. without thinking.

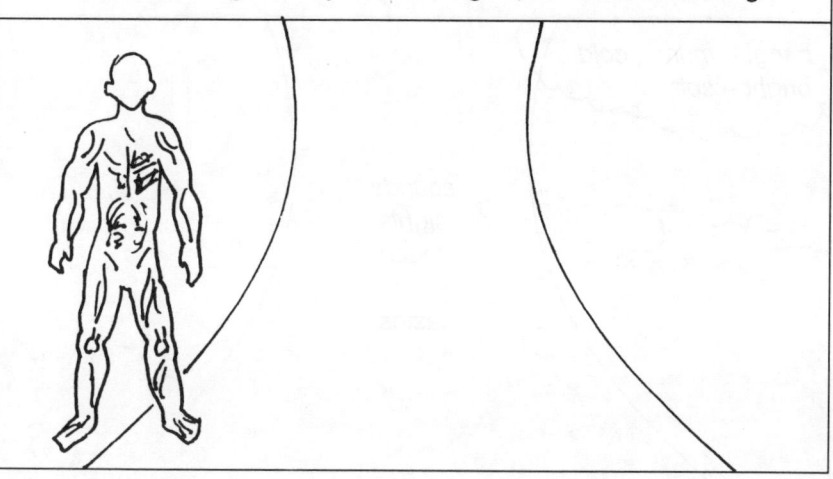

Other impressions are also embodied in our physical/thinking self. A good comparison is with food. By eating food I embody it within me. In this process I, the food and my relation to the environment all change.

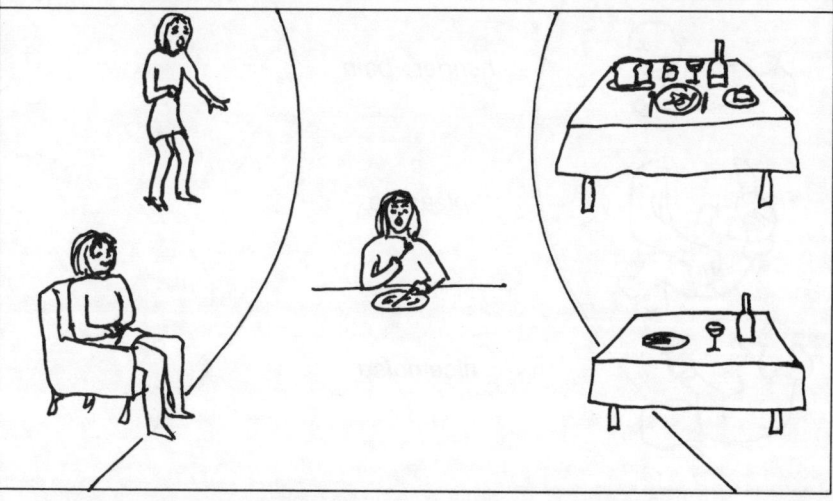

So - all impressions are embodied within us. In a baby this process is totally unconscious. As we develop, parts of it become conscious

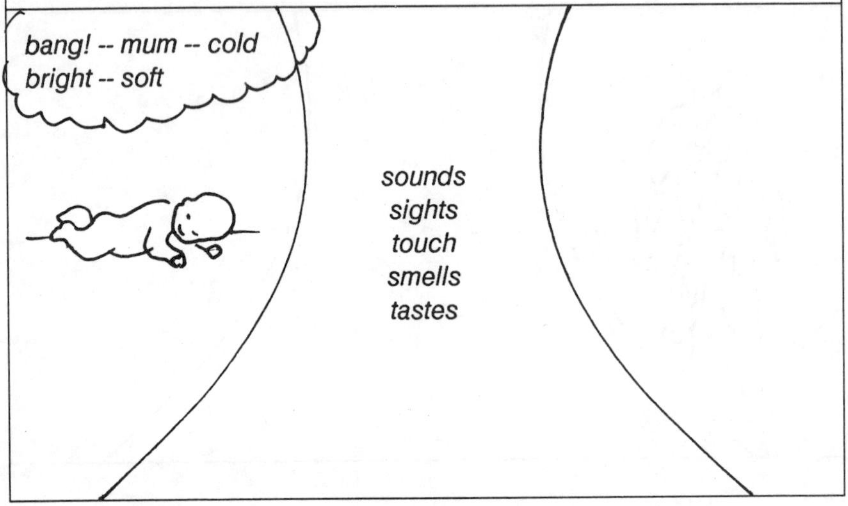

bang! -- mum -- cold
bright -- soft

sounds
sights
touch
smells
tastes

Like all creatures, we experience the world by association. This starts as a simple process but develops through qualitative changes to a very complex one.

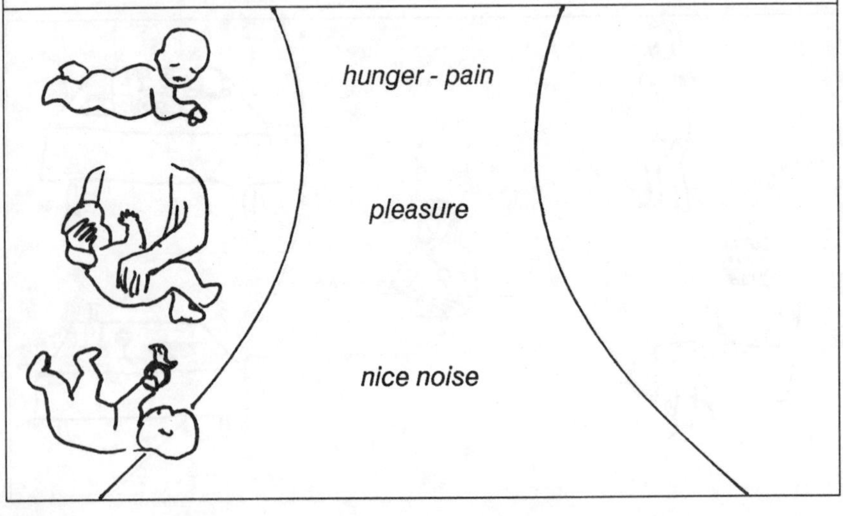

hunger - pain

pleasure

nice noise

This basic process takes place before the development of locic and conscious understanding and continues after it. **TRY THIS EXERCISE**. The assistant says any word that comes to mind. The worker responds with whatever thought or image occurs to him. Try this a number of times and check what the associations are.

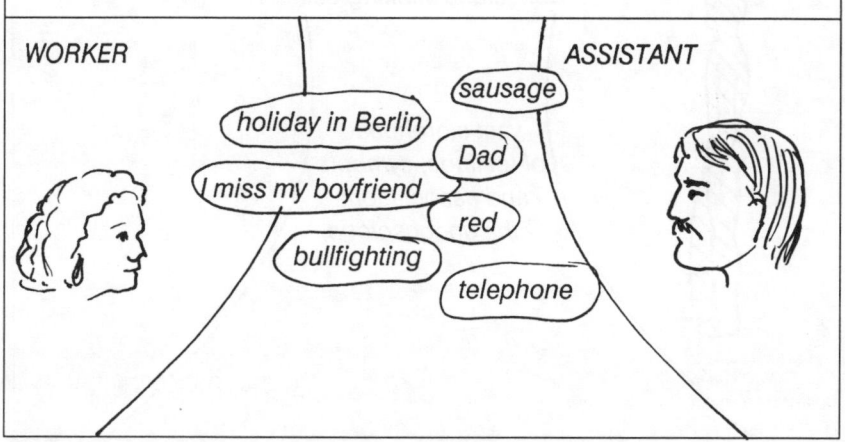

EXERCISE The worker talks letting the thoughts and images follow each other in an associative way. The assistant helps the worker to trace the connections - how did one image lead to the next? How is the chain of images built up? You can do this exercise by yourself - for instance while waiting for a bus.

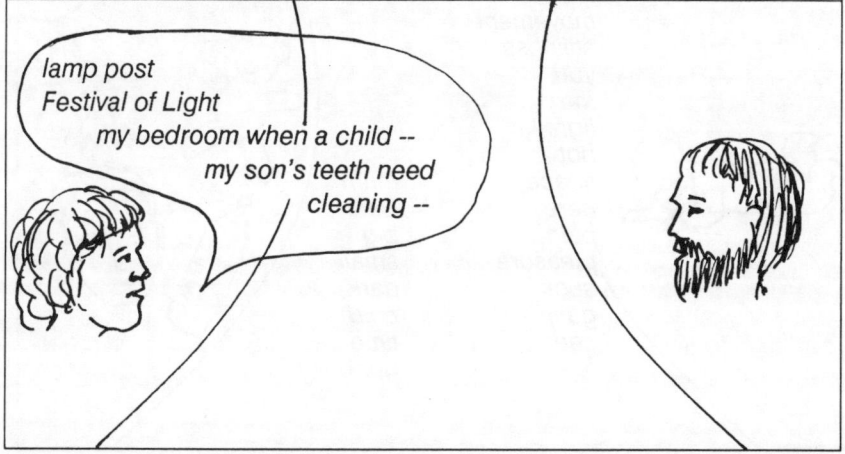

All the impressions, sensations and stimuli from the environment interact with that "vast storehouse of knowledge" that is our unconscious self. The unconscious is by far the larger part of the self.

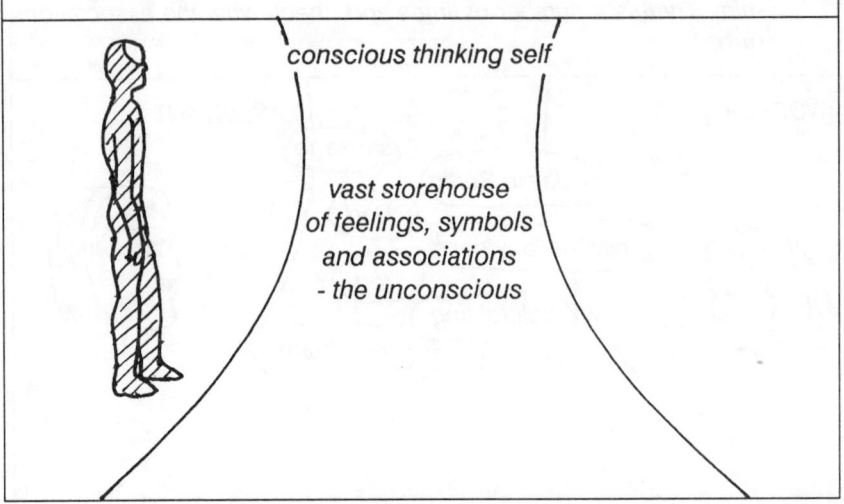

The extent of our unconscious intelligence is breath taking. To reproduce even some of the processes of one person electronically would cover the whole country with machinery. No wonder it has taken 8 thousand million years to evolve. A young baby can unconsciously take in more data than at any future time in its life.

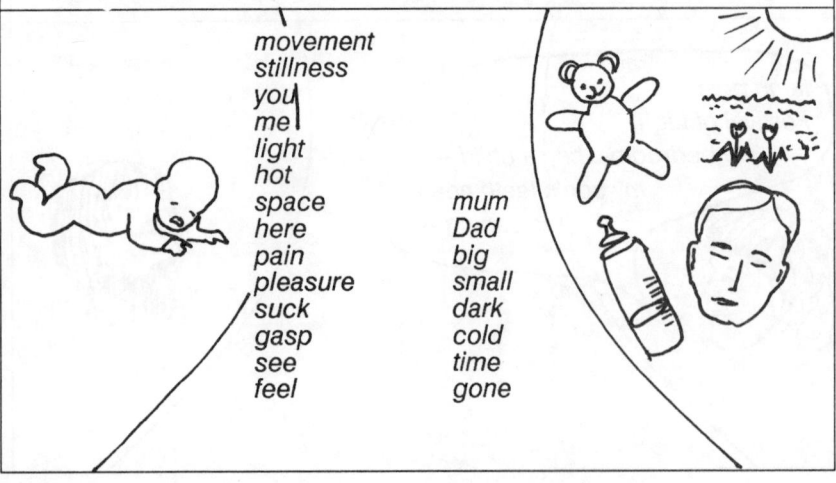

The unconscious is most clearly available to us when we sleep and dream. This was one of Freud's great discoveries. However it is not some hidden subterranean world. It is with us all the time, which is why it is called <u>unc</u>onscious, not <u>sub</u>conscious.

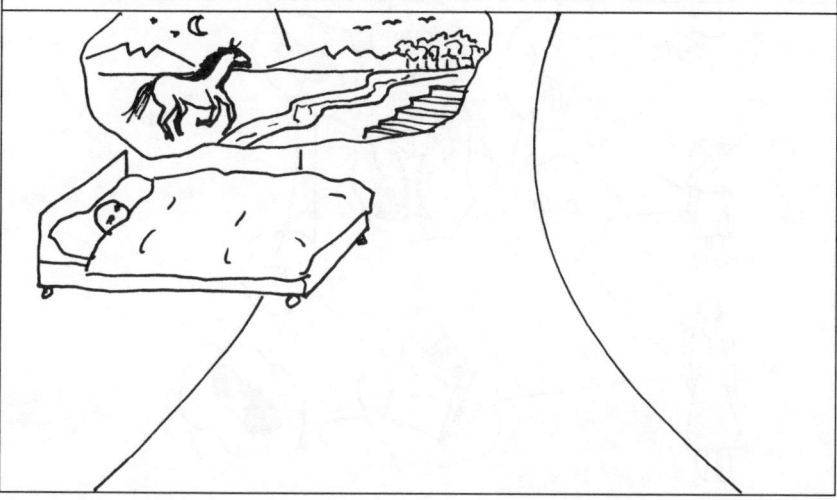

The unconscious is part of the material world, of nature. It exists just as our heart, kidneys or liver do, quite regardless of any theories we may have in our heads about whether or not the unconscious exists.

The language of the unconscious remains the same throughout life. It is a language of feelings, associations and symbols. It is not logical or rational in the ordinary sense.

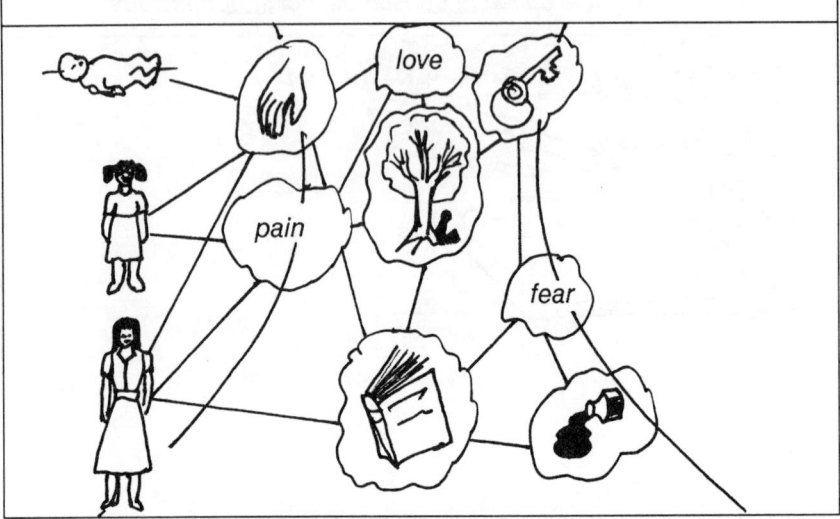

Most of our experience is contained within our unconscious. That is:

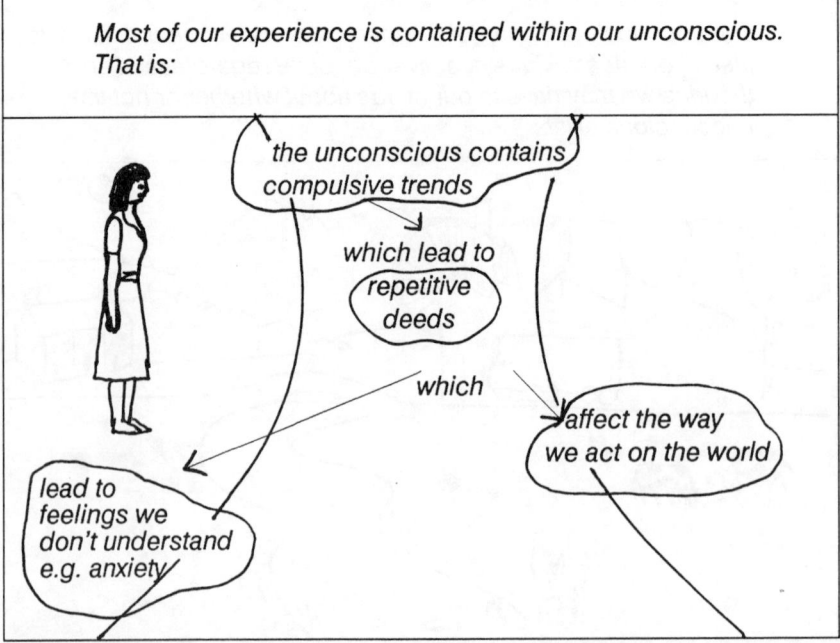

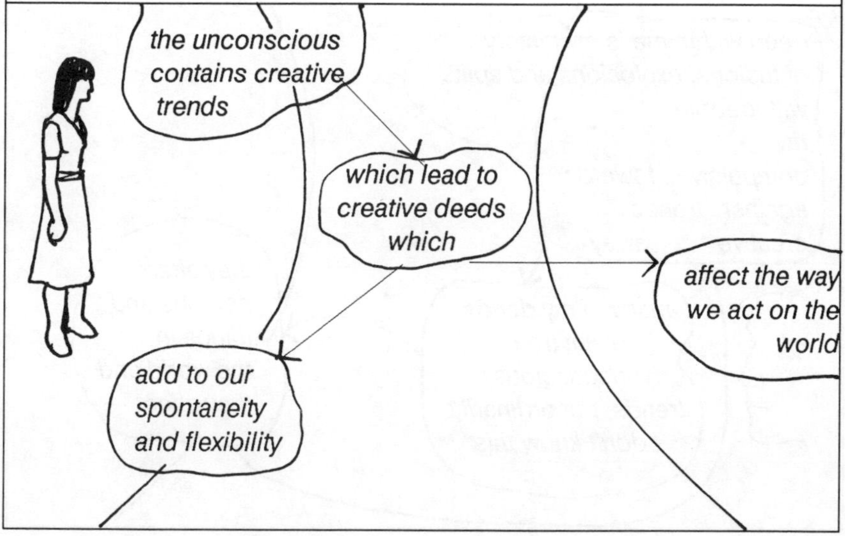

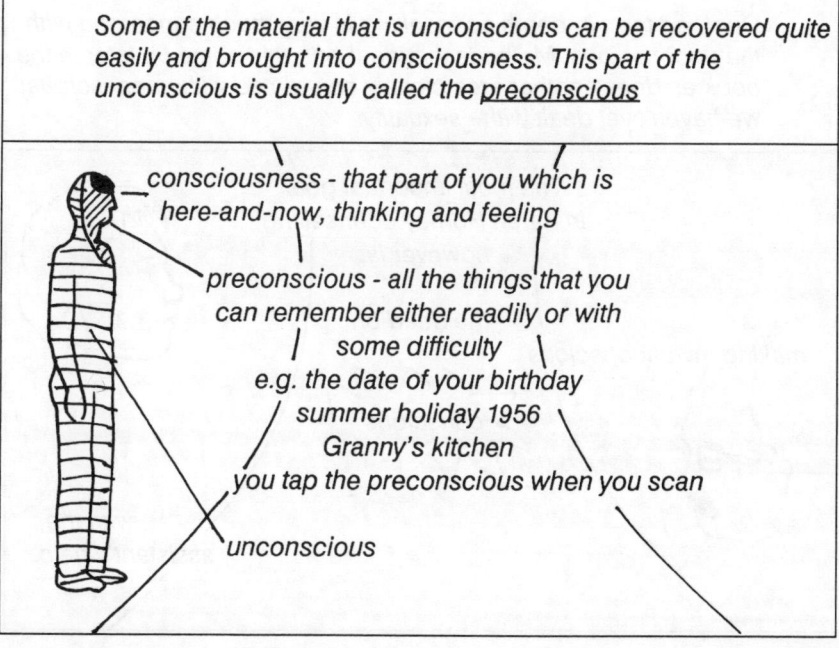

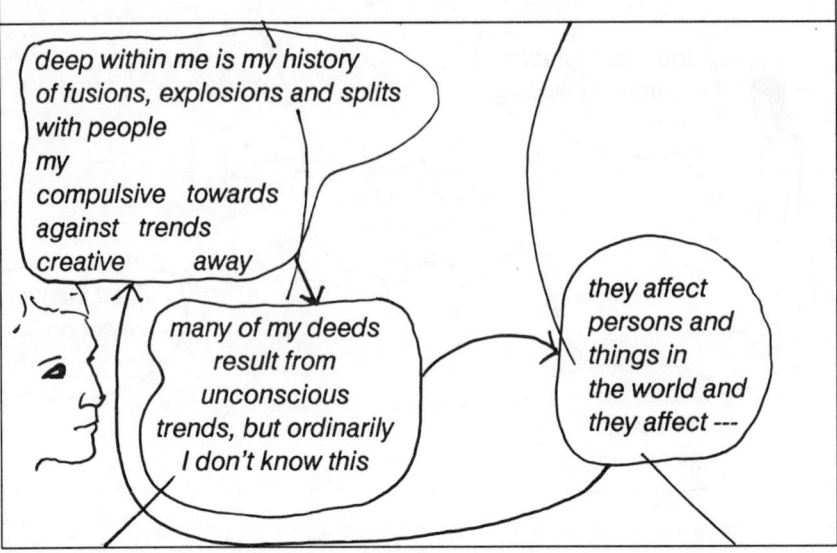

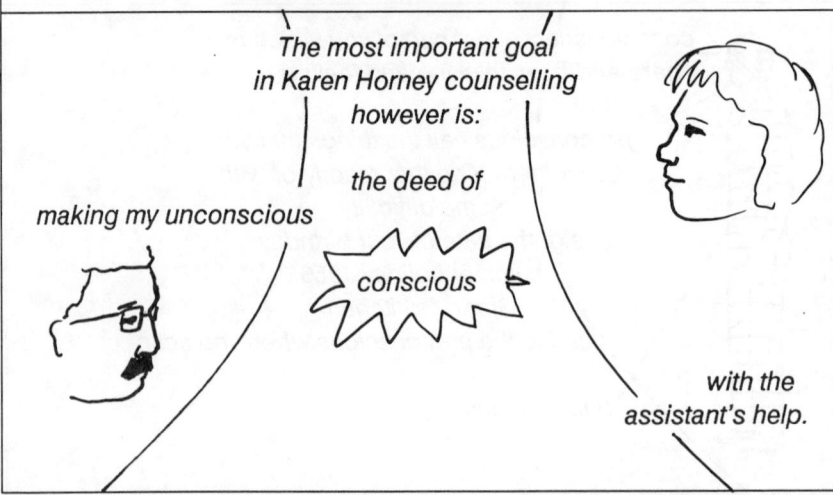

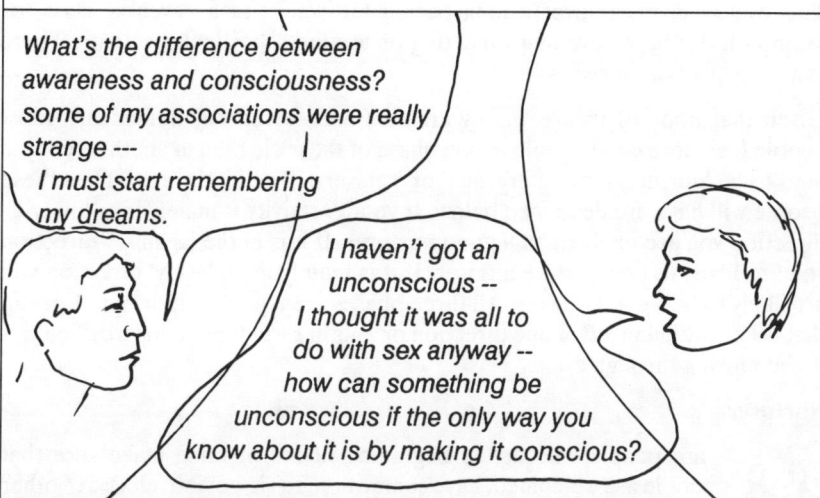

WORKING IN A GROUP

Most of the exercises in the book have been described as if for two people working on their own. Many people have found it more useful to set up a group in order to teach themselves counselling. More people means greater possibilities of support and discussion and a wider variety of potential partners.

The best size for a group of this kind is between seven and fourteen members. With more than fourteen of you it becomes difficult to relate adequately to everyone. With less than seven you hardly feel like a group.

The phases of a group

On p. 77 we talk about orgasmic drives of the baby and the phases of tension, charge, discharge and rest. This *orgasmic cycle* can be applied to almost any activity that is creatively performed and it can be useful to look at the activity of a group in these terms. A group that is working creatively will go through these phases. We have called them:

The nurturing phase

The energising phase - where a peak/climax is achieved and something 'new' is produced

The relaxing phase

This cycle can occur over a long period (10 weeks of an evening class for example), during an evening's meeting or around a particular activity. There can be cycles within cycles.

Given that none of us are wholly creative and sorted out individuals, most people feel more comfortable in one phase of the cycle than in another. People tend to be 'nurturers' or 'energisers' or 'relaxers'. The kinds of qualities these people will have are described below. If your creativity is mainly in a 'towards' direction you are likely to be a good nurturer. If it is in the 'against' direction you are likely to be a good energiser. If it is mainly in an 'away' direction you are likely to be a good relaxer. All three phases are equally important. A group that is heavily balanced in one direction or another will tend to have difficulties in the moving through cycle.

Nurturers

 are people who at the beginning of the meeting make sure that people are welcomed, have somewhere to sit, get introduced to other people, know what is going on. They are likely to be warm, friendly, approaching others, concerned to make sure that people feel OK and have what they need. They are usually good listeners. They help with the *warming-up* process of the meeting. They help to make people feel *included* in what is going on. Where this process goes on too long or is handled badly you may feel that the 'nurturer' is rather like a mother hen fussing over a brood of chickens. Other people may nurture the group in a more cognitive way. These are the people who offer the basic information that is needed for the discussion and make sure the people understand it. They explain things. They may suggest ways of going about things and offer a framework for activity. They offer 'tools' that may help people to grasp what is going on. Where this process goes on too long or is handled badly you may feel overwhelmed by the amount of information and ideas that are offered, stuck in the particular framework suggested, or inhibited from discussion and argument. A typical state of affairs when this has happened is a fruitless 'question and answer' session.

Energisers
are people who excite a meeting with their enthusiasm. They charge the proceedings with their energy, and move things forward. They are active and spark things off. They want to get things going, get people involved in activity and don't like too much sitting around. They are full of suggestions, good at arguments, quick at making connections and not easily put down. Their energy may be mainly at an emotional (affective) level. Examples would be the person whose rousing speech moves people to action; the clown or joker who stirs everyone up; two people who are angrily going hammer and tongs at each other. Or their energy may be mainly at an ideas level (cognitive). These are the people who develop and spark things off each other and create new possibilities of action. Where for some reason the 'energising' phase starts at the wrong point, goes on too long or is handled badly you may feel attacked or locked in endless argument, overwhelmed and frustrated by too many ideas and activities, or unable to get a word in.

Relaxers
are the people who help to cool out a meeting, bring it down from its peak and tie up the loose ends. They are usually calm and good at summarising things so that people feel they go away knowing what happened and what was decided. At an emotional (affective) level these are the people who chat easily, move away from the main subject, express people's satisfaction at the completion of the task, suggest ways of ending the meeting. At an ideas level (cognitive) they are the people who are good at drawing conclusions, making the final links and seeing the totality of the discussion that has gone on. Where the 'relaxing' phase starts at the wrong point, goes on too long or is handled badly you may feel dissatisfied that things weren't properly talked about, that people drifted away from the subject, that time was wasted or that things were all too neatly wrapped up. A typical situation of this kind is where you realise afterwards that the conclusions you've come to don't cope with the problems you were discussing.

Things to do in a group
Some exercises for nurturing a new group

The object of these exercises is to introduce people to each other and to get you to feel at ease as a group. You can probably think of other similar things.

Introduce yourselves (You'd be surprised how often people forget to do this!) and sort out your practical arrangements - what time you will start and finish - how often you'll meet, etc.

30 second conversation. Everyone stands up. One person keeps time. You have 30 seconds with each other person in the group to say whatever you like. When the time keeper calls: "All change" you move on to another person.

The exercises outlined for pairs can all be done in a group - you just have to break into pairs for each exercise. One important point is that you should come back to the group for the discussion rather than having it in the pair. If you confine your discussion to the pairs you may find the pairs tend to become rather exclusive. If you discuss the exercise in the pair and then try to discuss it in the group you will probably find that you have run out of things to say by the time you get back to the group. Keeping the discussions in the group will help you maintain group cohesiveness.

Changing partners

In the early stages of a group it is a good idea to do a lot of short five minute exercises and to change partners on each exercise. Make sure that everyone has worked with everyone else. This will help you to get to know each other and will break down barriers you may have about working with particular people.

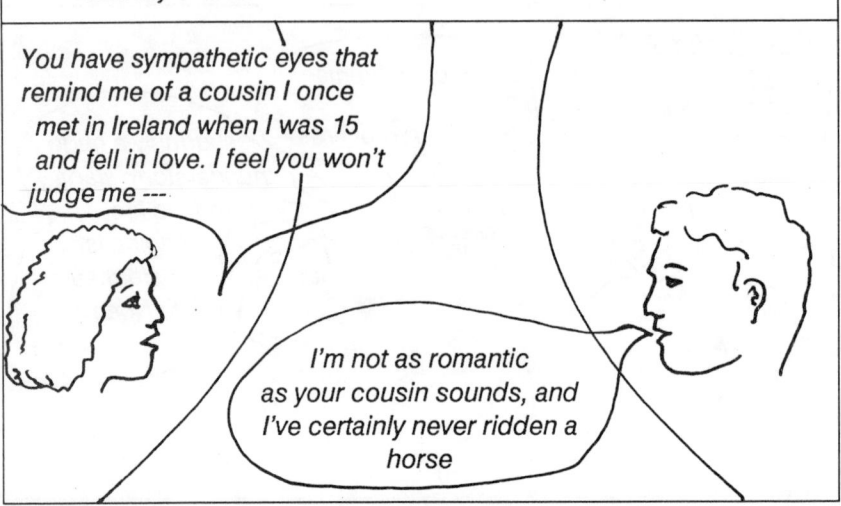

Projection

Projective processes always occur in groups. You project onto other people qualities, feelings and attributes that they don't have. Sometimes you project your own feelings onto them. Sometimes you simply behave towards them as if they were like someone else (mum, dad, granny, brother, wife, husband, kids, girlfriend etc). In a counselling group this often comes out as a desire to work with a particular person or a real antipathy towards working with somebody else.

It is of course true that you get on better with some people than with others and that in the long run there may be people who you feel can't help you or that you can't help. In the early stages of a group however it is important to try to be open to each other and test the reality of your projections. We deal with the problems of projection in more detail in Section Three.

Sorting out hassles

This isn't a manual on group dynamics so we're not going to go into details of all the things that can and may happen in a group and what you can do about them. If you get in a hassle in a counselling group however there are a few points that may be useful:

1) Having a hassle in a group may be a defence against the actual work of counselling.

2) The group may be heavily weighted towards a particular phase of the cycle making it difficult for work to be done. If you can identify this you can consciously try to put in the missing element.

3) You can use your counselling skills to try to defuse tension. Break into pairs to talk about the problem and let out individual feelings. When you come back to the group the problem may be easier to resolve.

4) Real differences exist between people and you may need to take some action - reorganise your meetings, split the group, agree to differ. Again you can use the counselling pairs to try to sort out what the issues are.

Section Two

Using interventions

and theory

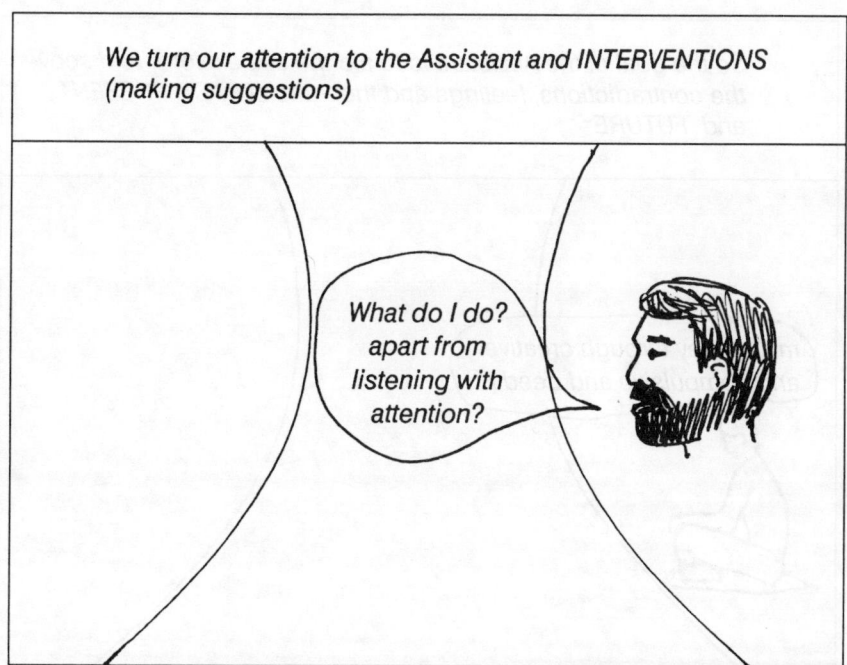

It is important to get a grip of the goals in counselling and of the roles of worker and assistant. An analogy may be useful.

WORKER
I am like an explorer going through familiar territory (myself) but looking for lost lands. I alone really know the territory.

ASSISTANT
I am like a friendly expert in navigation. I don't know the territory but I have a map and compass and can make suggestions about directions and how to overcome obstacles

So the goal of the Assistant is to aid the self explorer to discover the contradictions, feelings and thoughts of PAST, PRESENT and FUTURE

my journey through creative and compulsive and deeds

Before we get to some practical exercises we want to stress some GOLDEN RULES for interventions in counselling.

WORKER | **GOLDEN RULE NUMBER ONE** | **ASSISTANT**

all interventions are <u>suggestions</u> only

I will ignore or put aside any suggestion that doesn't seem right to me

I will always accept the worker's decision
usually I will say "try so-and-so" or "I suggest so and so"

GOLDEN RULE NUMBER TWO

<u>There are only 2 forms of intervening</u>

(a) I suggest you <u>say</u> something

(b) I suggest you <u>do</u> something

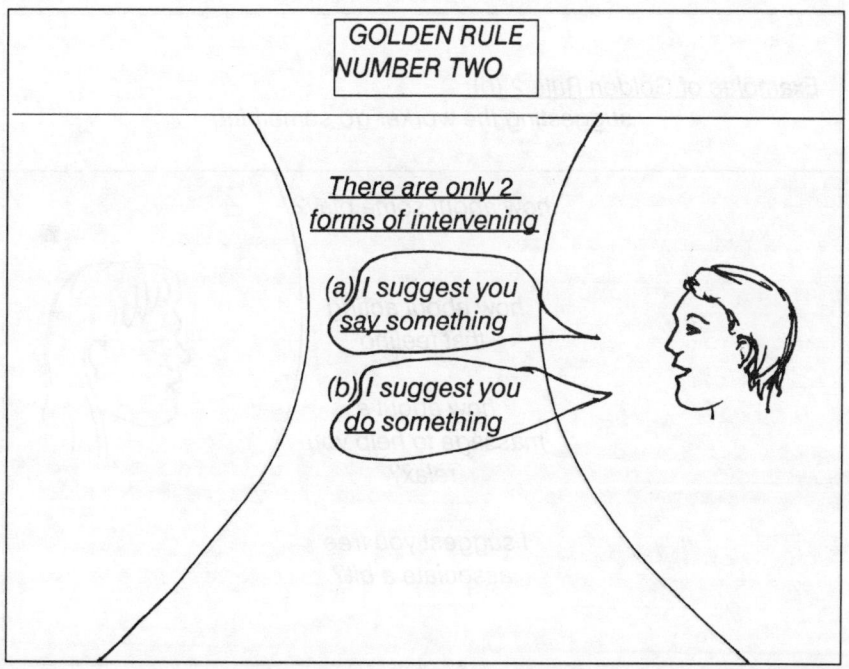

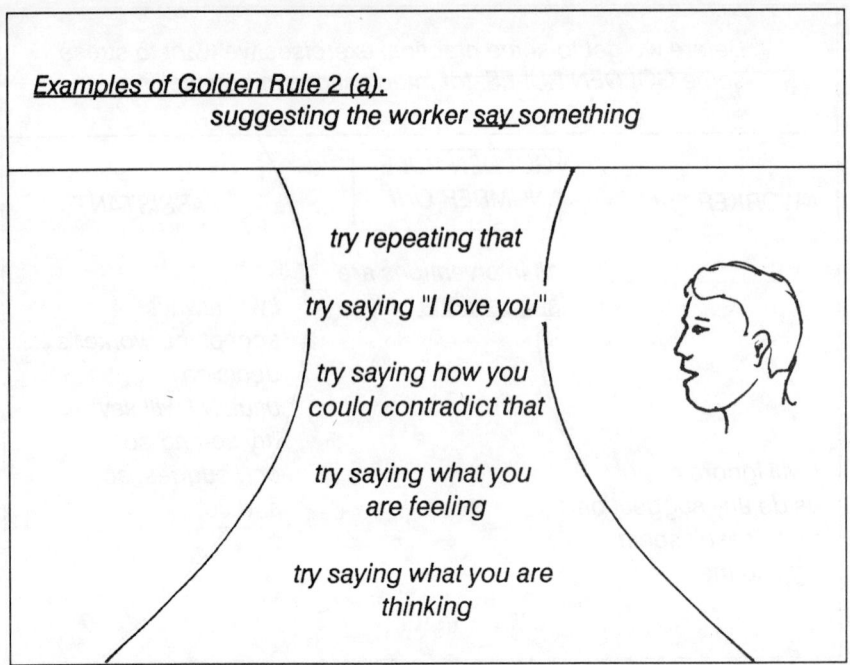

Examples of Golden Rule 2 (a):
  suggesting the worker _say_ something

- try repeating that
- try saying "I love you"
- try saying how you could contradict that
- try saying what you are feeling
- try saying what you are thinking

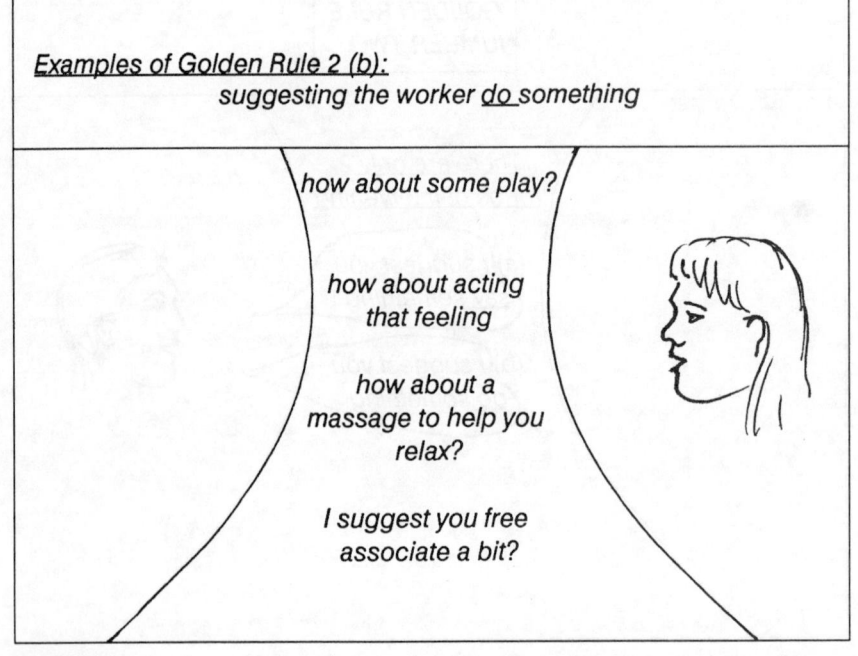

Examples of Golden Rule 2 (b):
  suggesting the worker _do_ something

- how about some play?
- how about acting that feeling
- how about a massage to help you relax?
- I suggest you free associate a bit?

What you DON'T DO during counselling

DON'T ask questions
DON'T offer advice
DON'T offer your experience
DON'T give your solutions
DON'T offer judgements,
criticisms or answers

*why did you do that?
my advice is --
well that happened to me
and --
why don't you --
how stupid!*

The reason for the two golden rules of
(1) interventions are suggestions <u>and</u>
(2) You may only suggest the worker <u>says</u> or <u>does</u> things are:

WORKER
is in charge. The
process should be
one of <u>selfanalysis</u>
not one of being
"social worked" or
"head shrinked" by an
expert.

ASSISTANT
aids the worker's
process, tries not to
spoil his "flow"
of consciousness.

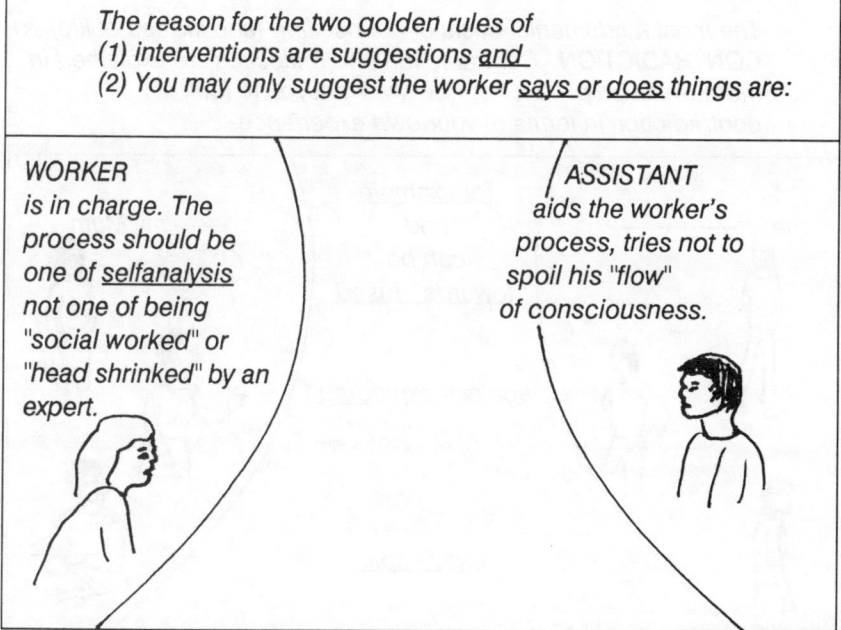

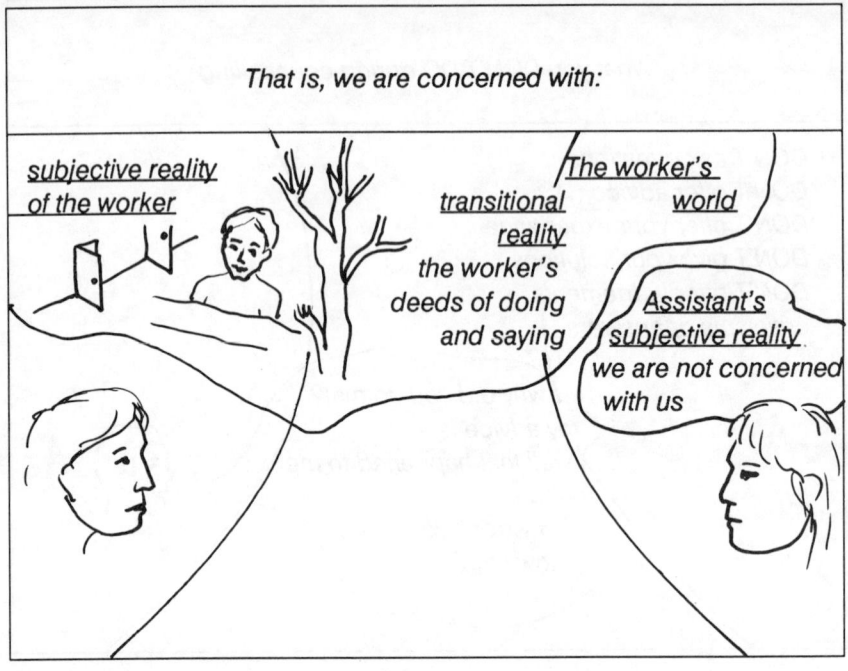

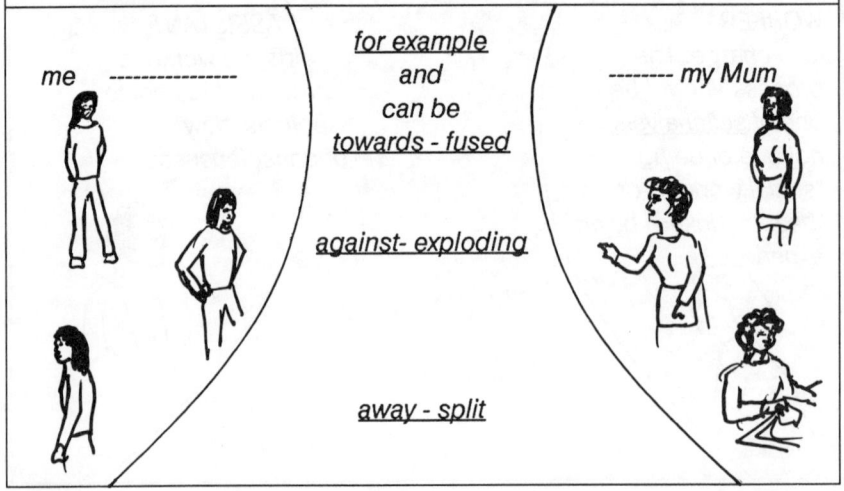

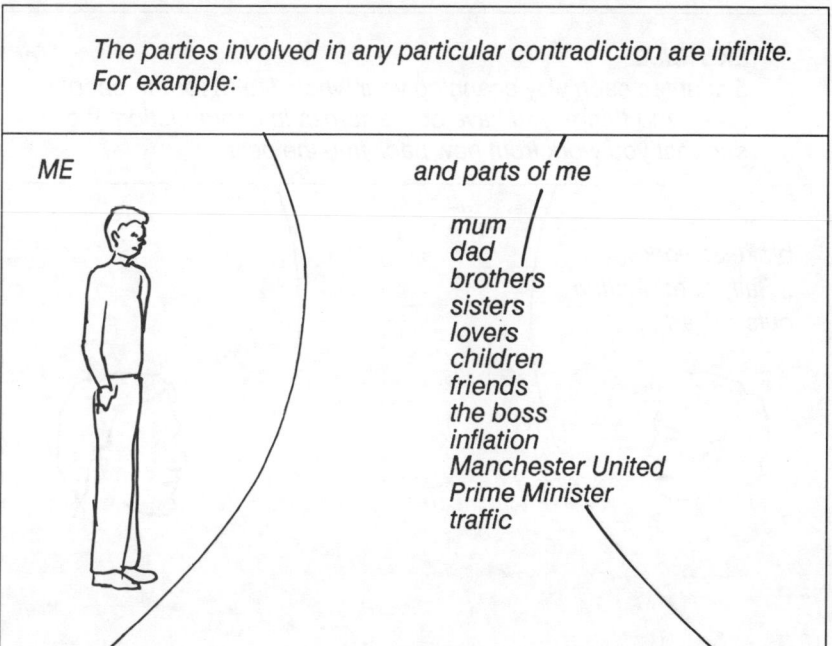

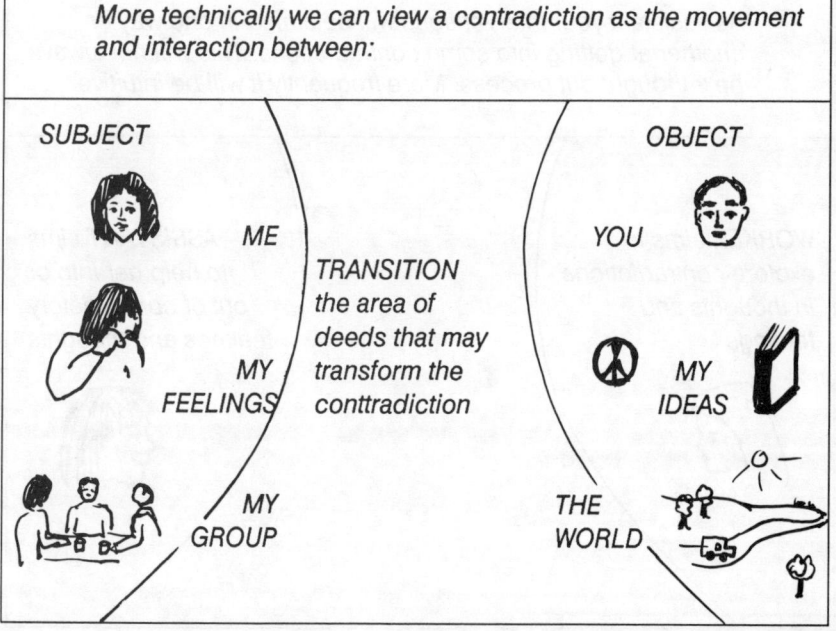

EXERCISE: *Try*
5 minutes each way scanning your whole life (!) for the people, ideas and things you have come across in contradiction. We suggest you work from now back into the past.

bloke at work ...
...Sally ... education ...
cuts ... Dad ...

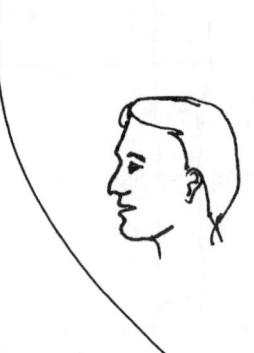

As assistant your interventions will be aimed in one way or another at getting into some contradictions. This will not always be a thought out process. More frequently it will be intuitive.

WORKER aims to explore contradictions in thoughts and feelings

ASSISTANT aims to help her into or out of contradictory feelings and thoughts

One of the ways of suggesting something to the worker is by REPETITION. In this case you will suggest she repeats her own words.

The reason for making this (or any other) intervention is to explore the feelings and/or thoughts involved in a contradiction. In this case you will be emphasising one side of the contradiction. This might be because you felt these were important feelings or because you felt that the worker was ignoring them, or that the whole process might be far more intuitive.

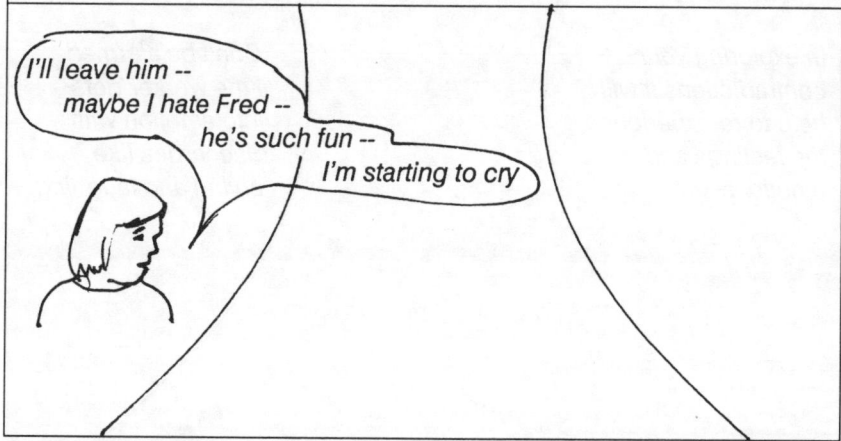

In this example the intervention has helped to bring out different aspects of the contradiction within the worker.

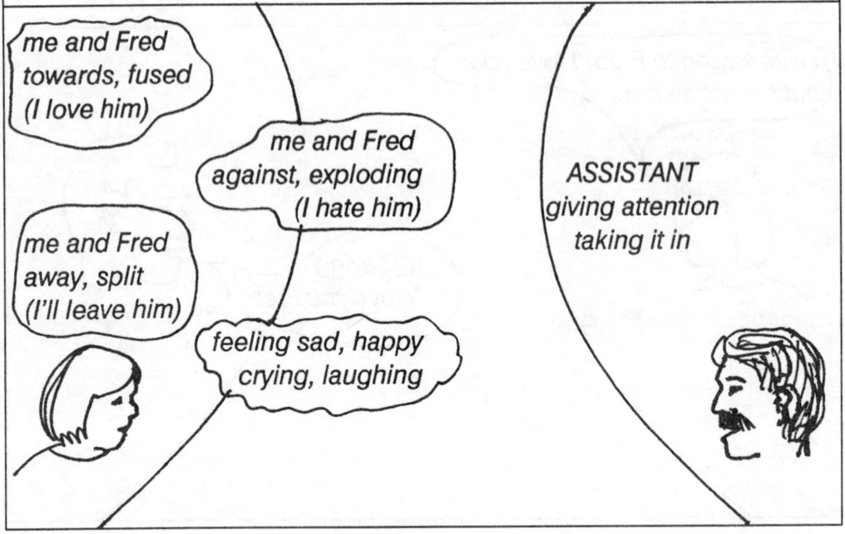

- me and Fred towards, fused (I love him)
- me and Fred against, exploding (I hate him)
- me and Fred away, split (I'll leave him)
- feeling sad, happy crying, laughing

ASSISTANT
giving attention
taking it in

We will go into more detail later about feelings and emotionality but ...

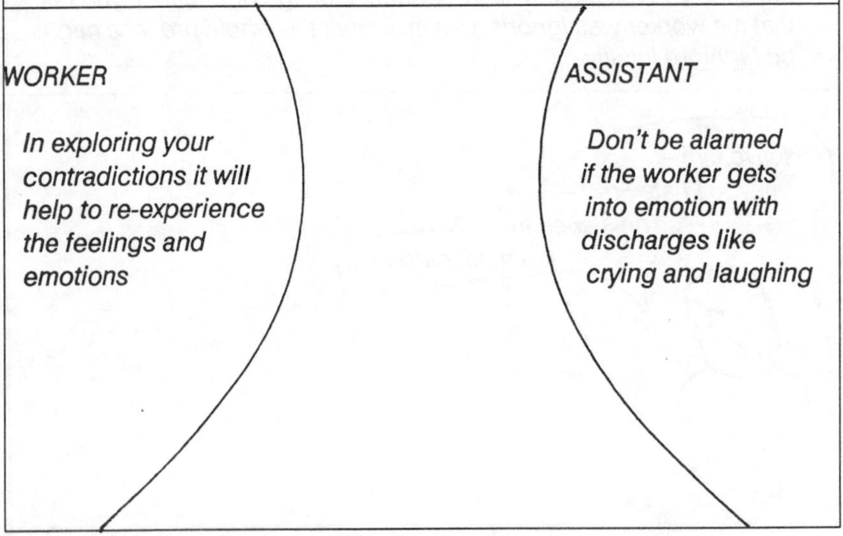

WORKER

In exploring your contradictions it will help to re-experience the feelings and emotions

ASSISTANT

Don't be alarmed if the worker gets into emotion with discharges like crying and laughing

In fact, repetition is often useful for reliving events and the emotions associated with them.

"I felt embarassed when I said "I miss you" Then I -"

"Try repeating "I miss you""

"I miss you"

"again?"

"I miss you --"

crying

EXERCISE:
In your first exercises you are not likely to get into emotional discharge - but in any case the goal is to explore -
CONTRADICTIONS

WORKER
Select someone important in your life (now or in the past) e.g. mum, dad, wife, husband, friend, teacher, etc.

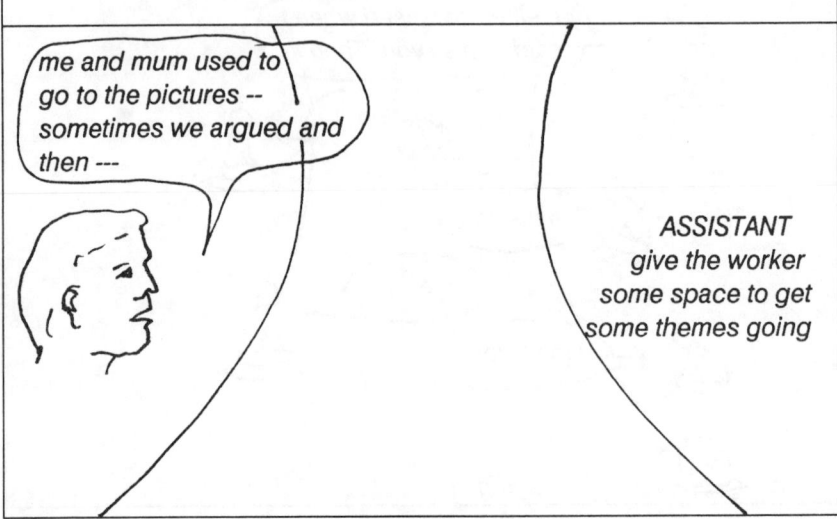

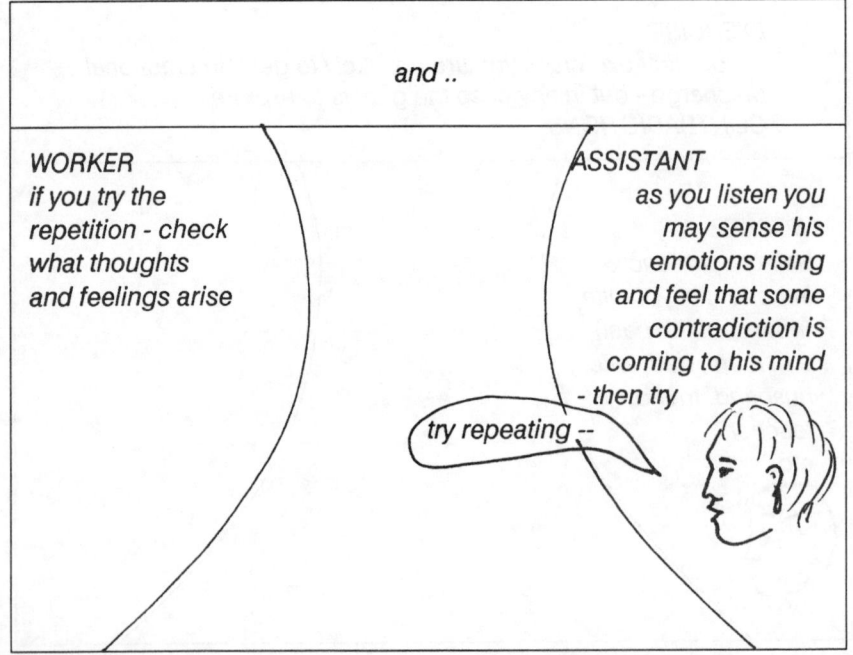

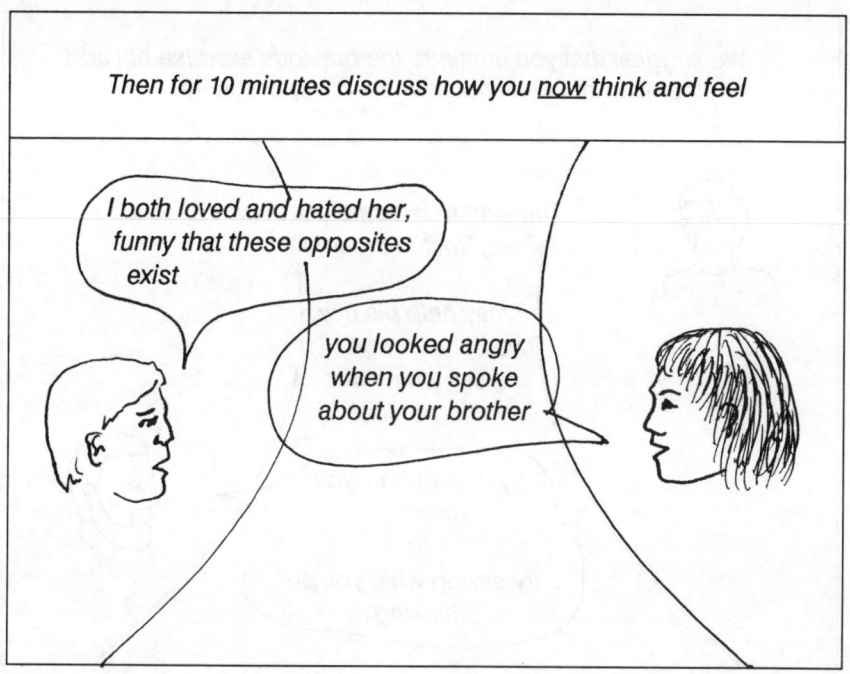

You can encourage the worker to explore opposite feelings and thoughts on some contradiction, for example:

- every time I see him I feel anxious
- try contradicting that, saying the opposite
- when I see him I feel fine ... well, I do ... sometimes I feel OK but ....

You can suggest that the worker does the opposite of how her body and stance appears. For example -

- when I see him I feel fine --
- try contradicting your stance ... try sitting up and looking fine
- I feel fine!

We suggest you do 20 minutes each way, with 10 minutes in between using the 3 interventions you now have. Again repeat the exercise a few times

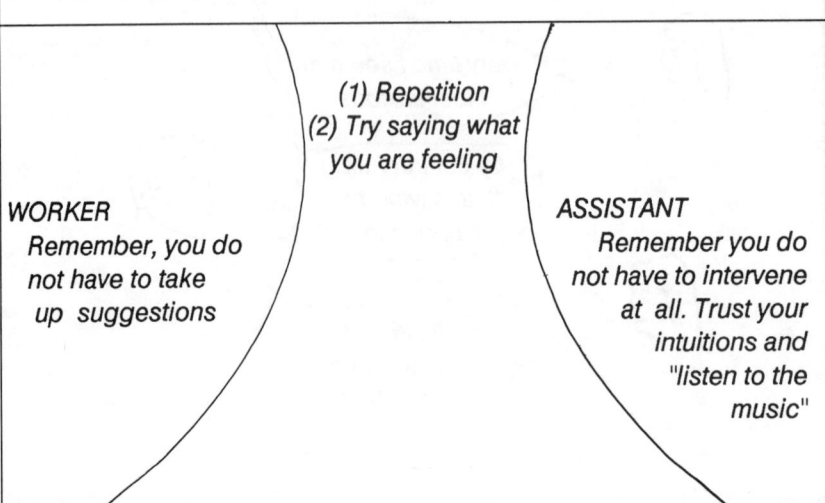

(1) Repetition
(2) Try saying what you are feeling

WORKER
Remember, you do not have to take up suggestions

ASSISTANT
Remember you do not have to intervene at all. Trust your intuitions and "listen to the music"

Often people find themselves inhibited about making interventions at first. This is an exercise for getting over this fear by "sending up" the whole process. The worker works in the usual way but encourages the assistant by taking up all interventions. The assistant keeps the Golden Rules but makes really SILLY interventions

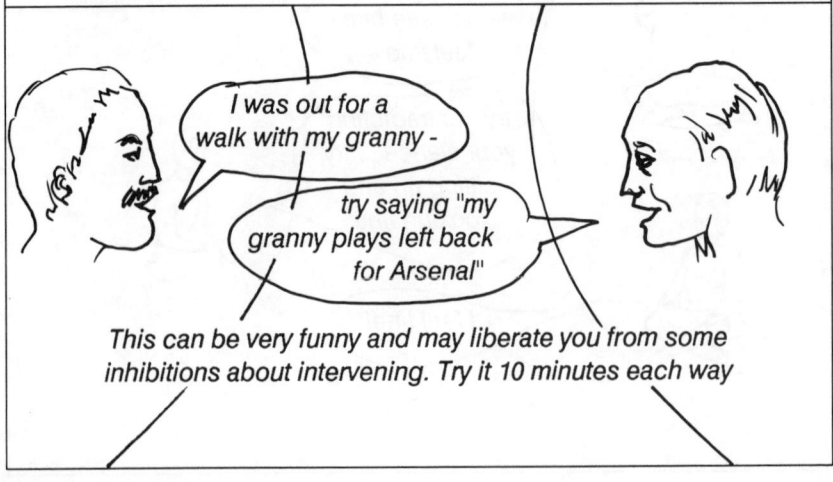

I was out for a walk with my granny -

try saying "my granny plays left back for Arsenal"

This can be very funny and may liberate you from some inhibitions about intervening. Try it 10 minutes each way

Another way of trying to overcome inhibitions about intervening is to take some time as the worker to explore how you feel about being the Assistant. What contradictions are involved for you? What does the situation remind you of? What are you afraid of?

When I played in the school orchestra I always came in in the wrong place --

I always have to do things right first time --

We hope that you are now ready for your first full counselling session. The next frames describe the whole process as it may typically happen. You will need about 3 hours consisting of:

(a) 15 minutes for coffee and chat
(b) 20 minutes - trivia of the day/play/exercises
(c) 45 minutes counselling session
(d) 15 minutes discussion
(e) 15 minutes coffee break
(f) repeat (b) - (d) with the roles reversed

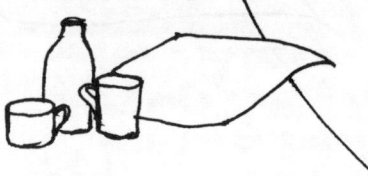

Just as a group follows a cycle of nurturing energising and relaxing, so does a counselling session. In fact this is a good way of looking at the whole process as it may occur

You will often have just come from work or be tired so we often spend 5 minutes "each way" talking about the trivia of the day. We call this "cleaning the top of the head".

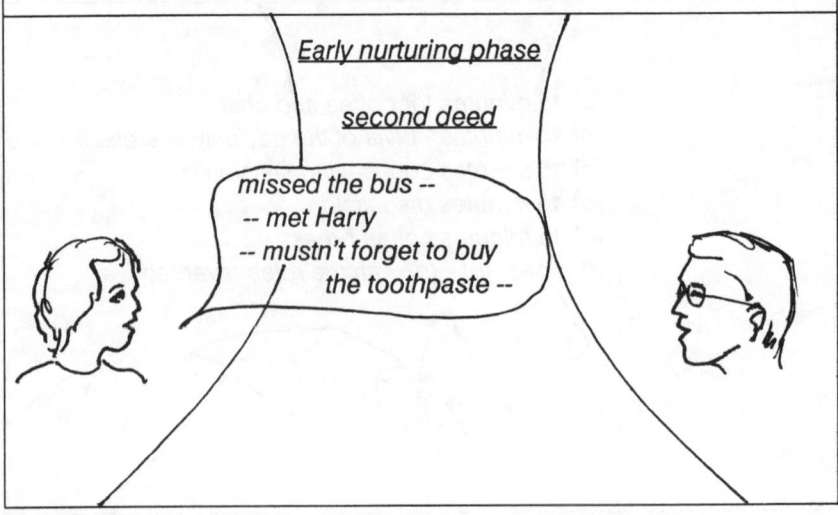

You might spend another 5 or 10 minutes in a "warm up" play or game

<u>*Early nurturing phase*</u>

e.g. reflecting each other's expression

<u>*Later nurturing phase*</u>
This covers the beginning of the counselling session itself

<u>WORKER</u>
Try not to be in a hurry, allow things to arise spontaneously. Stay with whatever thoughts and feelings you have, give yourself time and space. Be nice to yourself (You can nurture yourself too)

ASSISTANT You will make relatively few interventions in this phase. Concentrate on keeping contact with your partner and trying to stay with what is happening in her terms. Beware of non verbal communications and signals.

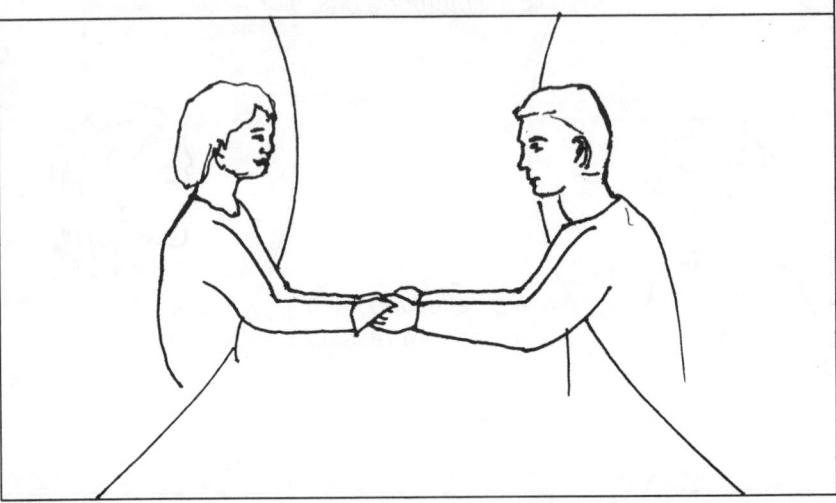

Interventions in this phase will probably be aimed at encouraging and drawing out your partner. You may need to alleviate her feelings of uncertainty; mistrust and anxiety give her permission to express such things and explore the connections.

SOME TYPICAL INTERVENTIONS

Try saying what you're feeling

Try saying what you're thinking

Try saying a bit more about ---

Try saying what you feel about this situation

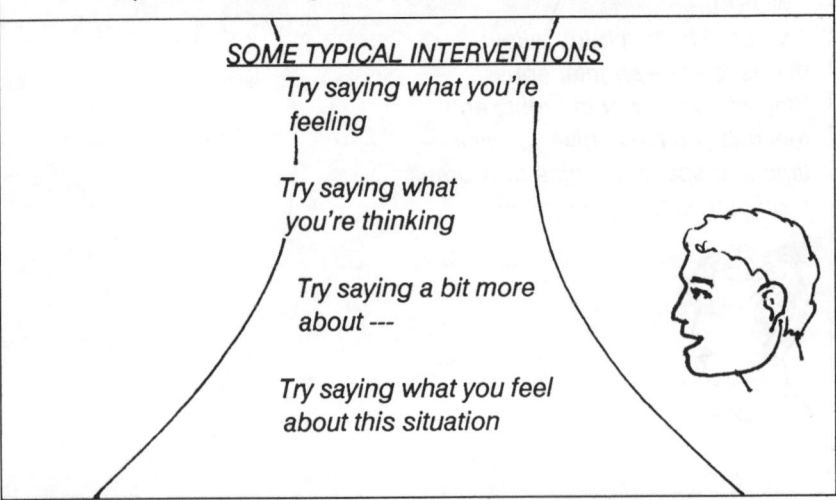

some more typical interventions:

Try saying what it reminds you of

Try saying where else you feel like this

Try saying what you would like me to do

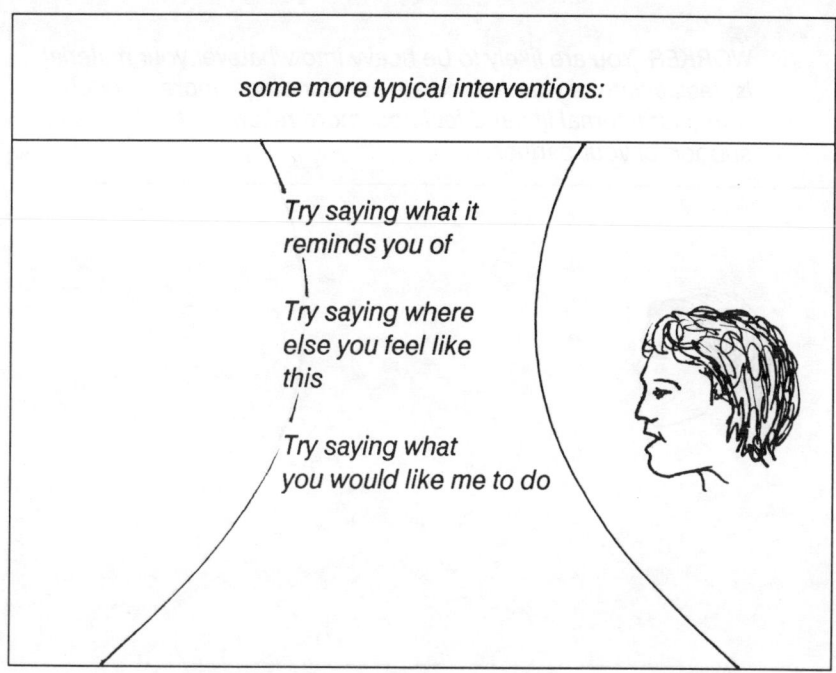

ENERGISING PHASE This is the phase people often value most highly, as it is the part where things "really come out" or you "get into something heavy". However important it is, remember its success is dependent upon the work of the other phases as well.

WORKER
This is a phase where you may get into some emotional discharge, though you can be highly energised and working creatively without this happening.

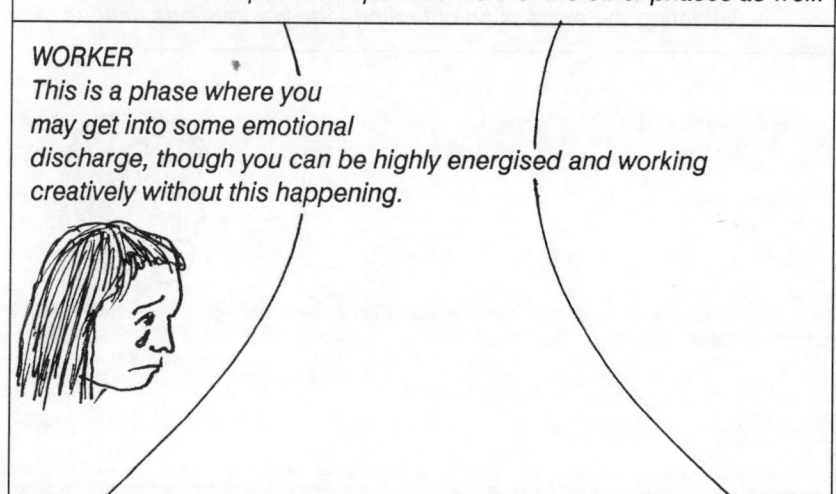

WORKER You are likely to be heavy into whatever your material is, less aware of your immediate surroundings, more in touch with your internal life and feelings, more reliant on the help and support of your partner.

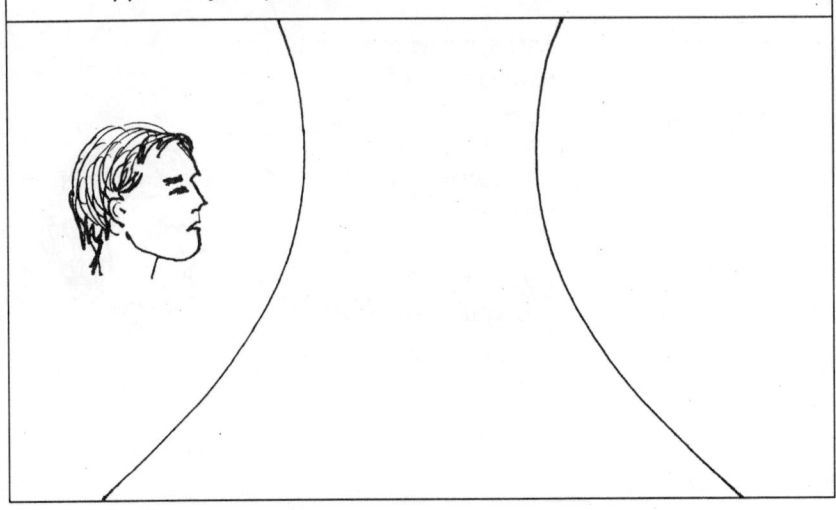

ASSISTANT You will become more active in this phase, using the knowledge and information you have built up to help your partner pursue his goal. You are likely to be more confronting, emphasising a focus that is being avoided and encouraging and validating the expression of feelings the worker finds difficult.

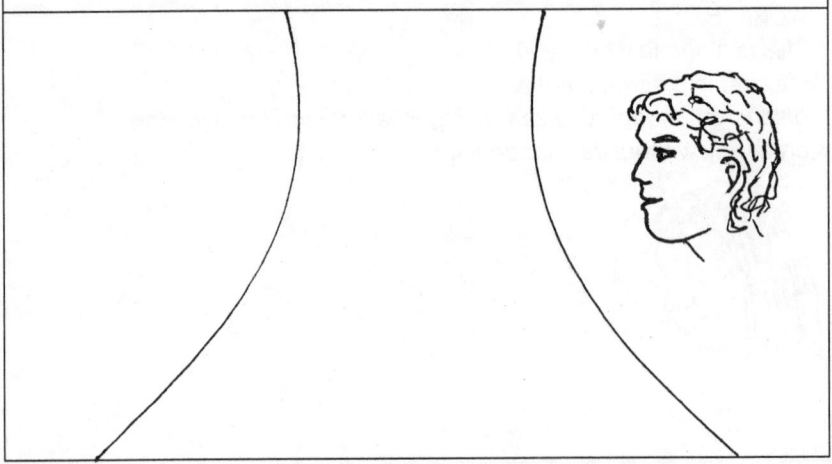

It is harder to give brief examples of typical intervention here as you wil be working far more closely and intuitively on the basis of what is happening. Remember that all interventions are suggestions however, the kinds of things used here might be:

Assistant thought/observation	Assistant Intervention
She doesn't sound as if she really means 'I was so angry I nearly walked out'. She sounds/her body looks frightened.	Try saying 'I wanted to walk out but I was too scared to'.
I think there's some significant emotion attached to the way Sue says 'I didn't want him to go'.	Try repeating 'I didn't want him to go'.
I think there is a lot of emotion Sue needs to discharge in order to understand her relationship with her dad.	Try repeating/contradicting (whatever the significant phrase is). Use her own words as possible.
Sue's been talking for 2/3 minutes about how she always gets covered in clay when she works in the pottery. I think she's talking symbolically.	Try saying 'I always get myself in a mess.'
I think Joe idealises his relationship with Mary.	Try exaggerating how good it is. Say 'we're the most perfect couple who ever met' etc.
Joe needs to look at the different parts of his feelings about that.	Try role-playing the different parts of yourself e.g. your 'head' and your 'gut'.
I think Joe is subject to anal-regressive fantasies with sado-masochistic tendencies.	You can't find a suitable phrase so keep the interpretation to yourself.

119

RELAXING PHASE   This is the phase when you "cool out" or come away from the material, come back into more ordinary frame of mind = connect, analyse and interpret what has been going on.

WORKER
You will be becoming less involved in your internal, subjective life. More aware of your partner as another different person; more aware of the meaning, significance and relationship of the things you have been talking about.

ASSISTANT   *You will be working to help the worker achieve this. If he has been into something very heavy, you will need to use your skill and judgement to bring him away from this at an appropriate point.*

<u>Some typical interventions</u>

Try looking at me
Try saying what I look like
Try describing the room
Try telling me what you are going to do when you leave here
Try telling me what you would like me to do

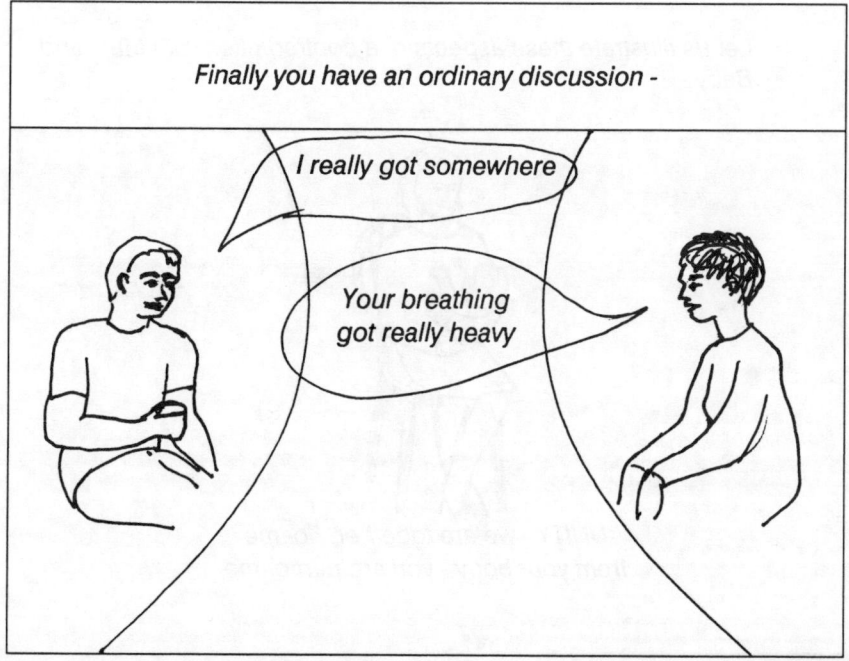

We now return to our main concern - CONTRADICTION and explain something about dialectics. The two main parties you might be concerned with in a contradiction can be in

UNITY:
for example we are towards, fused

OPPOSITION:
for example we are against, exploding

INTERPENETRATION:
for example we are simultaneously towards and against

TRANSFORMATION:
for example there is a new creative deed leading to new knowledge and the contradiction changing

Let us illustrate these aspects of a contradiction with Mum and Baby -

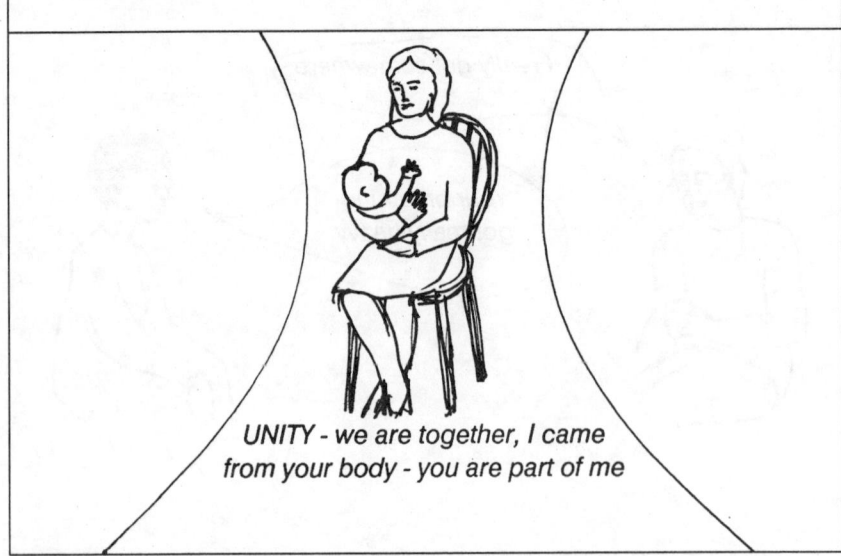

UNITY - we are together, I came from your body - you are part of me

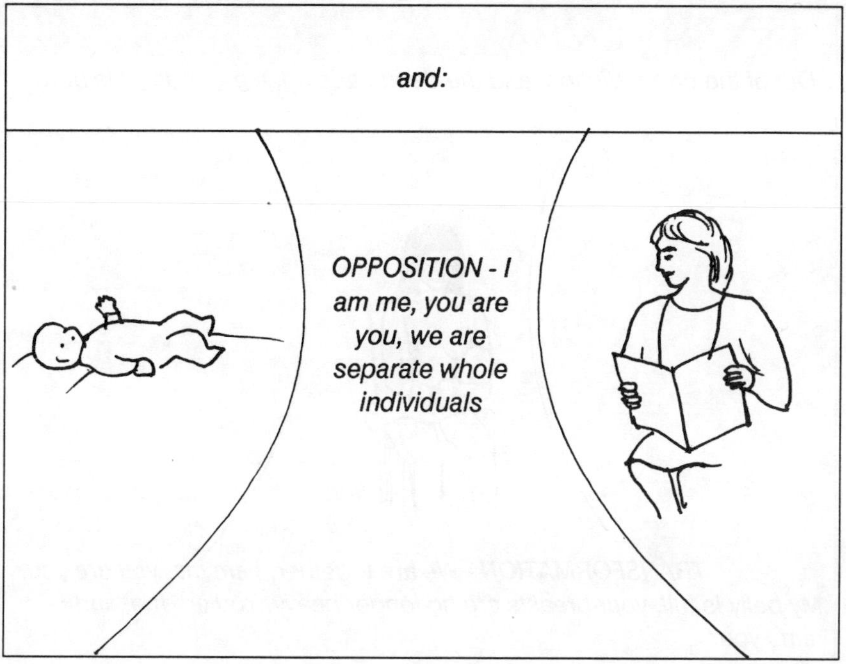

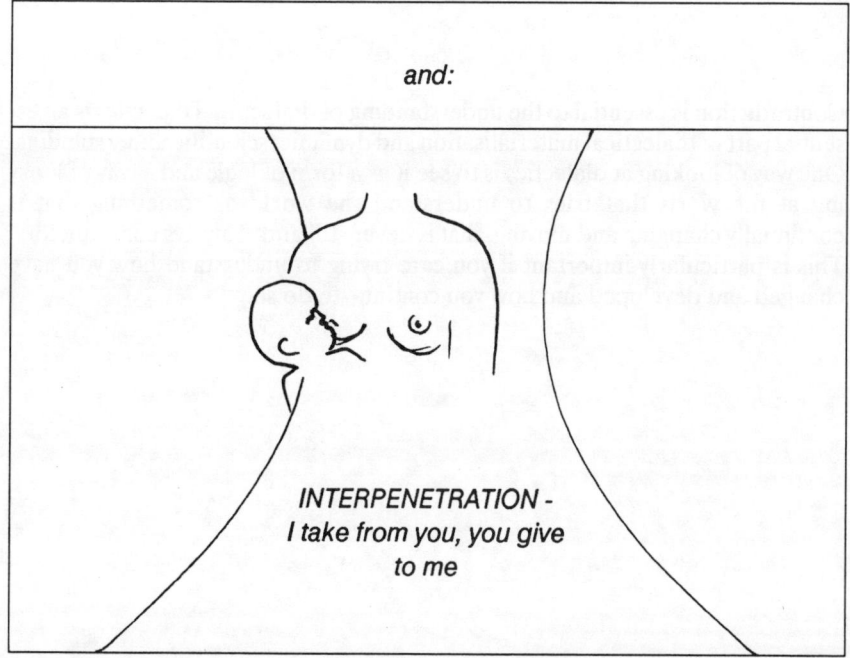

Out of the contradiction, and the deeds arising, a new quality is born -

TRANSFORMATION - We are together, I am me, you are you. My belly is full, your breasts are no longer heavy. You are me, and I am you.

Contradiction is essential to the understanding of dialectics. Dialectics is an essential part of dialectical materialisation and dynamic, scientific understanding. One way of looking at dialectics is to see it as a form of logic and a way of looking at the worls that tries to understand the world as something that is continually changing and moving, that is never still and is always contradictory. This is particularly important if you care trying to understand how you have changed and developed and how you continue to do so.

QUANTITY AND QUALITY (Never mind the quality feel the width)

One way of trying to understand this change and movement is to look at the changes in terms of quality and quantity. Sometimes a change will be quantitative, sometimes it will be qualitative and sometimes it will be a change from one to the other.

Here is an example taken from Hegel* which illustrates the change from *quantity* (something more or less) to *quality* (something different). A man finds that he is gradually losing his hair. Each morning when he wakes up a few more hairs fall out in the comb. Over the years his hair becomes thinner and thinner till finally he has only three hairs left... then two... then one. One morning he wakes up and his last hair has fallen out. He is bald. Over the years, as his hair was falling out *quantitative* changes were taking place. He was a man who was losing his hair - a man with gradually *less* hair but still a man with hair. When the last hair fell out a qualitative change took place. He could no longer be called a man with thinning hair. He became a bald-headed man. The change was one from *quantity* to *quality*.

Here is an example of the change the other way round - a change from quality to *quantity*. One day a baby who has only been able to crawl takes his first tottering steps. He can now walk. This is a qualitative change. Over the successive weeks and months he learns to take more steps. Gradually he can walk further. The qualitative change of being able to walk turns into the quantitative changes of being able to walk further, faster and steadier. Change can thus be seen as a continuous process of movement from quantity to quality and then from quality to quantity and so on in a never ending development.

Any change can be looked at in this way whether it is inside me or outside me, conscious or unconscious, emotional or physical, between people or things, organisations or society.

G.W.F. Hegel (1770-1831). Philospher who made the most detailed study and analysis of dialectics.

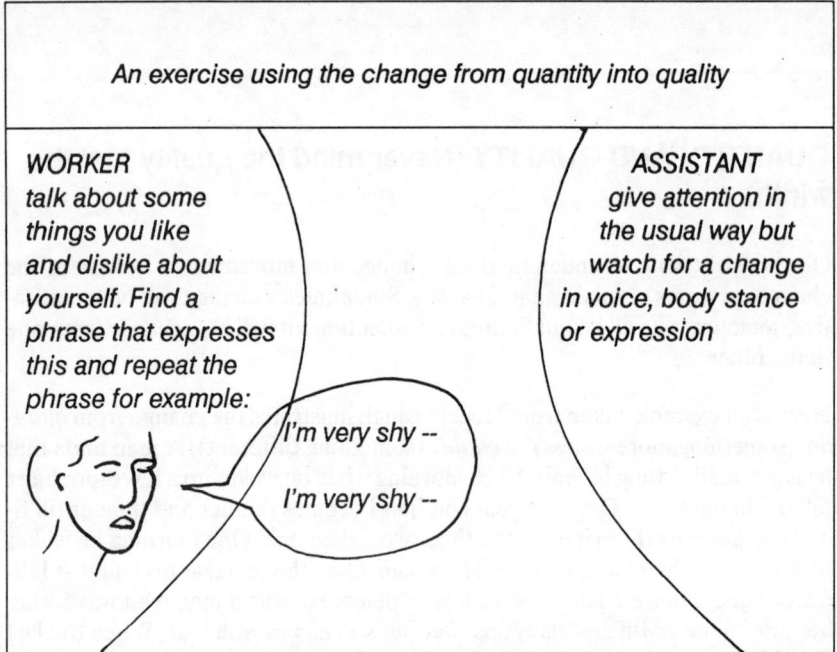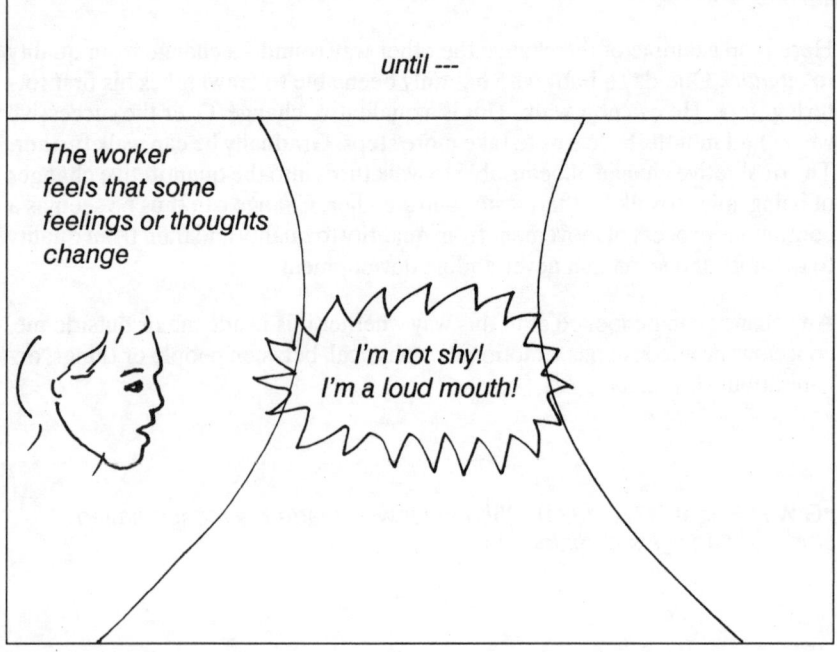

Stop and discuss the nature of the change (Reverse roles and repeat the exercise as often as you wish)

QUANTITY AND QUALITY - A group exercise
One person chooses a phase as previously. The group walks around and as each member passes the worker he repeats the phrase to him. Do this till the worker feels some change. Stop and discuss it.

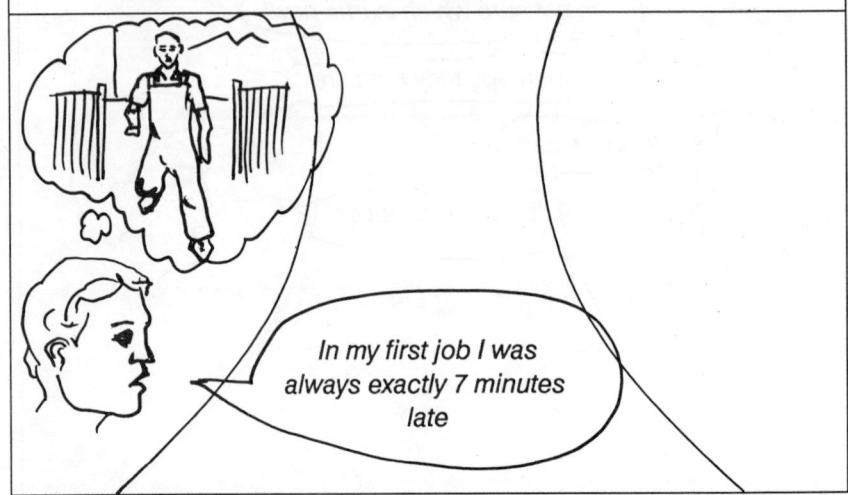

SOME EXERCISES OF CHANGES FROM QUANTITY TO QUALITY

"I was building a wall. I got one brick and then another brick and cemented them together and so on, more and more bricks on top of each other until finally I'd got a wall. It wasn't just a load of old bricks. It was a wall."

I always used to be early for appointments because I was terrified that people wouldn't wait for me if I was late. One day when I'd been standing around in the cold for the hundredth time waiting about twenty minutes for my boyfriend I realised how crazy it was since he was *always* ten minutes late. After that I started turning up on time."

"When I was pregnant I could feel the baby changing and growing inside me. It still felt like part of me, and I suppose it *was* literally. Once it was born though, there he was, different and separate, another little person, my son."

"First of all there was just me. Then Joe came along, and then Tom and Arthur and then Ian and Keith and Bob and Harry, and then Jim and Martin and John and we were a football team."

"I was trying to take the door off its hinges. I'm not quite tall enough to reach the top screws easily and it took me ten minutes of trying to realise that if I stood on a chair I'd be able to apply more pressure. I got it off in no time after that."

"When I was first married I had this ritual of saying to my husband, 'Look after yourself, won't you,' whenever he was going away for a few days. In the early days I really meant it. I really cared about whether he was alright or not. Then it gradually became an empty phrase. One day I found myself saying it because that was what I always said and realising that at the same time I was having a fantasy about his lorry being involved in an accident and him being killed. That was when I first admitted to myself that maybe there was something wrong with our relationship."

Of course dialectical materialism is not simply theory. It is also practice - action. It is only through our deeds and actions that theories and ideas arise. Theory is simply a summary or abstraction of our practice to date and is changed and altered by new deeds. The following cartoons try to show how contradictions change over time, giving rise to new theories and new actions.

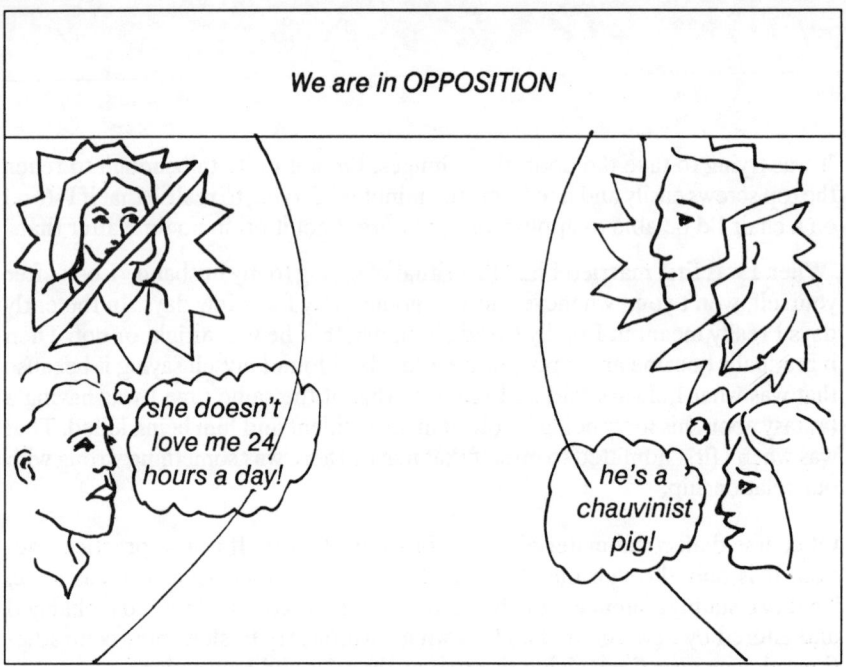

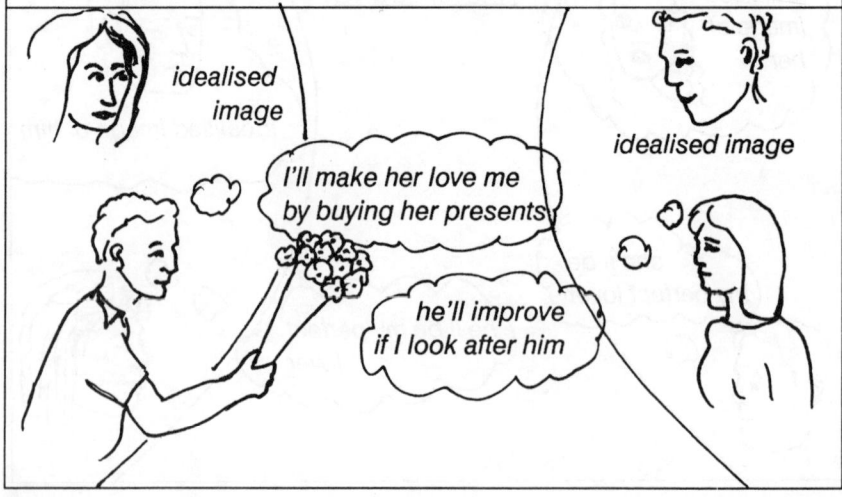

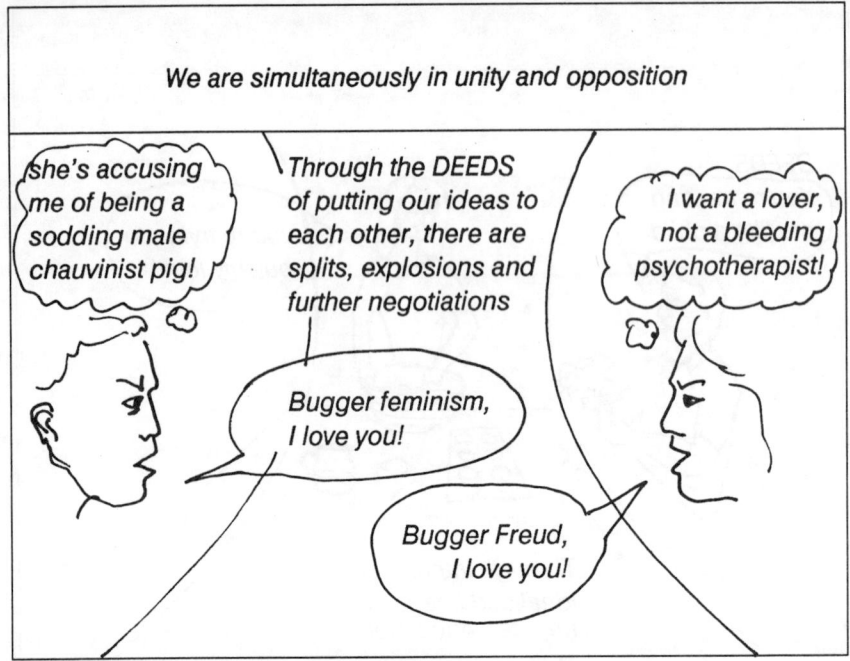

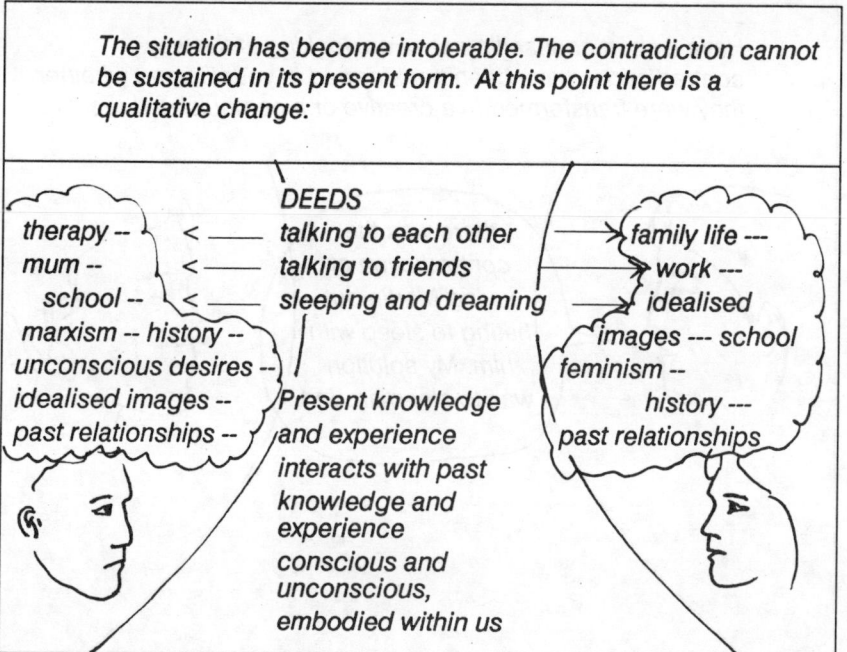

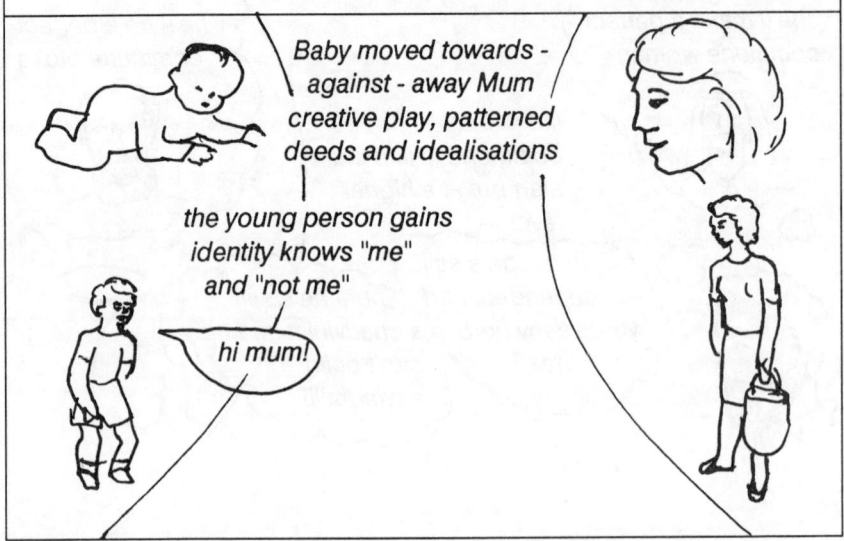

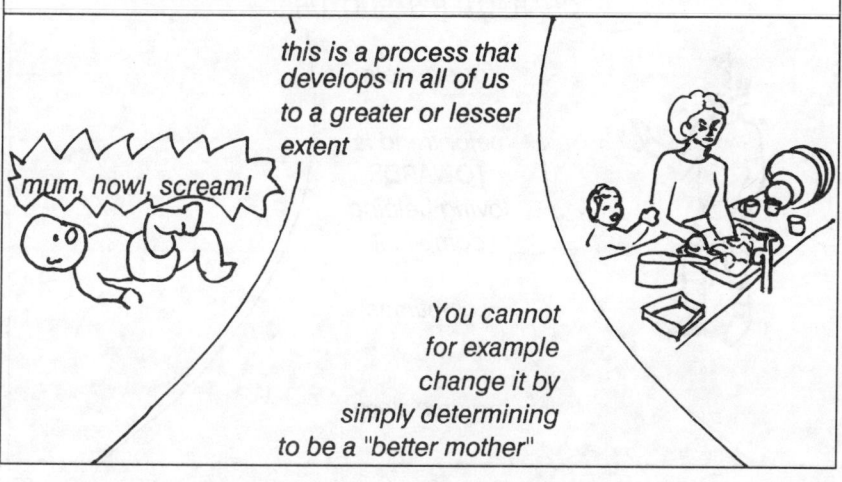

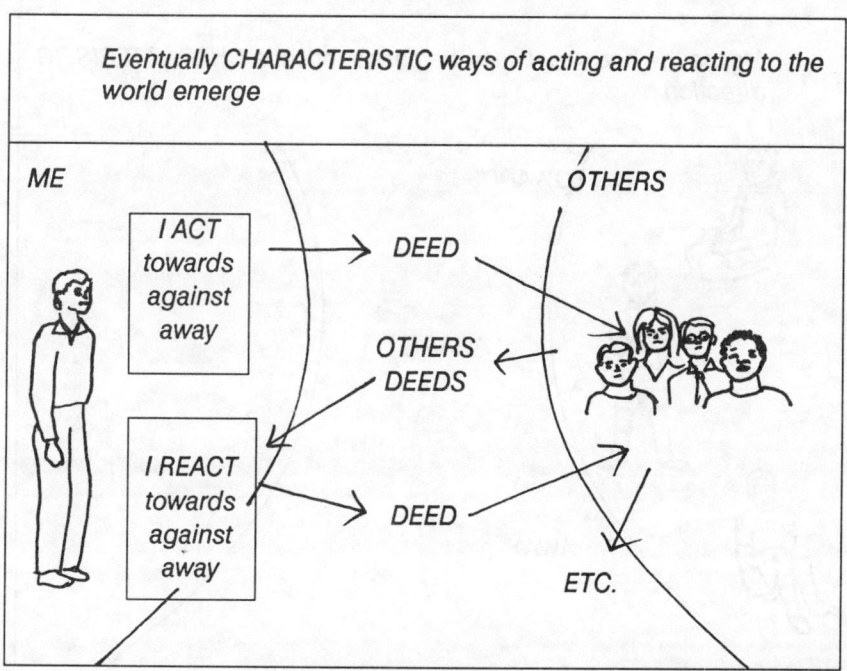

Although the young person will act and react with infinite variation, a CHARACTERISTIC direction and trend will arise with typical actions - reactions - feelings

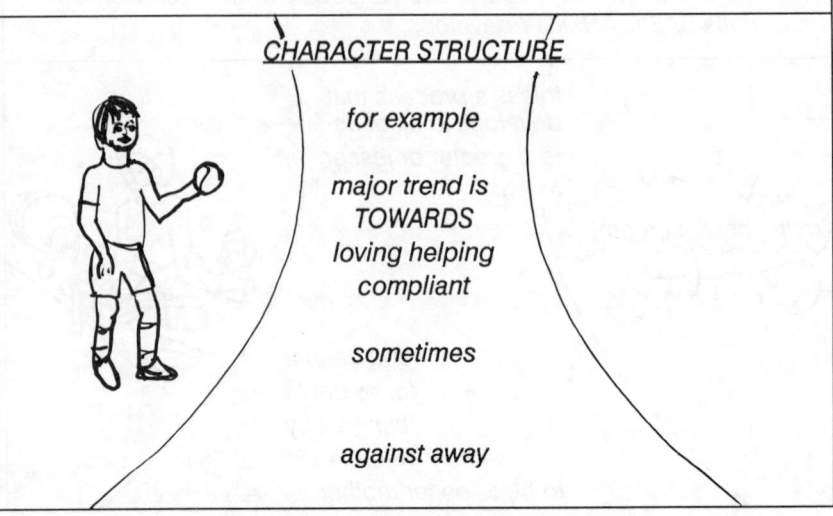

CHARACTER STRUCTURE

for example

major trend is TOWARDS loving helping compliant

sometimes

against away

Maybe the body itself also begins to reflect a CHARACTERISTIC direction

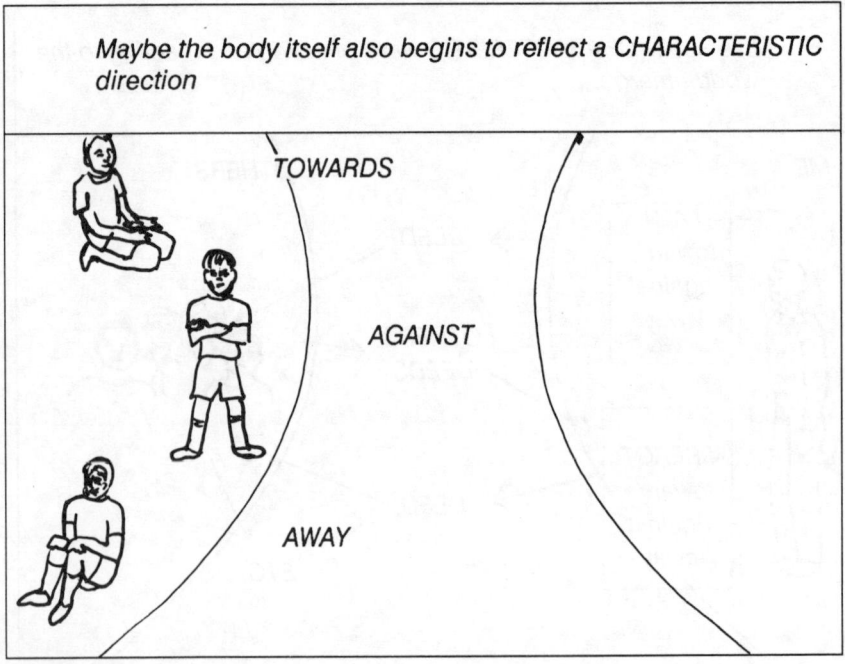

TOWARDS

AGAINST

AWAY

THE TYRANNY OF THE SHOULDS

What are the 'shoulds' and how do they arise? Why do people drive themselves as they do? What is the difference between the shoulds and the dictates of concience? What would happen if we didn't have shoulds? Wouldn't children grow up undisciplined and anarchic? Aren't some shoulds necessary? For instance I should brush my teeth because otherwise they'll fall out? I should go to work or I won't get paid. I should do work in my political group because I want to change the system.

To answer these kinds of questions it is necessary to go back a little and look at how the shoulds arise as part of the character structure. There are two crucial points to get hold of:

1) The shoulds do not necessarily bear any relations to the world of objective reality, to what is necessary, appropriate, reasonable or spontaneous. They are indiscriminate and tyrannous.

2) The shoulds do not necessarily operate in your own best interests. They may do so incidently and you may find that they operate in the interests of others. For instance 'I should go to work because it's immoral and lazy not to' is a very convenient should for the employees to have as far as their employers are concerned. The main function of the shoulds however must be seen in relation to yourself. The shoulds serve to maintain your idealised image and to protect your identity as your idealised self. This is one of the ways in which the objective, real world becomes mystified.

To understand how this process arises we need to go back to the baby or young child's early relationships. We explained earlier (p. 54) how idealisations first arise as a response to pain. Over time these experiences will develop into what Karen Horney called *basic anxiety* - a profound insecurity where the child is unable to relate spontaneously to others. The child's solution to this experience is usually to take one of the three ways of relating (towards, against, away) as a main direction. Which one he takes will be dependent on whatever seems to provide him with the greatest feelings of security. With this solution of a main direction, appropriate needs, values, sensitivities and inhibitions will develop. Real self-confidence is not developed because of the need to relate only in certain ways. Certain areas of the child's abilities to relate to others and the objective world are blocked and inhibited. The child's wishes and feelings cease to be determining factors in his behaviour. He does what he *should* do and his need for a feeling of identity, a feeling of what is *me*, what is separate from the world and others, becomes confused. You could say that he becomes alienated from himself.

As a response to this situation he creates in his imagination an idealised image of himself - a picture of what he should be like. This idealised self gradually becomes more important to him than the self which interacts in reality; it seems to solve all his problems in relating to the real world. Gradually his energies turn from trying to relate to the world as it actually is to trying to make himself and the world conform to his idealised notions of them. The emphasis in his life shifts from *being* to *appearance,* from spontaneity to compulsion.

The idealised image is in no sense a real image of the self. In order to hold onto it as real the individual has to drive himself cruelly to be and do impossible things. This is the function of the should. They are one of the ways of maintaining the idealised self.

The process described above, and indeed all the processes described in this book are processes that go on in everyone. No- one can escape them because they arise from the social relations in which we live. If they happen to you in an extreme way you may find yourself labelled neurotic or mad. If they happen to you in a less extreme or more socially acceptable fashion you will probably be termed normal. It is important to remember that everyone develops an idealised image of themselves of some kind. Yours may or may not interfere with your so-called normal functioning. It may be in line with what is considered normal in your culture. For example one stereotype of women is that they are passive, loving, submissive and unadventurous. If your own idealised image conforms with this you will probably not be seen as the least bit odd though you may be struggling to maintain your idealisation with just as much compulsion, pain and suffering as someone whose idealisation is more out of line.

Counselling is a way of reducing the power of our idealised selves and bringing ourselves more closely into relation with the world of objective reality through our creative deeds. Ultimately however we will have to look at the roots of these ways of living and experiencing in the social relations which cannot be changed by individual actions alone.

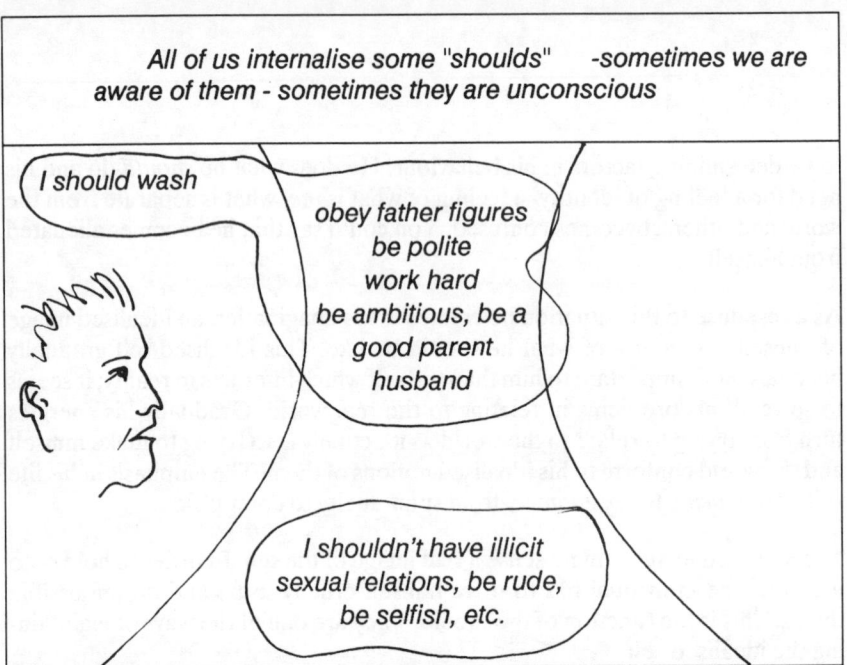

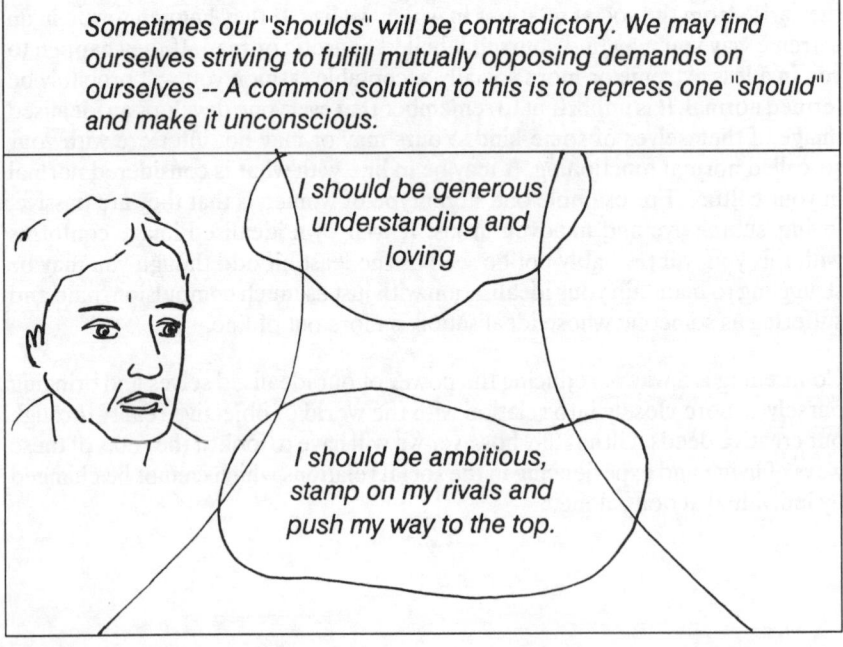

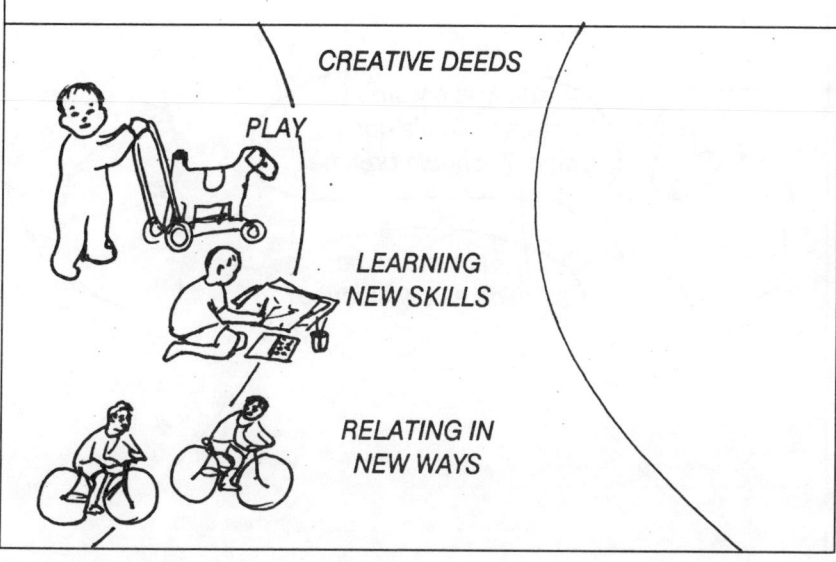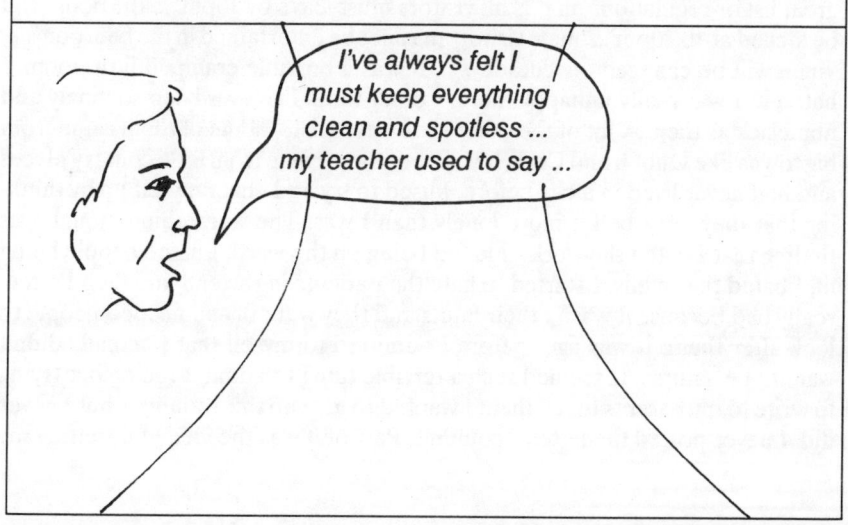

EXAMPLE OF SCANNNING ON SHOULDS

WORKER '...shoulds... the word reminds me of rules and regulations... the nurses' home when I was 18... there was a notice on the door of your room with a great list or regulations on it...' all visitors must leave by 10pm' ...'the doors will be locked at 10.30pm'... 'male visitors may not be entertained in the bedrooms'... 'linen will be changed on Tuesdays'... It was a horrible cramped little room. I hated it. I was really unhappy there. I don't think I've ever been so lonely and homesick as then. A lot of the other girls were Irish - some of them came from big towns like Dublin and Cork, but a lot of them came from little country places and had never lived in a city before. I used to try and cheer myself up by thinking that they must be far more lonely than I was. The worst thing though was finding that I hated the work - I hated being on the ward, I hated people being ill, I hated the smells. I started to hate the patients in the end and then I'd feel really bad because it wasn't their faults and they were ill and needed people to look after them. It was ages before I admitted to myself that I actually didn't want to be a nurse. It seemed such a terrible thing to admit. I remember trying to write to my parents to tell them I wanted to give up the training... but I never did. I never posted the letter. I couldn't. Part of it was the idea of upsetting my mum, feeling I'd let her down...that I'd failed in some way. It would have meant burning my boats... giving up opportunities she's never had... I couldn't do it... and it was all mixed up with the loneliness...

(Long pause)

ASSISTANT Try saying what you're thinking.

WORKER I was just wondering how I'd got onto all that. I was thinking that it didn't have much to do with shoulds but then I thought that perhaps it did - there's actually a whole lot of shoulds mixed up in that somewhere... you should stick at things. You shouldn't feel sorry for yourself... It's quite vivid actually... I get right back to that sick, gut feeling... guilt or something... I was so bloody lonely and I kept writing letters to my mum telling her what a marvellous time I was having. I felt I'd be letting her down if I didn't. I should be happy, shouldn't upset mum. The funny thing about not being able to tell her was that if I had she probably wouldn't have minded so much... she might have been a bit disappointed because it seemed like a big thing for her, me going to London and training for a nurse... but I can imagine her... she'd probably have said: 'Well, never mind. If you're not happy, there's no sense in going on with it. Come back home and we'll see what else we can do.' But I couldn't tell her. I couldn't go back like that. It was me really... I'd have hated myself so much if I'd given up... I had to put it all out onto her and say I couldn't disappoint her. I suppose in a way I was putting my shoulds onto her... (Long pause)

ASSISTANT Try saying how you're feeling.

WORKER Sad really. Just sad. I'm OK but it just seems so sad the things people do to themselves (sighing) It's really sad.

ASSISTANT Try repeating 'It's really sad.'

WORKER No. I don't want to get into all those feelings. I mean I am sad but I don't want to go into it. I don't want to feel sad. (Pause) I should go back to the shoulds! (Pause). No. I want to go back to the shoulds.

It's like the 10 Commandments, but inside your head... Thou shalt not commit adultery... thou shalt not covet thy neighbour's wife... thou shalt not steal... your own internal policeman... my uncle was a policeman... I've only ever stolen anything once in my life. When I was fifteen... I went on a shop-lifting spree with a girl from school and stole a silver brooch from a department store. I felt as if someone would know just by looking at me that I'd taken it. It wasn't a moral thing about stealing - it was this terror of being discovered... found out... the most awful guilt... thou shalt not steal... I never wore it. I threw it to the back of the drawer and tried to forget about it. I wanted to take it back... I almost wanted to be found out and punished... but it would have been so shameful.

(Pause)

I've got lots of shoulds about being a mother... like I shouldn't hit the kids, I should always be responsive, I shouldn't let them watch so much telly, I should be more interested in their schoolwork. It doesn't matter how I'm feeling - I could have a terrible migraine and they could be behaving like pigs and I'd still feel I shouldn't shout at them... It's like having all these people inside you - my uncle the policeman, the childcare books, the minister from the methodist church - I've got all those - and you can't get rid of them. You can know you've got them there, but you can't get rid of them."

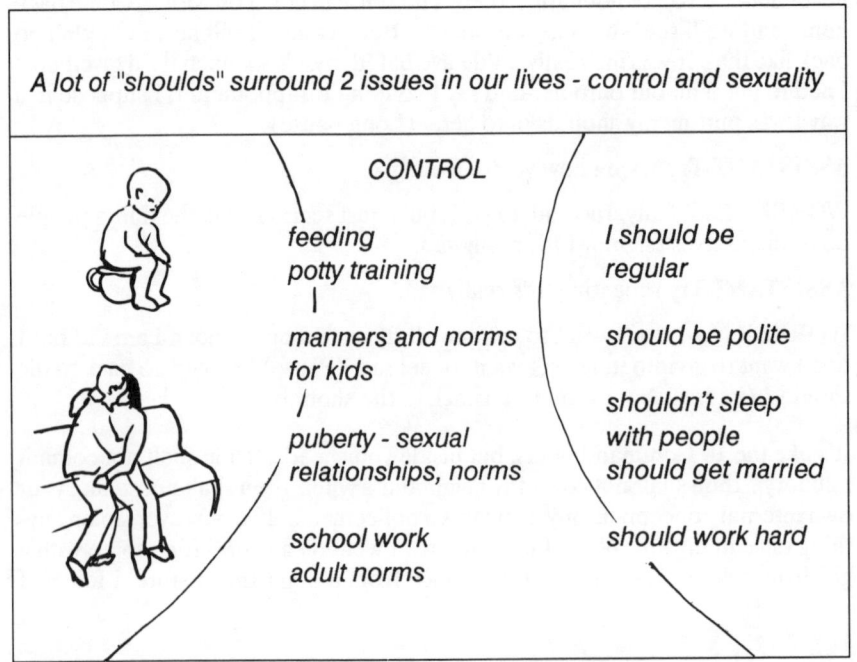

Our needs for towardsness and bodily-erotic comfort (orgasmic needs) are involved with control from babyhood to adulthood. Receiving love, anger or withdrawal (i.e. towards, against, away) has effects upon our character structure

EXERCISE we suggest a mini counselling session on should and sexuality. Many people are inhibited about this subject. By now we hope you have enough trust to do this exercise. In any case the worker is "in charge" and can reveal as much or as little as she likes

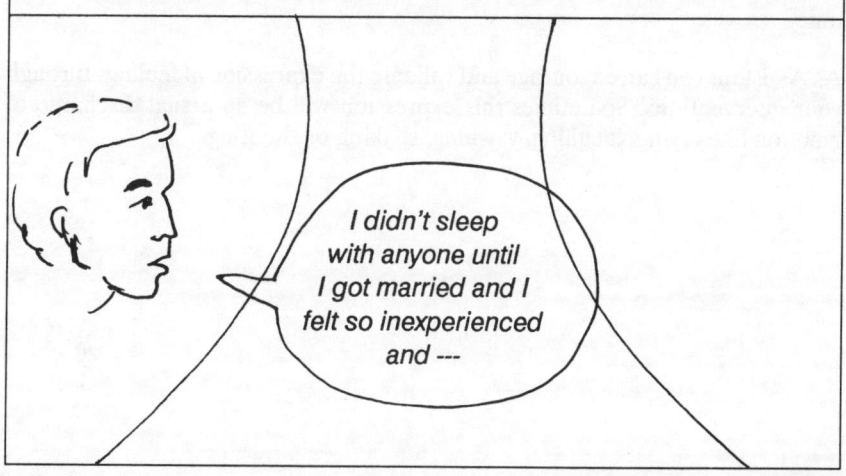

EMOTIONALITY

Section Two includes a lot of theory and a lot of ideas. We would like to emphasise that *this does not mean that counselling is an intellectual process*. In *practice* counselling is a feeling, intuitive, expressive, emotional experience. Good theories and ideas summarise that practice so that it can be passed on in an understandable form and used by other people so that they do not have to 're-invent the wheel.'

When you are actuallly counselling, let your unconscious take care of the theory. When you are the worker try to keep in touch with what you *feel*, let yourself experience whatever emotions arise. Intellectualising can be a way of shutting off from painful or distressing feelings. When you are the Assistant, respond intuitively, to your partner's feelings rather than her ideas. Gradually you should be able to integrate practices with theory and they will not seem split apart like this.

If you are really in touch with your feelings, you will not simply be talking about them but re-experiencing them, here and now, in the present. You may feel frightened, happy, sad, angry, bored and so on. Feelings may seem to well up inside you demanding expression. You may want to laugh, cry, shout, tremble or hit things. These feelings can be connected with events in your present life or things that happened way back in the past. You may start by crying for things that happened in your childhood, things that perhaps you never cried for at the time.

As Assistant you can encourage and validate the expression of feelings through your interventions. Sometimes this expression will be an actual discharge of emotion like crying, laughing, yawning, shaking or shouting.

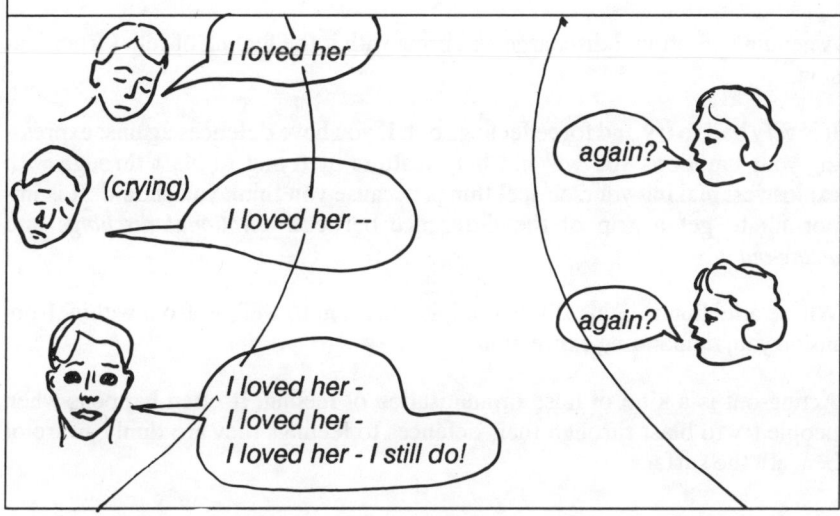

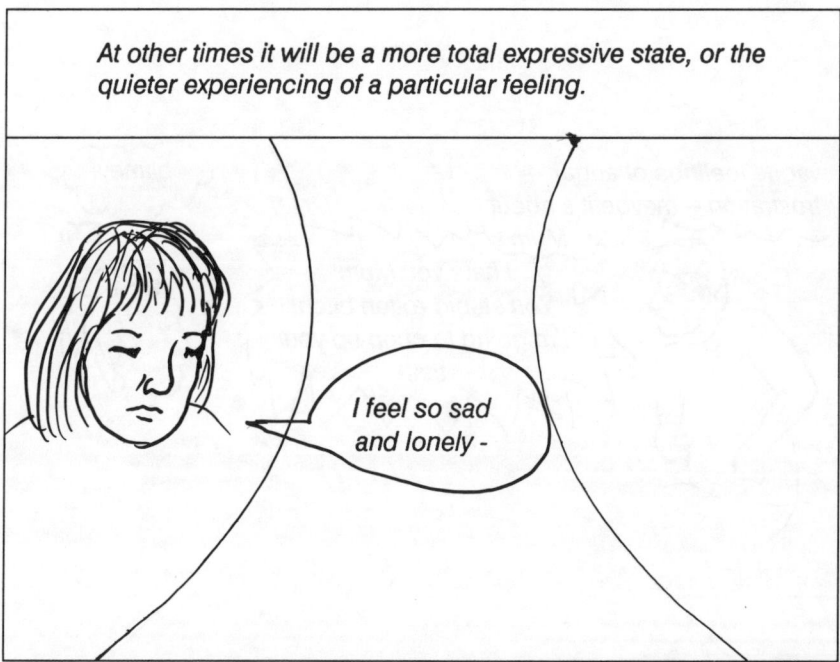

A genuine emotional discharge will bring with it the feeling of relief from tension.

It is very bad to try and force feelings out. If you have defences against expressing your emotions you will not help matters by trying to blast through with explosives, making yourself feel things because you think you should. It is important to get a grip of the difference between *emotional discharge* and *acting-out*.

Where a feeling is being discharged, it will seem to well up from within, from inside you, demanding expression.

Acting-out is a kind of false dramatisation of feeling. It often happens when people try to blast through their defences to feelings they are dimly aware of beneath the surface.

Acting out will only result in exhaustion not relief. There is nothing therapeutic about it and there is no point in encouraging it. It is usually a defence against other feelings.

At all times in counselling you need to maintain some free attention. As Worker, however involved in your internal, subjective life and feelings you become, you are doing this *in alliance with the Assistant.* Part of you is still aware of what is going on. You are not lost in subjective reality. If you do become totally submerged in your feelings (or equally sunk into an intellectual process) and this contact is lost, your work will have little therapeutic effect. As Assistant, one of your tasks is to help the Worker maintain this balance and contact, by suggesting he moves into or out of particular areas or experiences.

Remember too that emotional discharge should not be seen as an end in itself. It is the total experience of counselling in relation to the rest of your life that will produce change. Bursting into tears at the drop of a hat can also be a defence for example!

A final word on emotional discharge. People sometimes get very ANGRY in counselling when they get in touch with past and present hurts and injustices. They sometimes feel like hitting others, perhaps seeing them as present-day perpetrators of the old injuries. NEVER HIT ANOTHER PERSON, whether your partner or another member of the group. Black eyes and bloody noses are *not* therapeutic whatever temporary satisfaction they may give.

CLAIMS

The other most important way of maintaining the idealised self is by making claims, upon other people, on institutions and on life itself

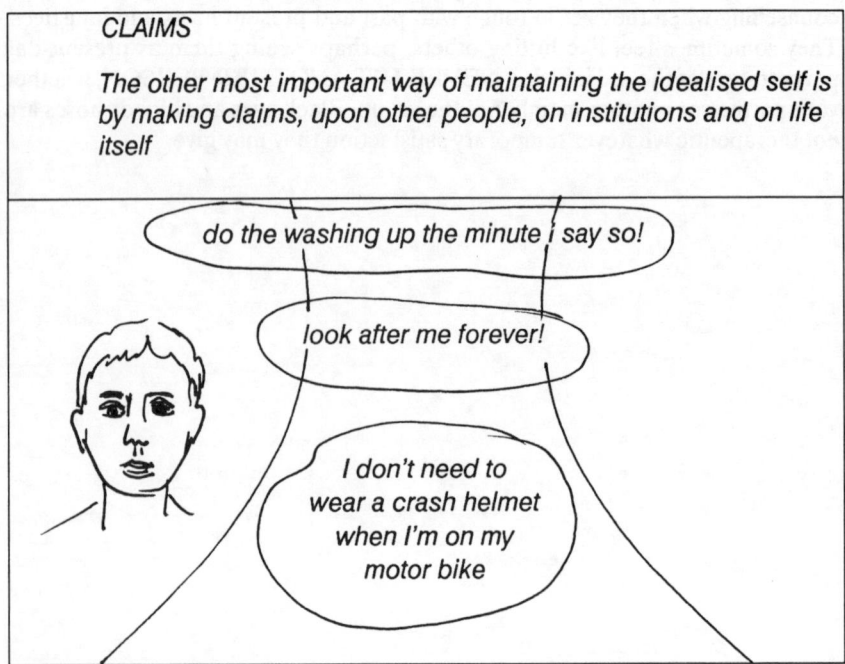

Behind every such claim is an attempt to make the idealised self real. As you find that your idealised image doesn't conform with the real world; so you try to make the real world conform with your idealised image.

Claims can be asserted in a number of different ways. For example I can impress with my importance -

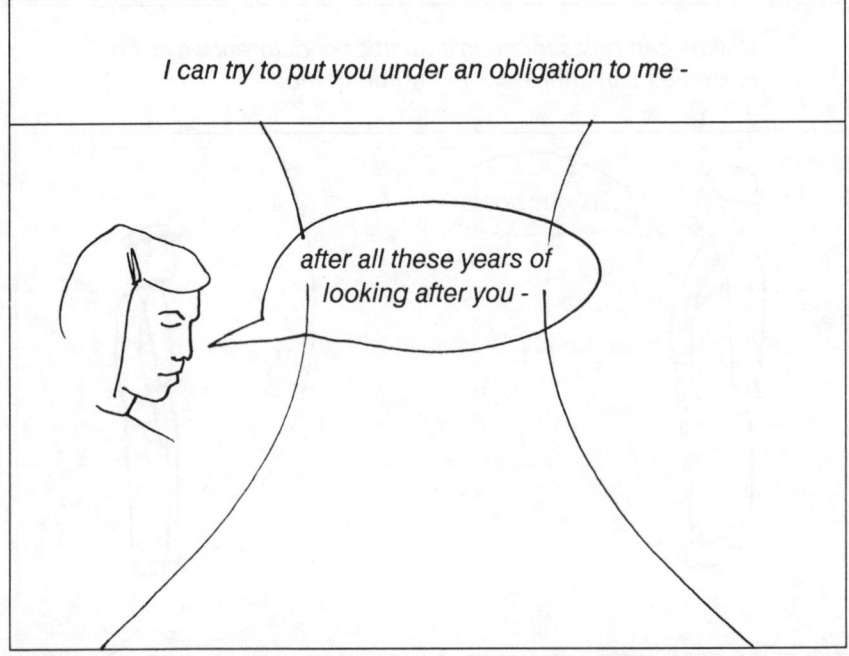

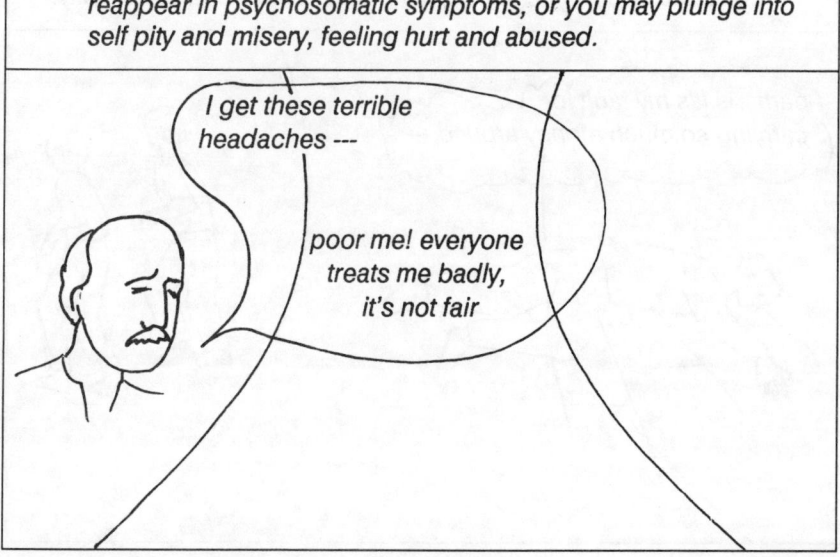

The effect of pervasive claims is to give you a diffuse sense of frustration and discontent. You will tend to concentrate on what is lacking in a situation.

You will probably feel very uncertain about what your rights actually are. The more you live in your private world, the more confused you will be about your rights in the world of actuality.

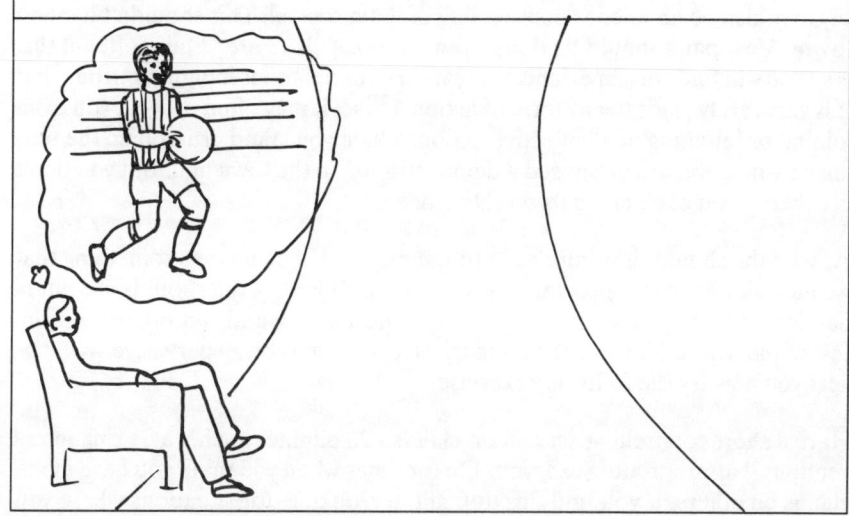

Inactivity and inertia is another common result of pervasive claims. Underlying this is the unconscious claim that intentions should be enough to bring about achievement.

As with the shoulds, these claims are unrealistic. There is little possibility of their fulfillment and the person making them has little consideration of whether they are in fact possible. They are almost always egocentric, arising from the individual's need to cling onto his idealisation. Frequently they contain an expectation that things will come to you without your making any effort. In general the reasons behind claims are unconscious. You are unlikely to be aware that some wish you have or demand you make is a claim. If someone points it out to you, you will probably have some plausible justification for why your claim is in fact a very reasonable demand and can even be seen as a positive quality. It is of course important to see that some demands you make have a basis in the real world and do not simply exist to help you maintain an idealisation. Frequently a demand you make can be a mixture of a compulsive claim and a genuine demand.

To take an example - conditions on the housing estate where you live are awful. Repairs aren't done and the council hasn't collected the rubbish for weeks. Your reaction is to feel that this is unjust, you have been badly treated and something ought to be done about it. You stand on the corner, full of righteous indignation, grumbling to your neighbour. It is quite true that you have a genuine grievance and it is reasonable to expect repairs to be done. There may also be an element of a claim in your demand however. Underneath what you say may also be an unconscious feeling of 'I am special. This shouldn't happen to *me*. *My* repairs should be done even if no-one else's are.' Quite often if this is so you will find you experience a great sense of righteous indignation, but that this very rarely leads to any form of action. In fact it may often prevent you from joining or initiating any collective action. While you stand grumbling, the tenants' association has organised a demonstration to the town hall. But you don't get there - you can't make the creative deed.

As with the shoulds it is important to remember that claims are something that we all experience to a greater or lesser extent. Whereas the shoulds are internal demands on yourself, the claims are external demands on others and the rest of the world. They may be quite trivial or they may be all pervasive. We suggest you now try the following exercise.

Have a short counselling session on claims - 20 minutes each way, using interventions if appropriate. Scan your life for times when you think you have made claims on others. If you find this difficult, try looking for situations where you have felt righteous indignation, vindictiveness, or uncertainty about your rights. Could there be an underlying claim? Spend some time discussing the exercise. As with the shoulds you may find it useful to do a repeat.

EXAMPLE OF SCANNING ON CLAIMS

WORKER "I find it easier to think of things that are claims from the past. One that seems funny now, though it certainly wasn't at the time, was when I broke up with my first girlfriend. I'd found out that she'd been seeing one of my friends and we had this big showdown. We were only 15. I remember we were at her parent's place and she kept saying - 'Ssh! You'll bring my mum down.' I was shouting so much. I kept saying to her - 'You betrayed me! You lied to me! I'll never trust anyone again!' Things like that - real romantic drivel as I'd see it now. But at the time it was all a great tragedy - I was sure I would never love anyone again because she'd two-timed me with my mate Bob. I think the claim was that she should love me regardless of what she actually felt. Mind you I think she made a lot of claims on me - I had to be smart, must wear a suit if I took her out, mustn't swear, must buy her chocolates in the cinema, must be polite to her mum. In some ways I suppose our claims fitted but in the end I was quite relieved. I could stop polishing my shoes every day....(Pause). One of my other claims is about people who leave the top off the toothpaste tube - it upsets me all day if someone does that... and leaving my records out of order... and not clearing something up the moment you spill it... I suppose that's a claim that other people should do things my way. They never do mind you... really gets up my nose... A lot of the things that I start to think of as possibly being claims are actually quite reasonable though. For instance, yesterday I waited half an hour for the No. 14 bus - and I don't think it's unreasonable to expect the buses to run on time - after all what do we pay our rates for? I mean it's ridiculous the way the bus service is at the moment. I'm sure that's not a claim.

ASSISTANT Try saying what you thought at the time.

WORKER Well... I thought... it's cold... and I'm tired... and I've had a hard day... and I thought *damn* London Transport, I'm going to be late home, and it's not fair... it's not bloody fair...

ASSISTANT Again?

WORKER It's bloody not fair. It's not fair .It really isn't fair. Well it's *not*. I work hard all day and I've got a right to be able to get home from work in time to see my kids... it's just not fair... and Pat gets annoyed if I'm late...it's not fair. It's not right. It's really not fair.   (Pause)

Well I suppose, maybe, it is a bit of a claim. There's the rational bit of me which says - well, it's bloody annoying the bus service is so bad, but there's no point in getting worked up about it because that won't make the bus come any quicker. Sometimes I even get around to thinking about *why* the bus service is so bad and what needs to be done about it. That's the rational part. The other part is that I do get worked up about it. I was cursing London Transport till I was blue in the face and I was so irritable when I got home I shouted at the kids. I couldn't stop thinking about it all evening. I guess that part's a claim of some kind. It's something to do with being exempt, being special - a 'this shouldn't happen to me' kind of thing. Because I wasn't in the least bit bothered about any of the other poor sods and some of them had been waiting much longer than me. There were two old ladies who'd been there ages and I didn't care a fig about them (Pause)

ASSISTANT Try saying what the feeling is.

WORKER Well, I'm starting to feel guilty about the two old ladies now!! I was so busy worrying about myself I never gave a thought to how cold they must have been... I feel really selfish now...

ASSISTANT Try saying I *shouldn't* be selfish. I *should* always be concerned...

WORKER I shouldn't be selfish...(laughing) Yeah, I shouldn't be selfish... (more laughter)... It's what my mum always used to say..."   etc, etc.

One final word now about shoulds and claims. We have the assumption that undoing compulsive trends and patterns that have built up over many years is a slow and difficult process and involves working with unconscious material that can be painful and distressing. It is quite common in the process of counselling to start to develop new shoulds and claims in an attempt to deal with this. For example - I should change all these things immediately. Is this happening to you yet?

The "shoulds" we internalise and the claims we make form a unique caracteristic pattern of moving towards - against - away. Karen Horney called this:

THE PRIDE SYSTEM

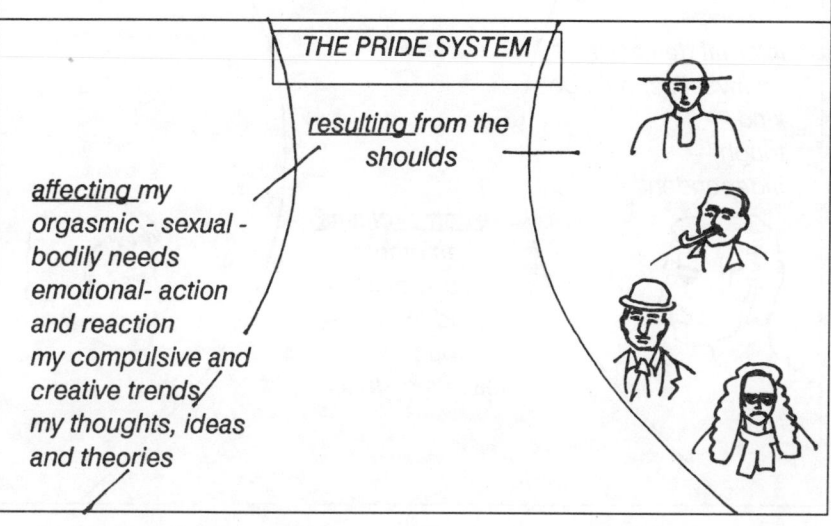

resulting from the shoulds

affecting my
orgasmic - sexual -
bodily needs
emotional- action
and reaction
my compulsive and
creative trends
my thoughts, ideas
and theories

We will work upon the unconscious trends later. For the moment we want to stress that:

most of the pride system is *unconscious*

for example:

unconscious
pride defends
a compulsive
against trend

conscious

I never apologise!

159

We can think of the pride system as a kind of defence system - defending me internally and externally

<u>internal demands</u>
on myself: should be
kind ---
tough ---
independent ---

<u>external claims</u>
on others:
you should be
kind to me ----
tougher ---
leave me alone ---

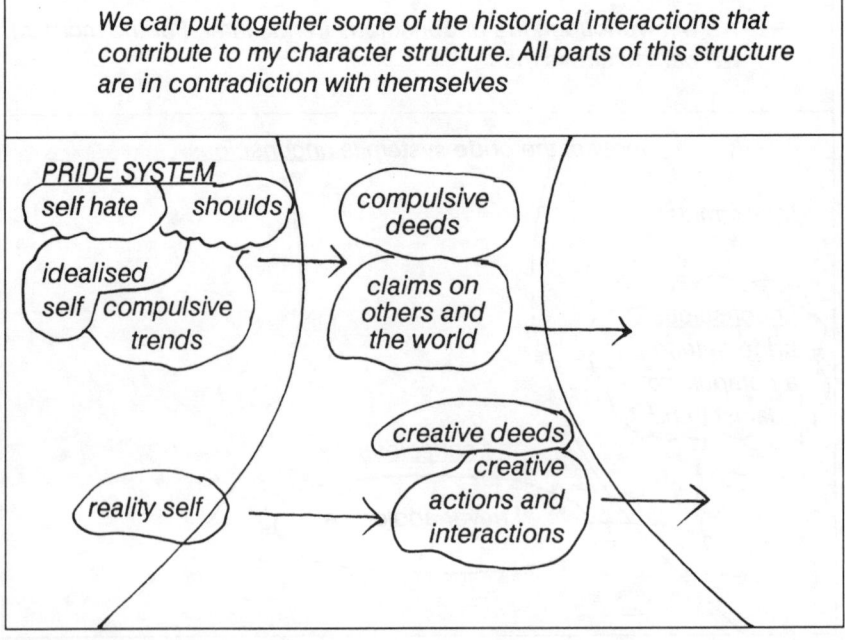

We can put together some of the historical interactions that contribute to my character structure. All parts of this structure are in contradiction with themselves

> *The result of constant internal demands (the shoulds) can lead to SELF HATE. This takes all kinds of forms, but in extremis might end in suicide.*
>
> *everyone's nicer than me*
> *I'm useless*
> *If I really knew myself it would be a horror movie*
>
> *I can't do anything*

THE PRIDE SYSTEM AND SELF HATE

At this point some definitions may be useful:

The idealised self. This is my idea of what I am or what I should be. It is unrealistic, glorified, impossible to attain. It exists in the area of subjective reality although I will probably perceive it as existing objectively and it will crucially affect my deeds in relation to the world.

The reality self. Karen Horney calls this the real self. We have changed her definition slightly because whereas she sees the real self as an innate potential for growth, we see it as the part of you that is in genuine contact with objective reality and can operate spontaneously in relation to others. We see this as arising from deeds and not from an instinctual force.

The actual self. This is the sum total of your being at any one time and includes both the reality and idealised selves.

The pride system consists of two conflicting forces - pride and self-hate. The pride is in no sense real pride in your actual capabilities. It is perhaps what is usually called 'false pride' and stems as we saw earlier from the need to maintain an idealisation. Anything can be invested with pride but in particular you may find that your most compulsive needs are turned into assets that you should be proud of. Thus for example, appeasement becomes goodness, dependency becomes love, inconsistency becomes freedom.

One effect of this is to make you very vulnerable as your idealised image becomes a measuring rod with which you measure your actual being, and, insofar as your actual being seems to interfere with your idealisation, so you hate it. You start to hate yourself. Pride and self-hate are absolutely inseparable. They are the two sides of the same coin of misery and suffering.

Self-hate is an extremely powerful and tenacious phenomenon. It is not only the result of self-glorification but also one of the ways in which it is maintained as we saw with the shoulds. For example, I should be a good mother. If I'm not then I flood myself with blame and criticism in an attempt to drive myself to ever higher standards of perfection.

Awareness of self-hate is often very slight although the results of it may be more evident in feelings of guilt, inferiority, shame or torment. It is essentially an unconscious process and because of this it is often externalised. This can be an active externalisation where instead of consciously hating myself I direct my hate outwards against other people, other ideas, institutions or life itself. The things I hate most in others will probably be the things I hate most in myself. Alternatively the externalisation can be passive. In this case I will feel the hate as directed against myself but will see it as coming from other people. For instance - no-one likes me, everyone despises me, I'm always the victim.

Self-hate can operate as part of two different conflicts. The one that is most apparent is the conflict within the pride system between pride and self-hate. Less apparent is what Karen Horney calls the central inner conflict. This is the conflict between the whole pride system and the reality self. As you proceed with your counselling and particularly when you begin to work with unconscious material you will begin to undermine the pride system. As this happens you may experience self-hate in its worst and most forceful dimensions - turned against your reality self which in the process of counselling should be becoming stronger and more directive.

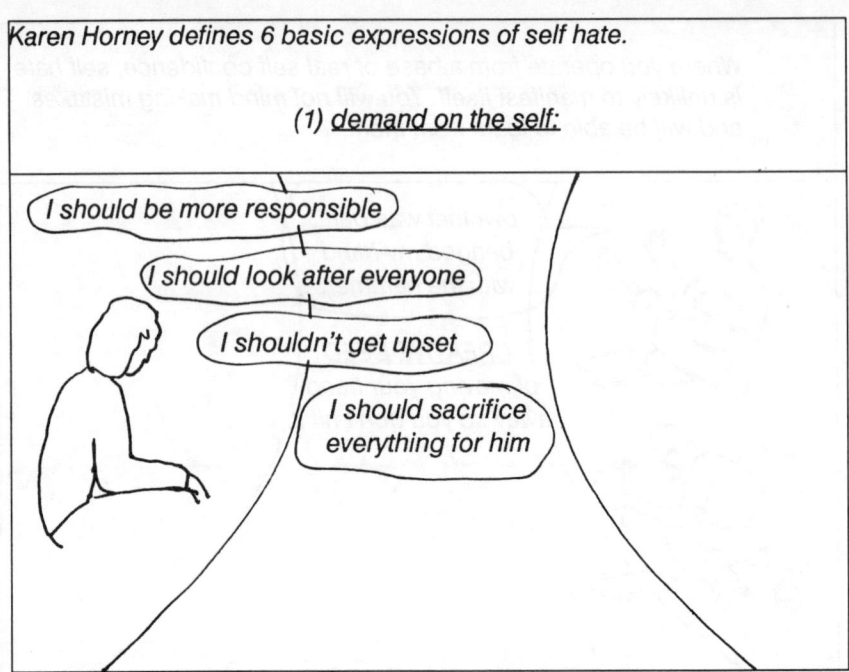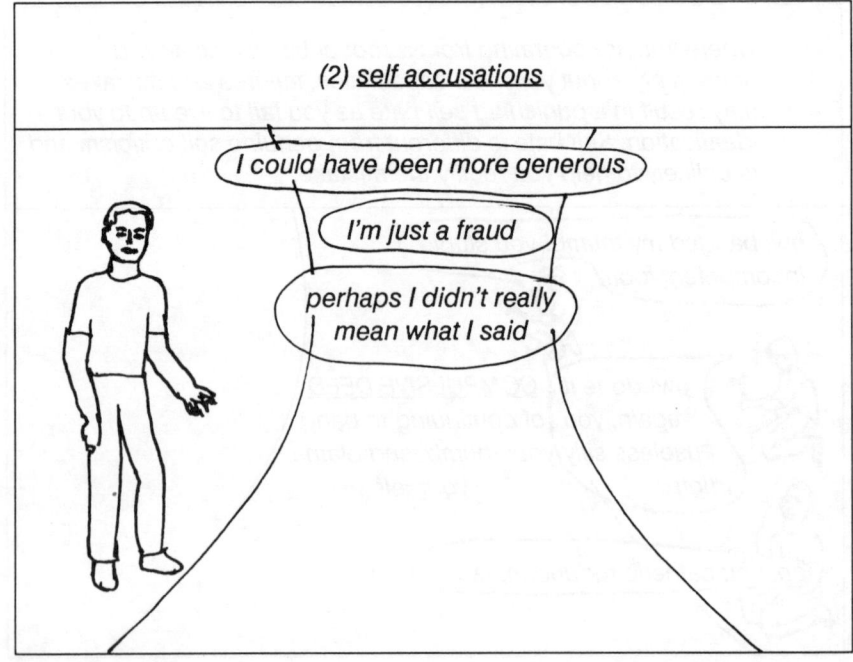

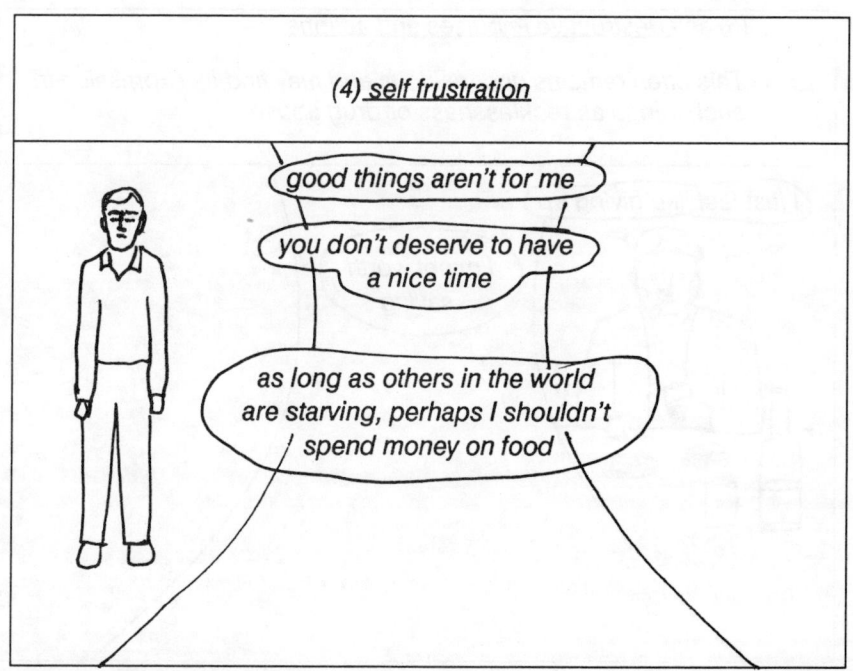

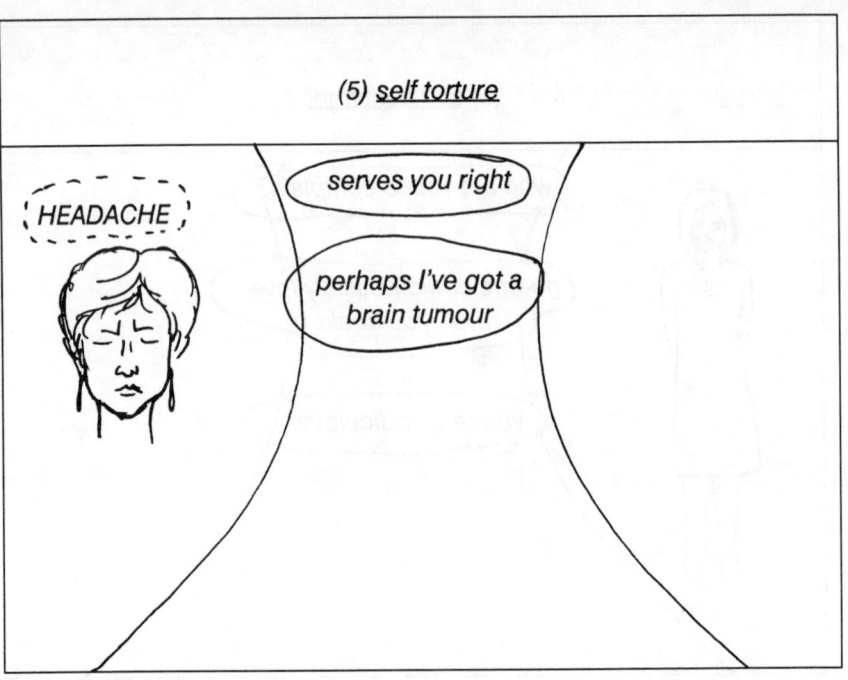
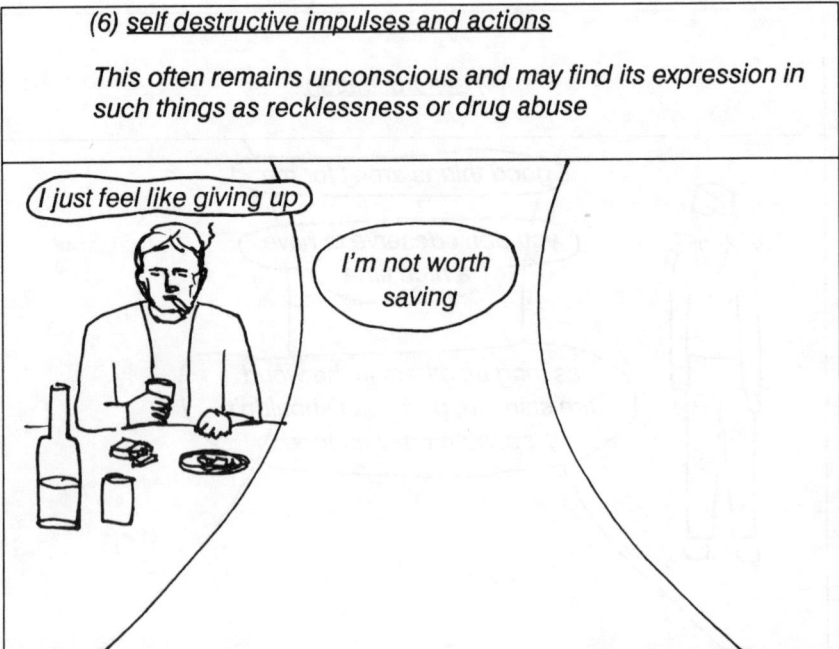

If you've done all the exercises and counselling so far it's probably a good idea to do another full session of 3 hours. We suggest ---

WORKER

Free wheel and work "as it comes" - let your unconscious worry about Karen Horney deeds and theory

DEEDS
chat
trivia of day
play
counselling
discussion
repeat

ASSISTANT

Similarly let your unconscious worry about Karen Horney listen to the music - trust your intuition

We suggest you both skim through the preceding parts and discuss what you think about it in the light of your counselling work.

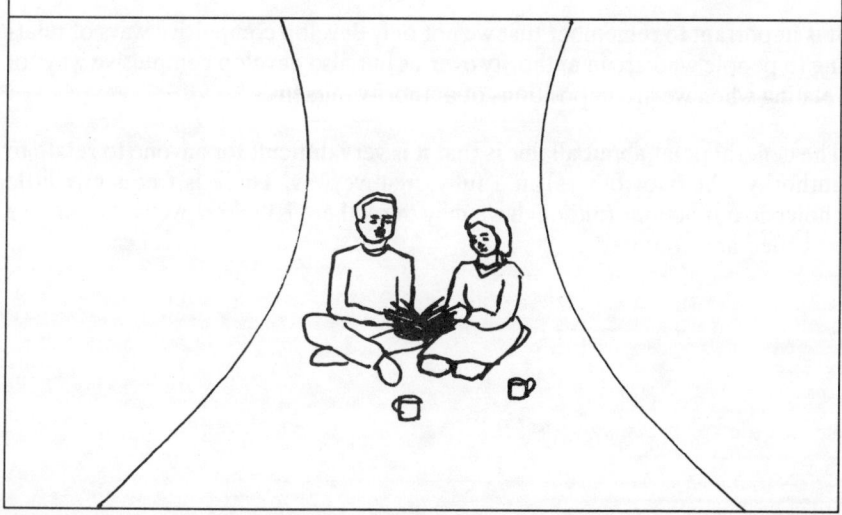

THE PATRIPSYCH

The patripsych is a short term for what we have called the 'internal constellation of patriarchal patterns'. By this we mean all the attitudes, ideas and feelings, usually compulsive and unconscious, that develop in relation to authority and control. This development is closely related to learning about sex-roles - learning about whether you are a little boy or a little girl. We do not believe that children know instinctively which sex they belong to. We argue that this is something which is learnt in the family. If you compare our culture with other cultures or other periods of history, for instance, you will find that being male or female has very different meanings.

We said that these feelings are generally compulsive and unconscious and that they relate to issues around authority and control. Some examples of this would be:

1) I have compulsive feelings of dependence on authority figures. I will do whatever they say and assume they know best.

2) I have a compulsive need to fight authority figures. If someone is in control I will argue and oppose them regardless of what they do.

3) I have a compulsive need to flight from authority figures. If I feel someone is in control I will try to leave or withdraw into myself and ignore what is going on.

It is important to remember that we not only develop compulsive ways of relating to people who are in authority over us but also develop compulsive ways of relating when we are in positions of authority ourselves.

The general point about all this is that it is very difficult for anyone to relate to authority (theirs or others) in a fully creative way. There is frequently little choice in our actions (although we may think there is) and power relations are mystified and confused.

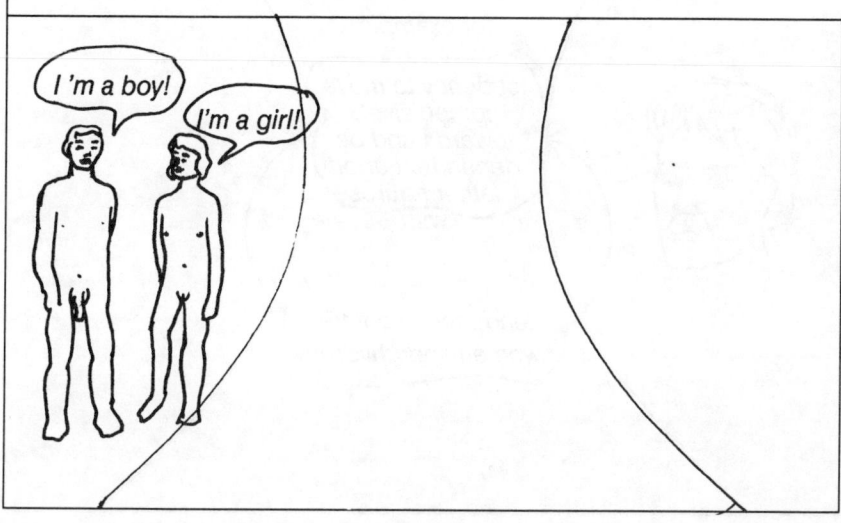

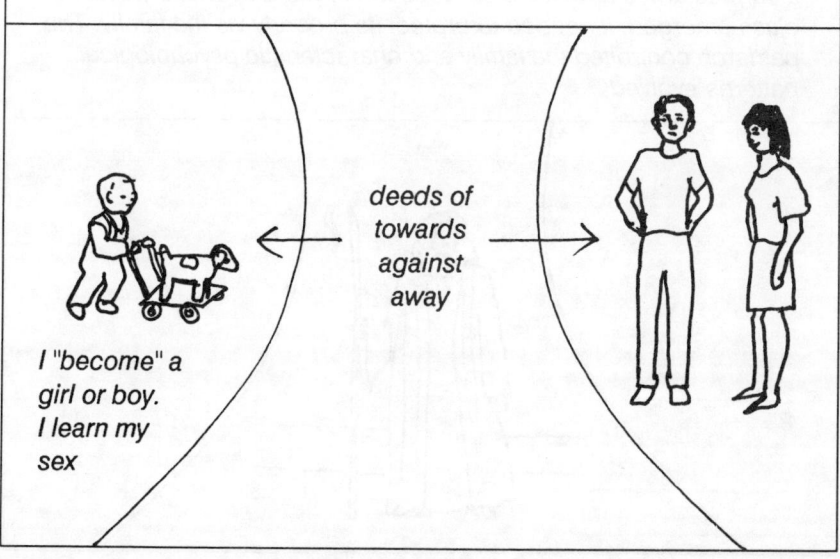

Within me certain emotions and norms arise around my sex role. Many of these feelings are unconscious

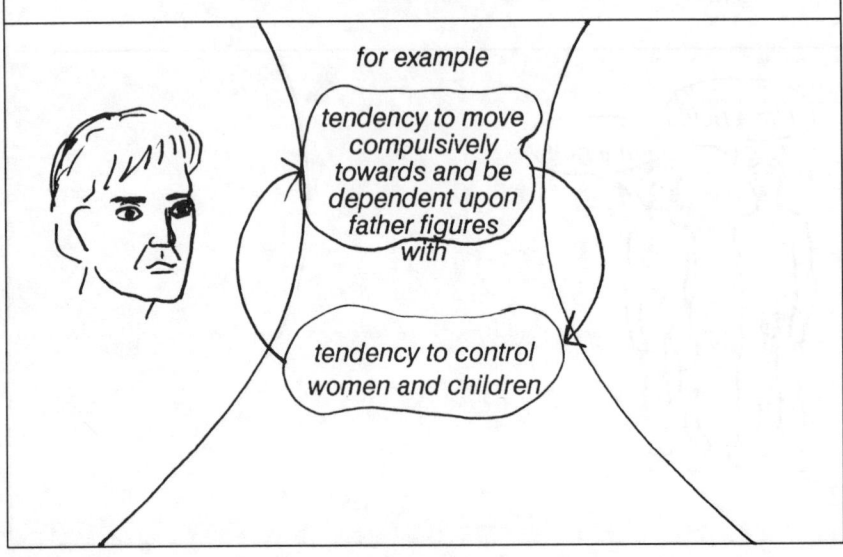

General trends of this sort exist in each of us without exception. We call these trends the PATRIPSYCH - because 5/6000 years ago when a surplus arose above the production of food and shelter, a ruling class emerged. It needed to protect its property via the family. The patriarch controlled the family and characteristic psychological patterns evolved

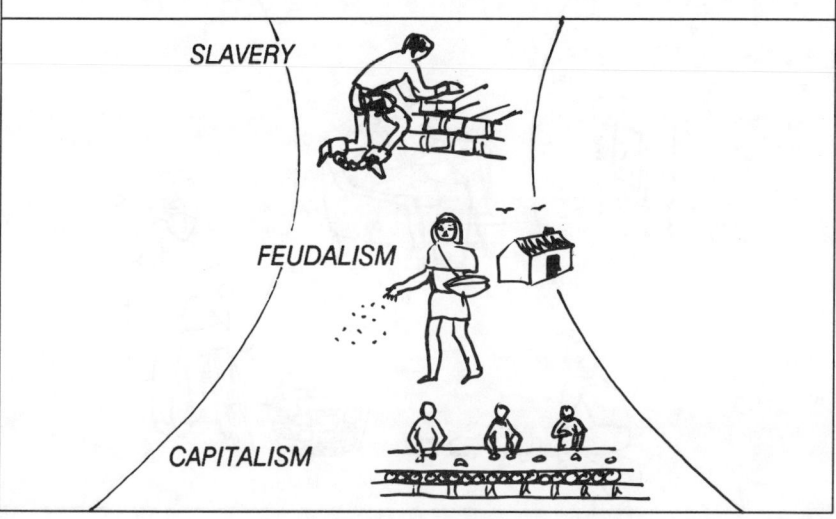
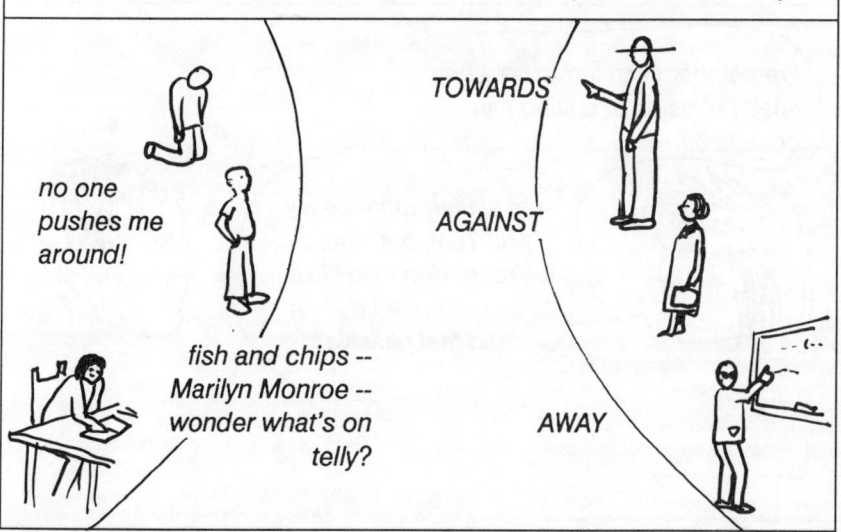

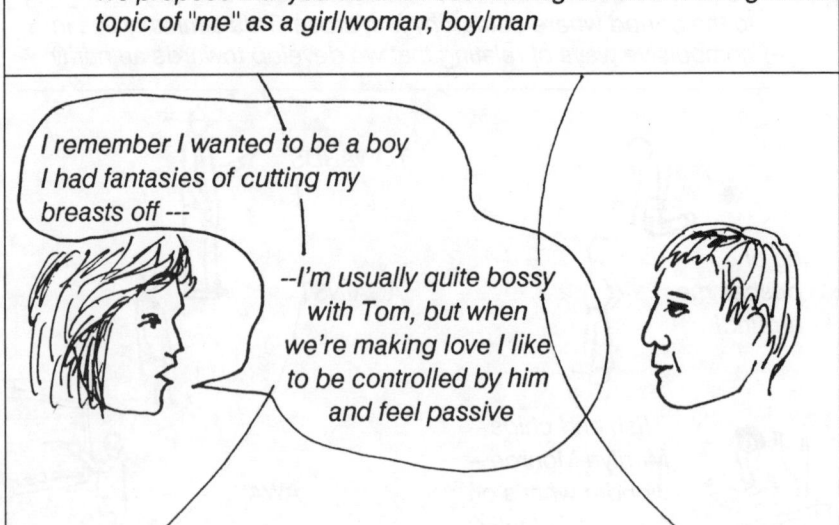

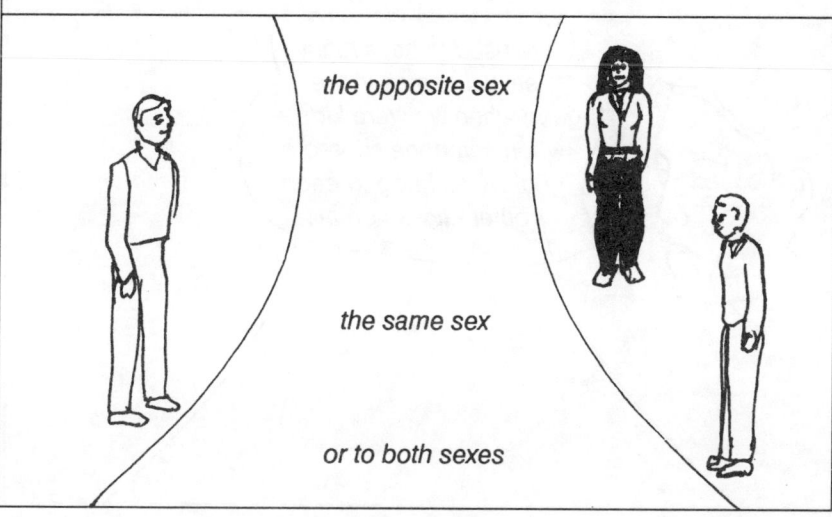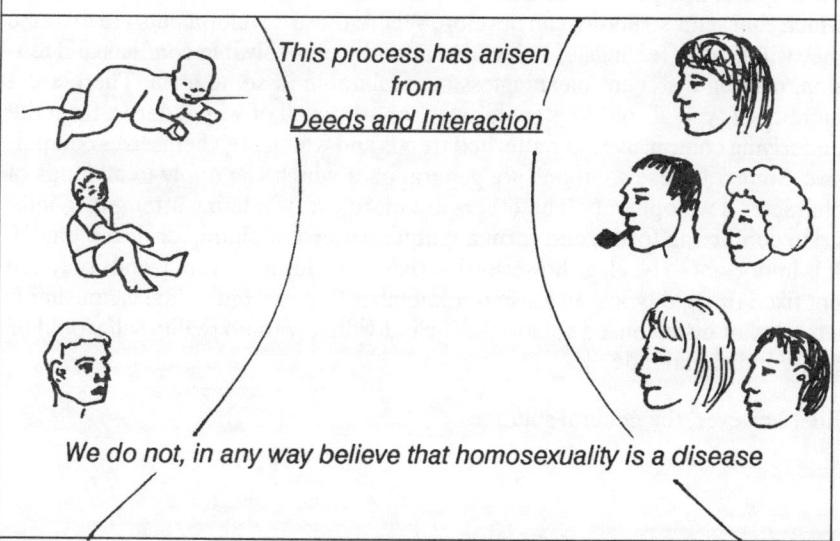

ATTEMPTS TO RELIEVE TENSION AND COMPULSIVE SOLUTIONS

Throughout this part of the book we have talked about a number of ways in which character structure can develop. Where these developments are extreme they will lead to feelings of being torn apart by unresolvable conflicts and tension, making life seem meaningless or intolerable in some form. There are a number of typical solutions to this state of affairs all of which derive from the underlying compulsive anf patterned trends and which are themselves compulsive. Some of these solutions are general ones which can apply to all kinds of character developments. The others are more overwhelming attempts to integrate conflicting forces and form a unique pattern of character development. It is important to be clear however that these developments are trends only and not fixed or rigid types, and also to remember that any individual is not simply a totality of his idealised solutions. The individual with no reality self would be a rare individual indeed.

First however, the general solutions.

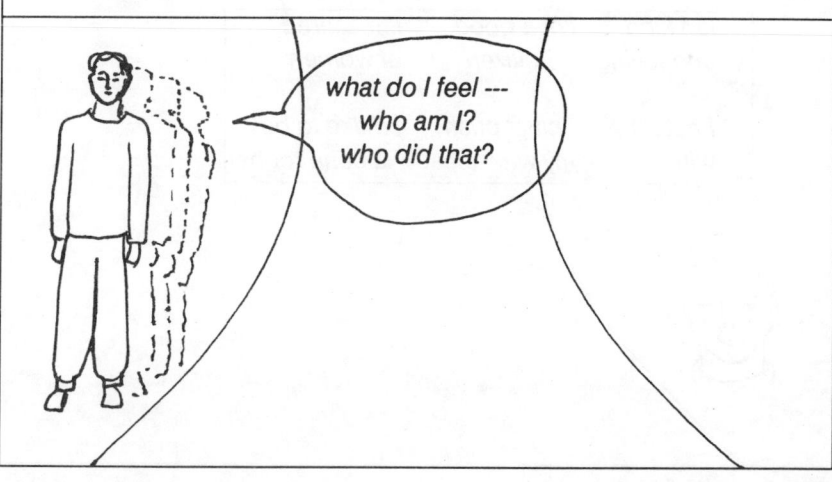

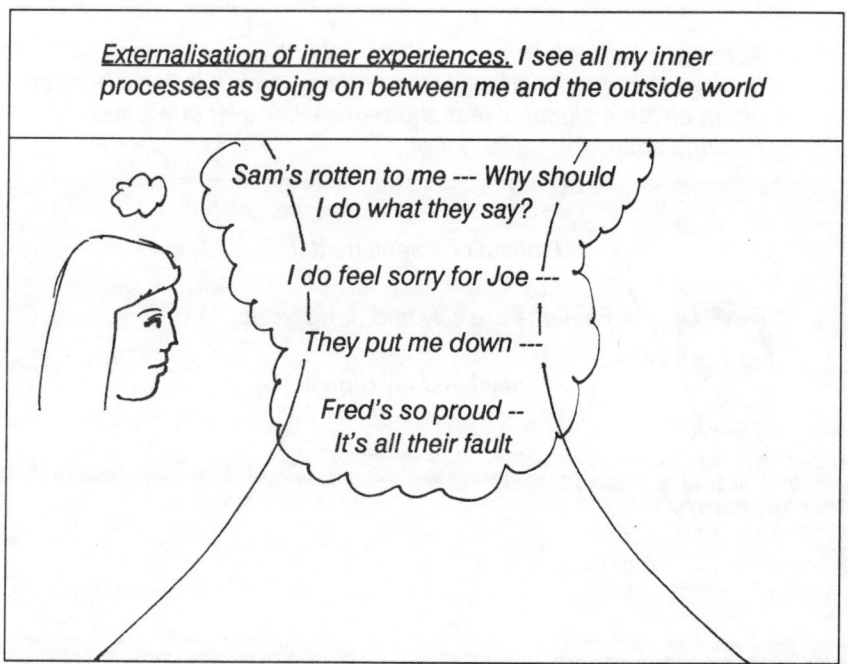

Compartmentalisation This is like keeping parts of yourself in different boxes so the conflicts are never apparent and you never see cause and effect. If this is one of your solutions, you may find it difficult to understand dialectics at a personal level.

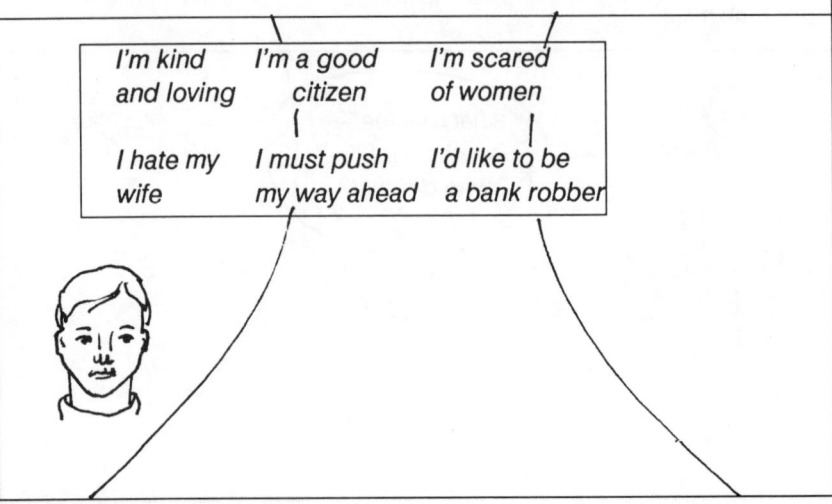

Automatic Control This is a solution of putting a check on all feelings that might endanger the pride system. It is like a burglar alarm giving a signal of fear and panic whenever unwanted feelings arise. You never "let go"

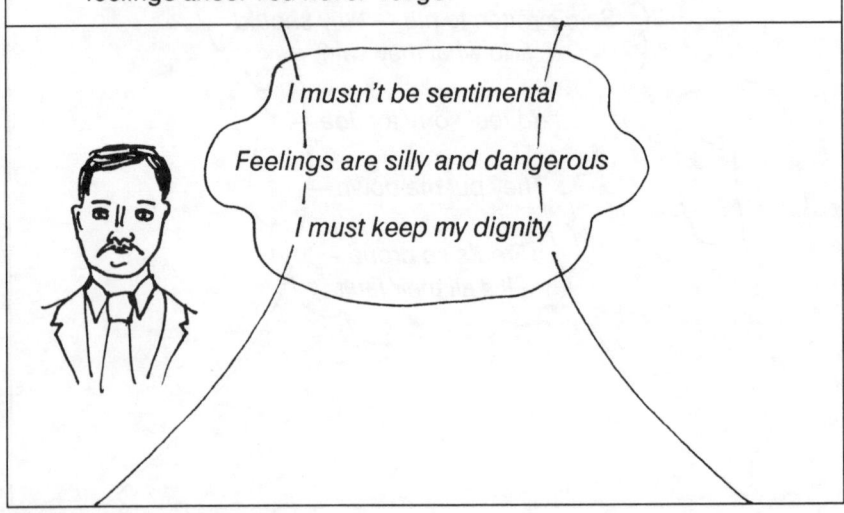

Supremacy of the Mind I live in my head and resolve all my conflicts in the abstract. I watch myself live. My logic will save me.

mind over matter --- --- if I wish for it strongly enough it will happen --- intelligence can solve anything

We suggest you do a counselling session trying to look at where you have taken any of these solutions. Have a discussion afterwards

at school I was always small and weedy - but I was clever and I think that became a solution for me

Looking at the specific solutions or character developments we can see how all the factors we have so far enumerated operate together. The crucial question for any of us as an individual here is 'how do I experience myself'. If the idealised self makes up for the larger part of experience you are likely at various times to have experienced profound feelings of uncertainty about your identity, perhaps unconsciously rather than consciously . As Karen Horney herself puts it, the question that torments you is 'Am I the proud superhuman being - or am I the subdued, guilty and rather despicable creature?' The two sides of the pride system operate in unity and opposition (See P.120). They are in unity in that the one is dependent for its existence on the other. They are in opposition in that the conflict between them threatens to tear you apart. At different times you are likely to feel totally identified with one side or the other. The solution to this is usually to move in the direction of identifying with one or other part of the contradiction or alternatively of removing yourself entirely from it.

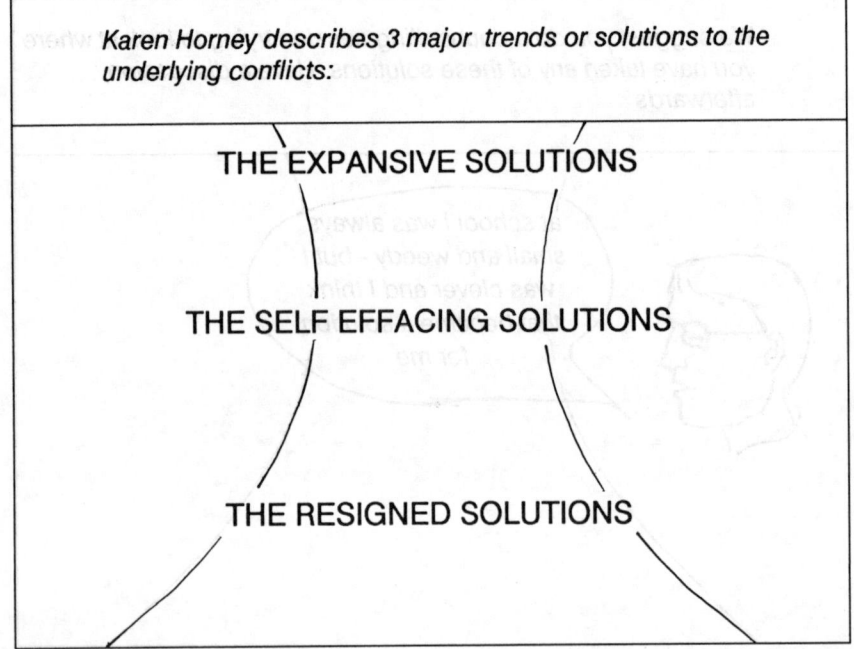

Karen Horney describes 3 major trends or solutions to the underlying conflicts:

THE EXPANSIVE SOLUTIONS

THE SELF EFFACING SOLUTIONS

THE RESIGNED SOLUTIONS

In the EXPANSIVE SOLUTIONS you identify prevailingly with your idealised self. You are engaged in a compulsive, never ending search for glory.

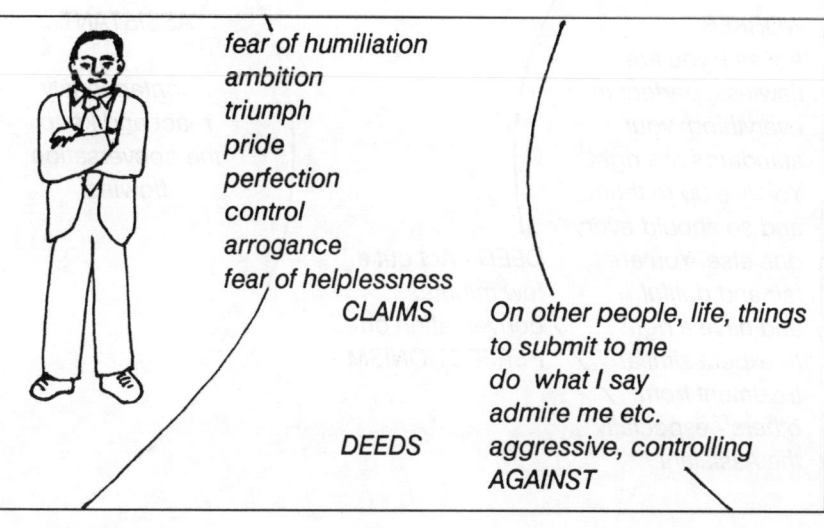

fear of humiliation
ambition
triumph
pride
perfection
control
arrogance
fear of helplessness

CLAIMS   On other people, life, things
          to submit to me
          do what I say
          admire me etc.

DEEDS   aggressive, controlling
          AGAINST

It is easier to learn this by role play. We will look at 4 subdivisions of the Expansive Solutions. The first is NARCISSISM. You identify with your idealised self. Use any topic that comes to mind. Repeat with roles reversed.

WORKER
Act as if you are supremely selfconfident in all your marvellous attributes. You are glorious and intelligent and to be admired. The assistant should devote her life to you. You are charming and delightful Others should love you, uncond itionally

DEED - Act out a few minutes conversation on NARCISSISM

ASSISTANT
Spontaneously react and keep the conversation flowing

181

Second role play: PERFECTIONISM
Here you identify with your standards

WORKER
Act as if you are flawless, perfect in everything: your standards are right. You live up to them and so should everyone else. You are fair and dutiful and have a right to expect similar treatment from others - especially the Assistant

DEED - Act out a few minutes conversation on PERFECTIONISM

ASSISTANT
Spontaneously react and keep the conversation flowing

Third role play: ARROGANT VINDICTIVENESS
Here your motivating force is the need for vindictive triumph

WORKER
Act as if you are proud competitive, ruthless. Everyone else is hypocritical. Be arrogant, offensive and rude. Frustrate others: you are invulnerable; you have a right to hurt others. Enjoy your sadism

DEED Act out a few minutes conversation on ARROGANT VINDICTIVENESS

ASSISTANT
Spontaneously react and keep the conversation flowing

Fourth role play: AGGRESSIVE MASTERY
This is a less extreme version of arrogant vindictiveness

WORKER
Act as if you must master and control everything and every one, particularly the Assistant, her life, loves, mind and baby

DEED Act out a few minutes conversation on AGGRESSIVE MASTERY

ASSISTANT
Spontaneously react and keep the conversation flowing

After doing a role play you may need to "derole". Separate yourself from the role you have just played.

"I don't really hate you and want to control you"

"I'm glad to hear that - some of what you said made me feel quite upset"

We suggest you now have a discussion about these kinds of solutions and try to look at the following topics:

1) The contradictions involved in these solutions. What is the effect for example if any of these idealisations is smashed? Karen Horney suggests that in the perfectionist solution the effect of recognising an error or failure or finding that life is not as perfect as your demands will plunge you into undiluted self-hate.

2) What general attitudes and defences towards life accompany these solutions? Karen Horney argues for instance that in the case of the narcissisitic solution the individual is generally optimistic, turning outwards to joy and happiness, yet often at the same time, sensing a discrepancy between expectations and experience.

3) What are the effects of these solutions on human relations? Work situations?

In the SELF EFFACING solutions you find a never ending search for reassurance, protection and love. You identify prevailingly with your subdued self and have taboos on all that is presumptuous, selfish and aggressive.

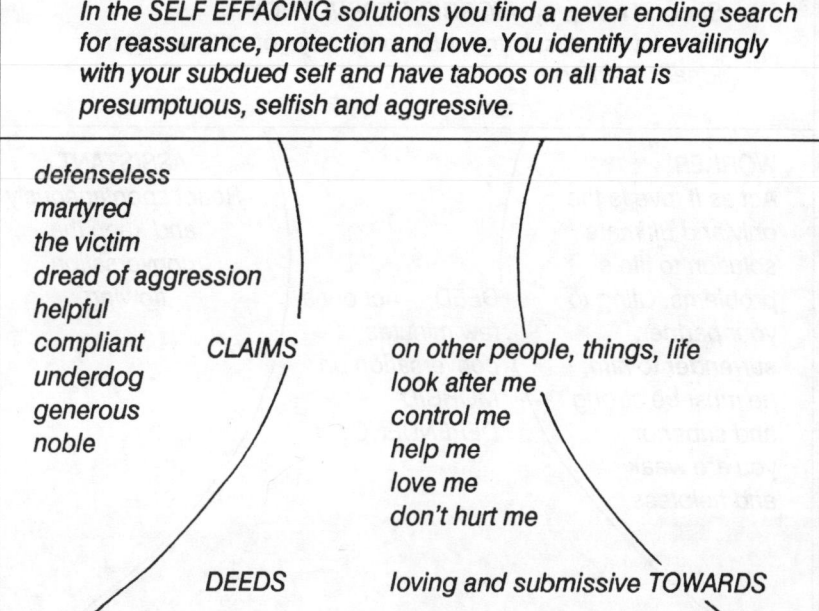

defenseless
martyred
the victim
dread of aggression
helpful
compliant
underdog
generous
noble

CLAIMS on other people, things, life
look after me
control me
help me
love me
don't hurt me

DEEDS loving and submissive TOWARDS

Karen Horney divides this type of solution into 2 main trends. Again we suggest you try a role play. First SELF EFFACEMENT. Repeat with roles reversed.

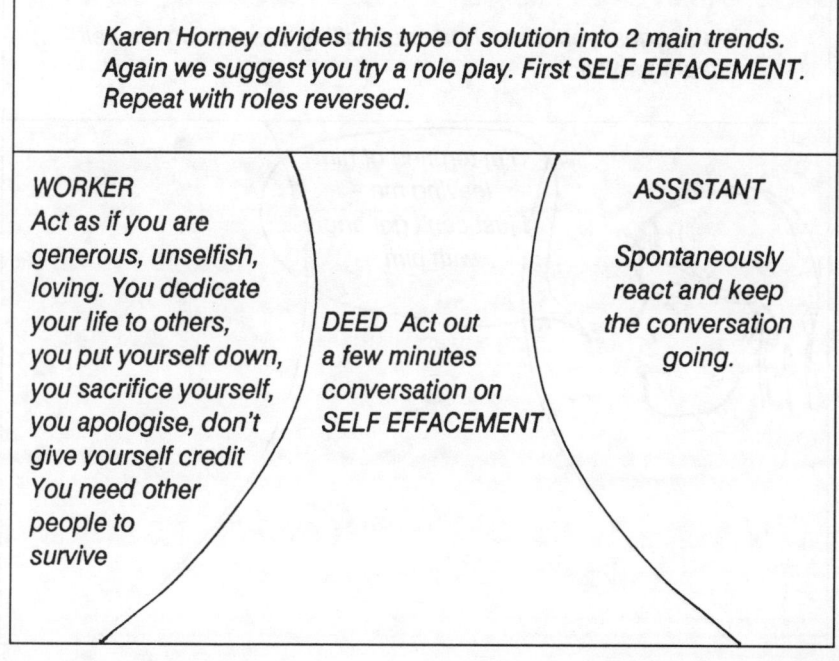

WORKER
Act as if you are generous, unselfish, loving. You dedicate your life to others, you put yourself down, you sacrifice yourself, you apologise, don't give yourself credit You need other people to survive

DEED Act out a few minutes conversation on SELF EFFACEMENT

ASSISTANT

Spontaneously react and keep the conversation going.

185

Second role play: MORBID DEPENDENCY
Here love and surrender become ways of actualising the idealised image.

WORKER
Act as if love is the only and ultimate solution to life's problems. Cling to your partner, surrender to him; he must be strong and superior. you are weak and helpless

DEED - Act out a few minutes conversation on MORBID DEPENDENCY

ASSISTANT
React spontaneously and keep the conversation flowing.

We suggest you do a short counselling session on the self effacing solutions.

I'm terrified of him leaving me ---
I just can't get angry with him ---

We suggest you now have a discussion about these kinds of solutions and try to look at the following topics:

1) The contradictions involved in these solutions. How for instance can hostility and vindictiveness be expressed? Karen Horney suggests this can happen through extreme demands on others that attempt to make them feel guilty.

2) What general attitudes and defences towards life accompany these solutions? In what ways are these solutions more typical for women?

3) What are the effects of these solutions on human relations? Work situations? Karen Horney suggests that frequently relationship form between a man with arrogant vindictive tendencies and a woman with morbid dependent tendencies as up to a point they complement each other.

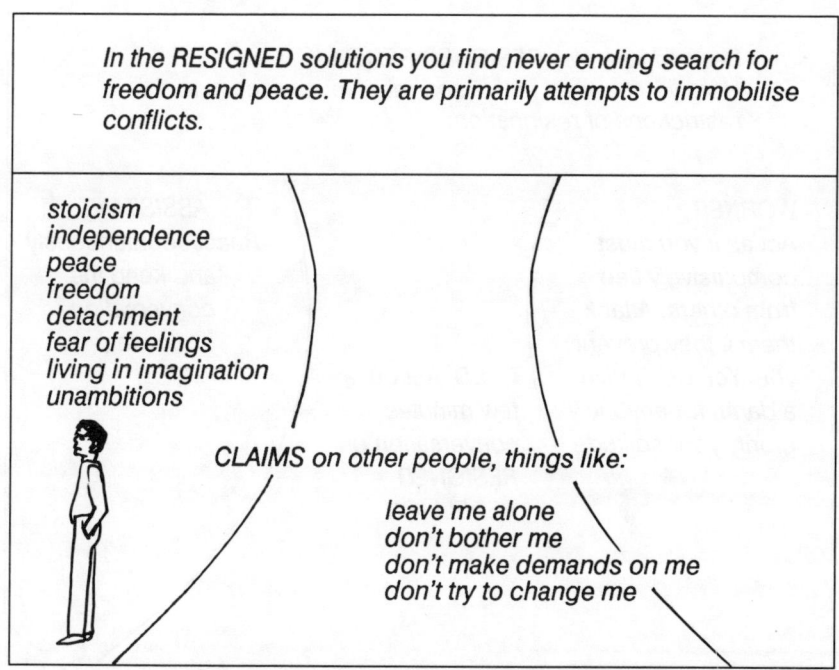

Karen Horney divided this type of solution into 3 main trends.
Again we suggest you try a role play.
First PERSISTANT RESIGNATION.

WORKER
Act as if you must be free of all feelings and ideas. You don't want to use any energy - be aloof, self sufficient, detached and private. You have no closeness or strong feelings at all.

DEED Act out a few minutes conversation on PERSISTENT RESIGNATION

ASSISTANT
React spontaneously and keep the conversation flowing

Second role play RESIGNED REBELLION
Here you have an active and rebellious reaction to the restrictions of resignation

WORKER
Act as if you must compulsively flee from others. Attack them if they prevent you. You don't give a damn for anyone - glorify your solitude

DEED Act out a few minutes conversation on RESIGNED REBELLION

ASSISTANT
React spontaneously and keep the conversation flowing

Third role play on SHALLOW LIVING
Here you find a retreat into trivia, fun or automated living

WORKER
Act as if all that matters is distraction; do any thing to stop yourself feeling, thinking or acting seriously

DEED Act out a few minutes conversation on SHALLOW LIVING

ASSISTANT
React spontaneously and keep the conversation flowing

We suggest you now do a short counselling session on the RESIGNED SOLUTIONS

I've always wanted to be able to live without other people ---

I thought of joining the Foreign Legion

Sometimes I watch TV to get away from it all

We suggest you now have a discussion about these kinds of solutions and try to look at the following topics:

1) The contradictions involved in these solutions.

2) What general attitudes and defences towards life accompany these solutions? What, for example, are the social implications of trivialised, automaton-living? How and why is it encouraged?

3) What are the effects of these solutions on human relationships? Does the emotional deadness and alienation involved prevent relating?

ROLE PLAYING TRENDS

The role-playing just outlined for pairs can also be done in a group. This exercise can be energising and fun. Each member writes below the numbers 1 - 9 in random order. Have a short enteraction of two minutes only with every other member of the group and act into the trends one by one in your random order. If there aren't many of you you'll find you meet some people twice. You can pick any subject for your conversation - something you have done together in the past, some aspect of your relating since the session started, or a completely imaginary topic. When you have role-played all the trends have a discussion in the group. What ones felt most like your own experience? What happened when, for example, someone playing a morbid-dependent trend, met someone into arrogant vindictiveness? What if you were both into resigned rebellion? It is usually useful when doing this exercise if someone acts as a time-keeper as it can get quite hectic.

Towards-major trend of self effacement

1) Self effacement

Be compulsively loving. Put yourself down all the time. You're small and a martyr, self-sacrificing, there's nothing you couldn't grovel about.

2) Morbid dependency

You're totally helpless, ill, need looking after for ever. Everyone must love you or you'll die.

Against-major trends of expansive solutions

3) Aggressive mastery

Master and control everything and anyone. Master the other's life, loves, ideas, body... absolutely everything.

4) Narcissistic

You are glorious and wonderful and the other has to confirm your intelligence, beauty and glory in every small degree.

5) Arrogant-vindictive

You're absolutely ruthlessly proud; attack and be vindictive; you must triumph. Enjoy your sadism.

6) Perfectionist

You have to be totally perfect in everything, intellectual, emotional, whatever. The other person has to be perfect too.

Away - Major trend of resignation

7) Persistent resignation

Be free of all feelings and ideas about anyone or anything. Don't put any energy out if avoidable. Be totally self-sufficient, aloof, detached, private. No closeness.

8) Resigned rebellion

Be very active about getting away from everyone and everything.

9) Shallow living

Get into constant activity and distraction; any kind of fun or action which will avoid you thinking and feeling.

We can now put all of this together:

TRENDS

TOWARDS → self effacing solutions → self effacement
morbid dependency

AGAINST → expansive solutions → aggressive mastery
narcissism
perfectionism
arrogant
vindictiveness

AWAY → resigned solutions → persistent resignation
resigned rebellion
shallow living

Remember these are trends only - i.e. moving and changing directions in living AND IN ANY CASE WE ALSO HAVE:

CREATIVE DEEDS

discriminating loving

principled struggling

taking time and space for yourself

We propose that you now have several full counselling sessions to explore these avenues in your own lives

WORKER
still let things "flow" -as it comes- your creative unconscious will have taken much of this in

ASSISTANT
Remember that one trend on the "surface" may hide other trends. see if your interventions can help the worker to uncover her own trends. Check out that you use the "Golden Rules" though.

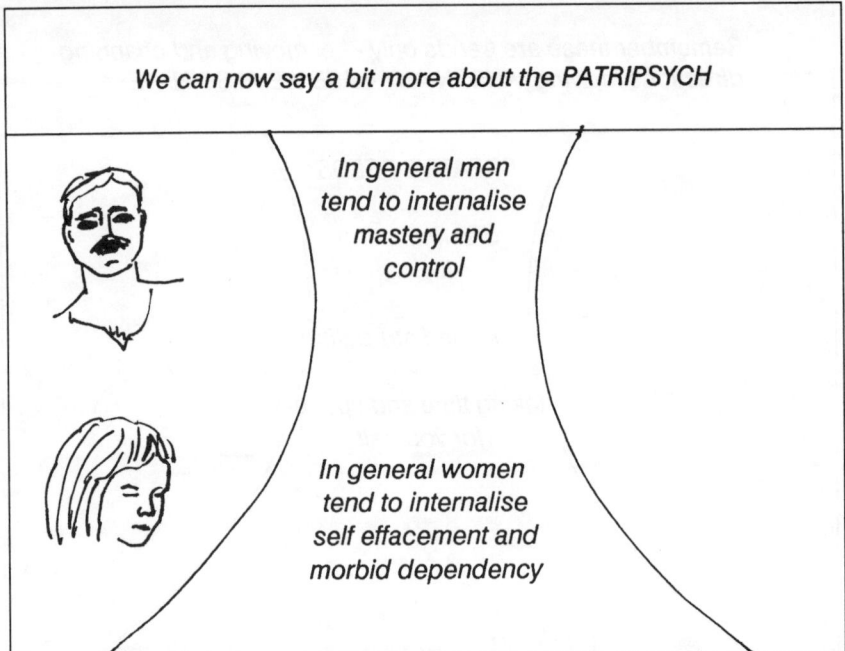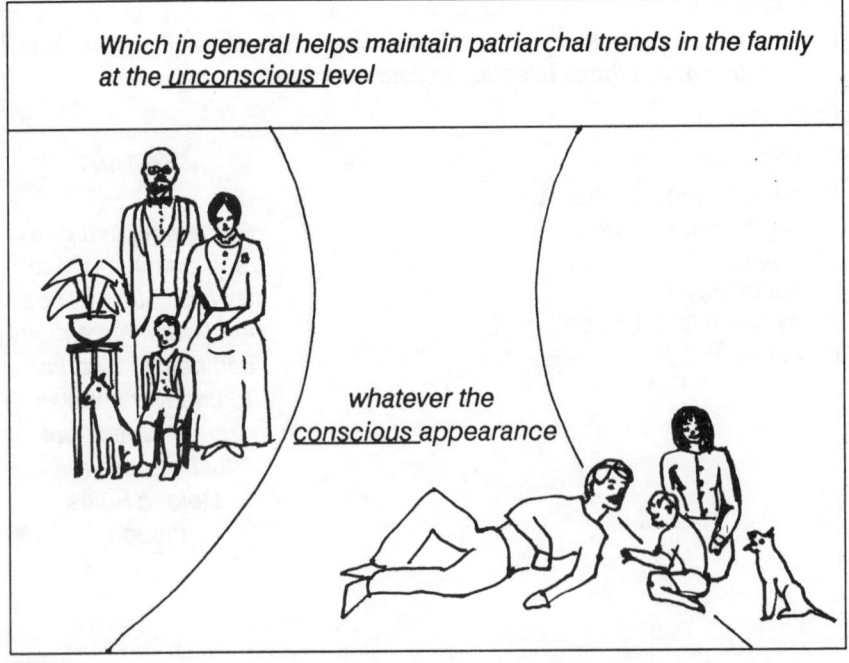

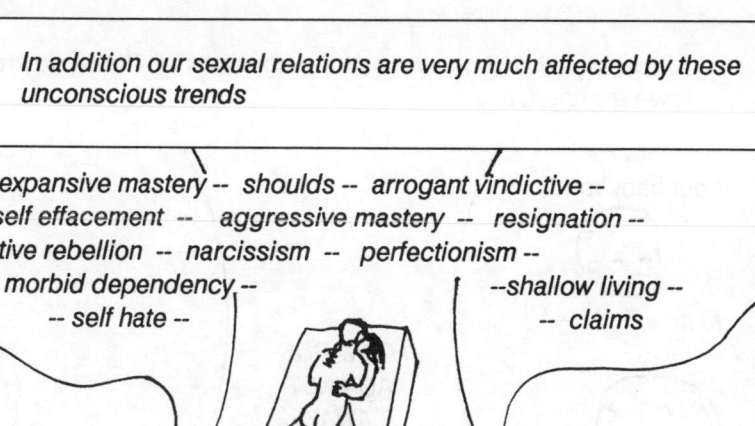

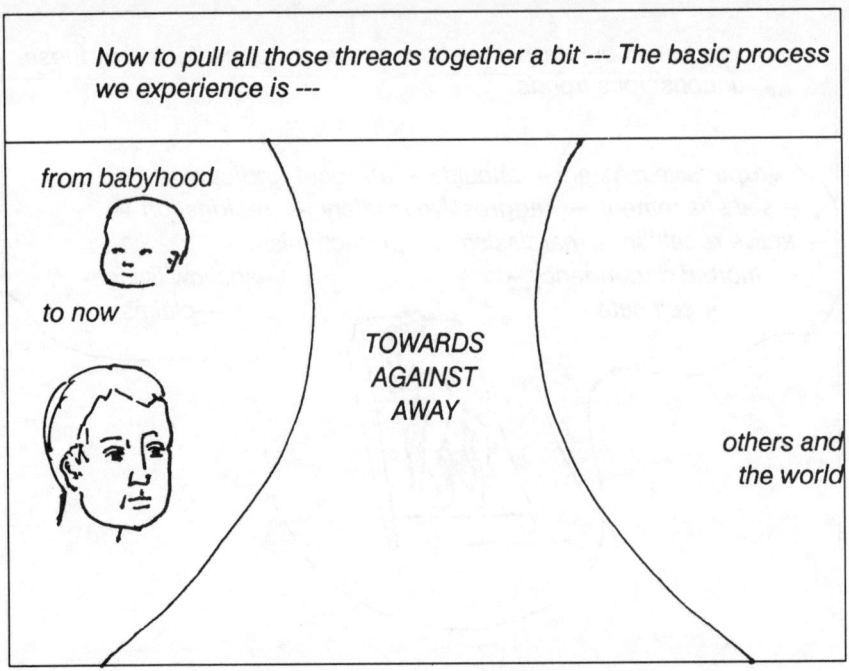

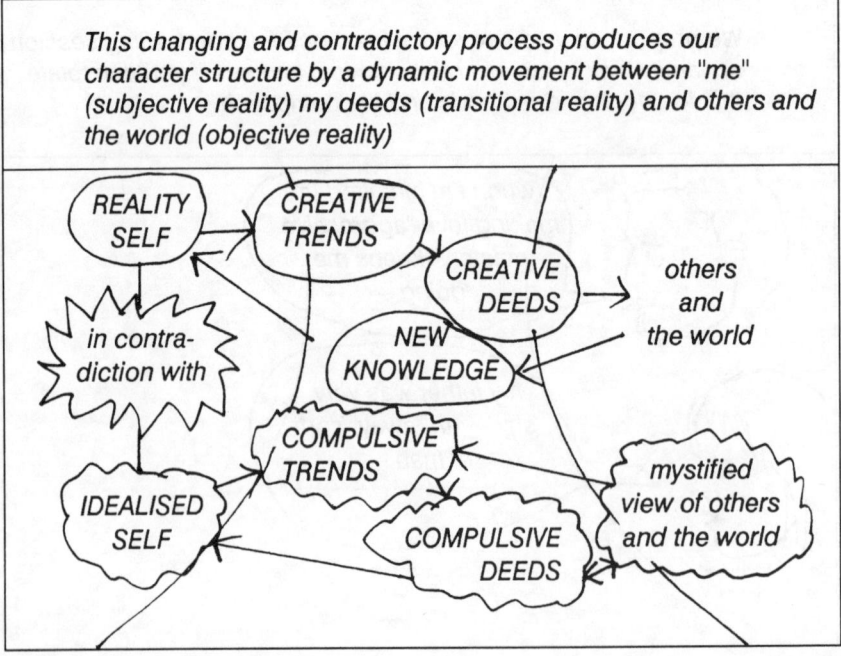

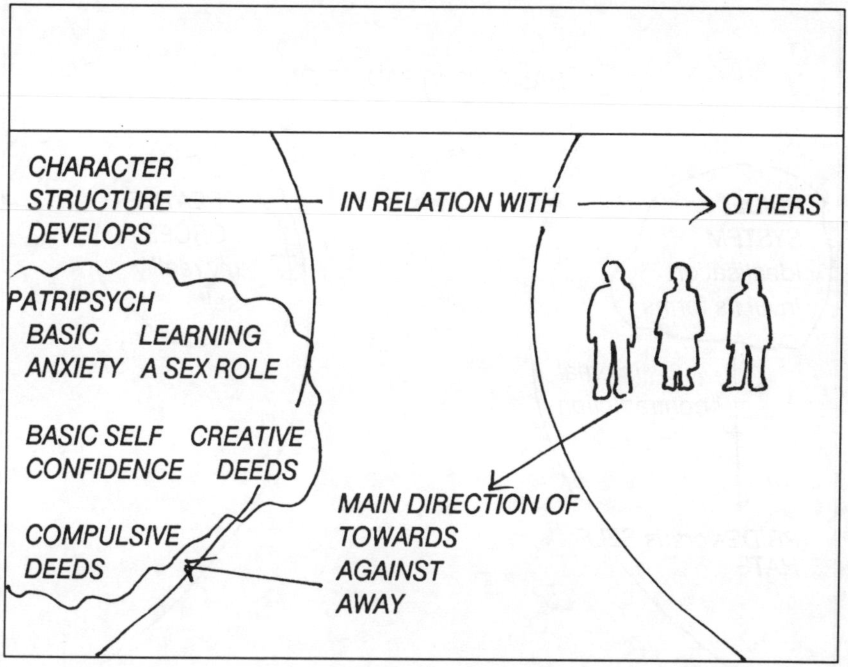

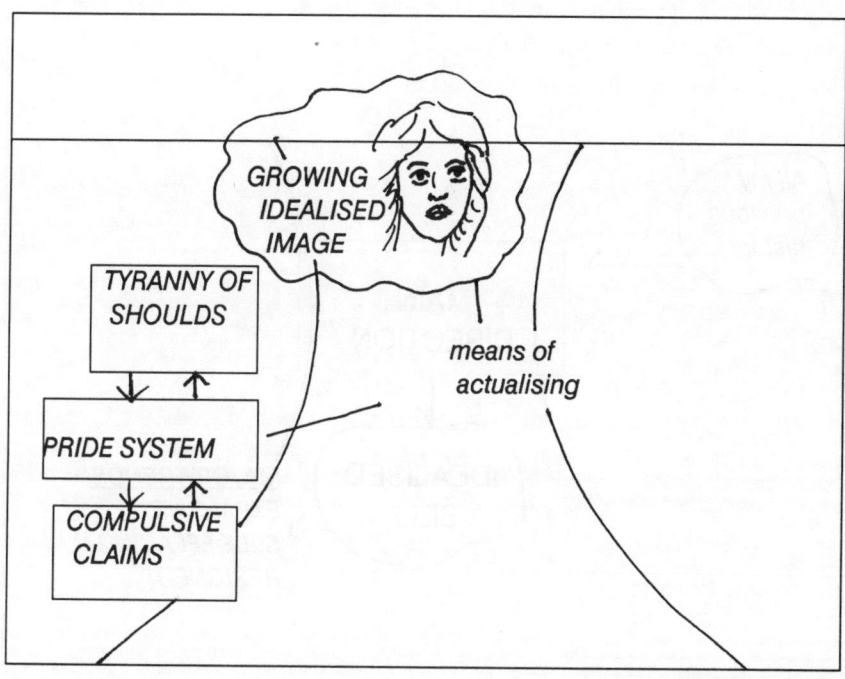

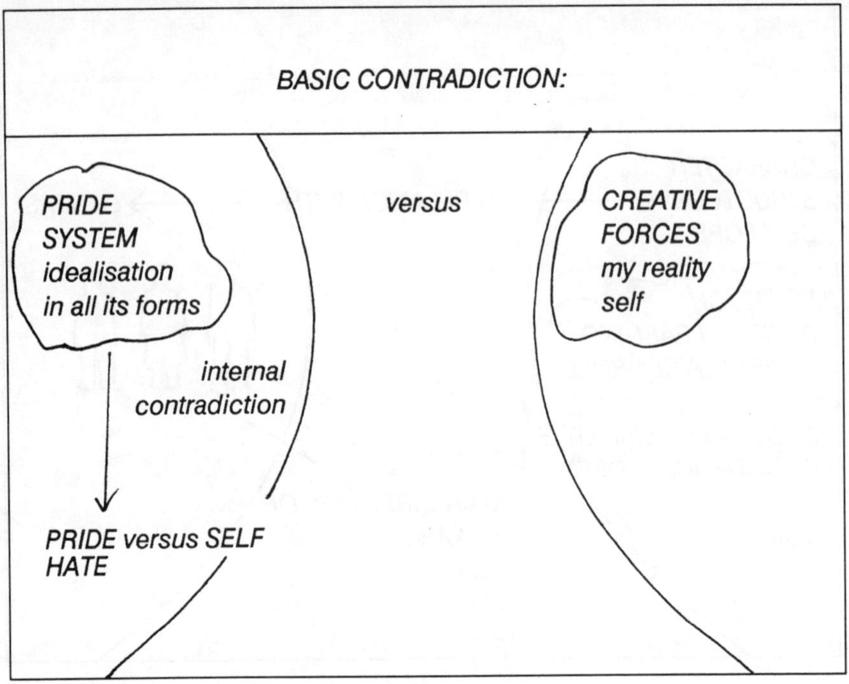

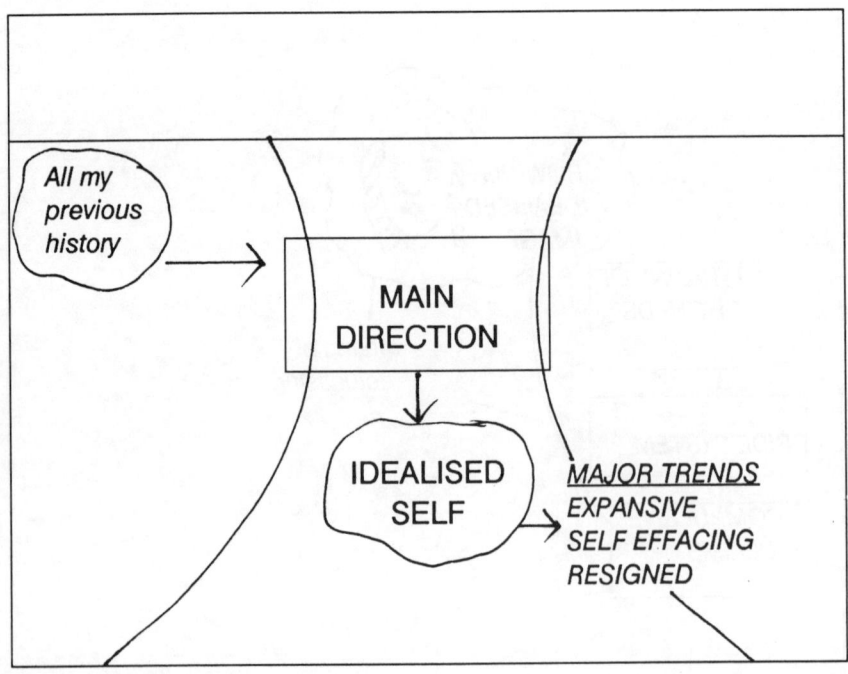

Usually the existence of compulsive trends is unconscious. In your self analysis you can start to uncover them. It is useful to remember that:

IDEALISATIONS COMPULSIVE TRENDS AND DEEDS

are, or were a rational *defence* against some pain, fear or anxiety

They have a *function* even here-and-now, they *do* something for us.

It often helps to ask yourself - "what function does this solution/trend have for me?" - the Assistant can help - for example:

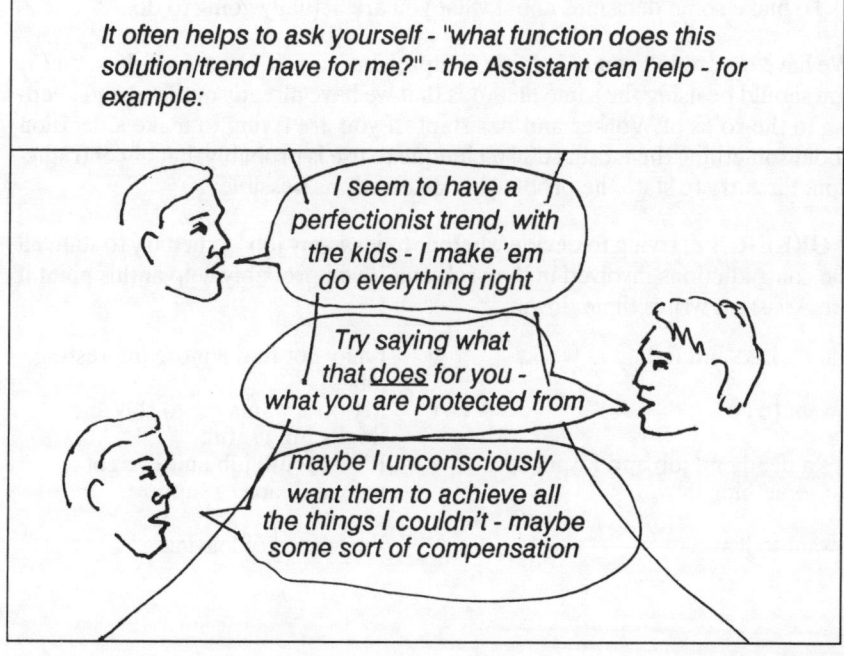

— I seem to have a perfectionist trend, with the kids - I make 'em do everything right

— Try saying what that *does* for you - what you are protected from

— maybe I unconsciously want them to achieve all the things I couldn't - maybe some sort of compensation

COUNSELLING ON SPECIFIC PROBLEMS AND WIDER ISSUES

In much of this section of the book we have presented counselling as a process of self exploration that concentrates on the past, using this to understand and change the present. There is a contradiction involved here in that of the many reasons people often want to start counselling one is frequently that they have a problem here and now in their lives that they need to do something about. For instance: 'I'm depressed.' 'My marriage is breaking up.' 'I feel my life is empty.' 'I'm lonely.' The other part of the contradiction of course is that changing how things are now, is also a means of understanding the past.

In any counselling session you may find yourself dealing with the immediate effects of such problems - your own and your partner's. You may want to use a session in all or any one of the following three ways:

1) To explore the situation, its history and contradictions.

2) To gain relief from the immediate stress of the situation, probably by talking and getting into emotional discharge.

3) To make some decisions about what you are actually going to do.

We have covered (1) and (2) fairly comprehensively. If you are working on (3) you should be using the same methods that we have already outlined and keeping to the roles of Worker and Assistant. If you are trying to make a decision about something the most useful technique to use is probably that of contradiction. First, try to state the problem as succinctly as possible:

WORKER "I'm trying to decide whether to leave my job." Then try to state all the contradictions involved in the problem. It will probably help at this point if the Assistant writes them down.

I am bored and fed up at work.	v	I may not find a more interesting job.
I want to go.	v	My boss wants me to stay and thinks I'm useful.
It's a dead end job and I want to do something new.	v	It's a secure job and I've got a wife and kids to support.
I want to leave.	v	I'm scared of leaving.

List as many contradictions as you can. Then take each of them one by one and try to get into each side of the contradiction separately.

For example:

"I'm bored and fed up at work. I do repetitive things all day. The people there get up my nose..." etc, etc.

When you have exhausted this, move to the other side of the contradiction: "I may not find a more interesting job. There's a lot of unemployment at the moment. I haven't got any qualifications ..." etc, etc.

Try to explore all the thoughts and feelings involved. You may find that you tend to jump from one side of the contradiction to the other. If this happens try using two chairs. You sit on one when you are talking about one side of the contradiction and on the other for the other side. Physically moving from one to the other may help sort out your confusion.

You may also find it useful to look at the contradiction in terms of:

- contradictions within me

- contradictions between me and other people

- contradictions in the situations around me and in society

- the inter-relations between these contradictions.

At the end of this process you should be in a better position to make some kind of decision. You may well find that it is not the decision you came to the session trying to make. In fact, it is often better to think in terms of small steps, small deeds that might transform the contradiction rather than coming down on one side or the other. In the example we've just given, you might decide on the deed of:

- buying the evening paper

- talking to your wife about how she felt about it

- using the next counselling session to work on why you're always scared of starting something new.

As Assistant there are two interventions you may find useful.

1) Try saying what that could be a solution to?

This is useful in exploring the parts of a contradiction. For example, being bored at work could be a solution to any or all of:

- the tedium of work
- the need to retain my sanity
- hating finding life interesting
- the need to maintain an idealised image as someone who doesn't care.
- the need to avoid confrontation with the boss.

2) Try saying what you are going to do.

This will be most useful when you are into the analysis.

Questions to ask yourself as Worker might be:

What actions could I take?

What would be the consequences of doing that?

How about stating that as something concrete?

Who would I have to interact with to achieve that?

What new contradictions will that solution lead to?

etc., etc.

We have also put a lot of emphasis in this section on the internal life of the individual and the small group or family of which he/she is part.

Most of the contradictions from which we suffer however have their origins in the larger society and there are many problems which we can do nothing about by working on ourselves. There is a complex relationship between the histories and lives of individuals and the contradictions of society.

For now it is as well to keep in mind that there are many things which you may need to tackle in society rather than in your psyche. It may be useful in any problem to look at where the contradictions arise from -

- within me

- between me and people I relate to face to face.

- in the situations around me, like work, family, politics, society.

(In reality of course these three aspects are intertwined and mutually interact and contradict).

It is also useful to remember that the less you are in contact with objective reality the less able you are to see the real root of the contradiction. You are more likely to be mystified and understand the world as it appears to you, rather than as it is. This is sometimes called false consciousness. Often you can tackle the effects of a problem by working on yourself. Tackling its origins will mean tackling society and this requires different tools.

We have reached a point where you could counsel regularly and develop your unique self analysis through mutual counselling

We suggest the DEED of meeting say once a week

Before you move on to the next section (advanced counselling) you need plenty of practice.

The time of course varies, but we recommend at least 20 full counselling sessions

Section Three
Advanced counselling, tools and theories for working on the unconscious

INTRODUCTION

So far, the methods introduced are ones which should enable you to gain greater understanding of yourself and other people, and to change certain aspects of your life and behaviour, hopefully increasing your creativity and decreasing your reliance on stultifying, uncreative patterns of relating. Making major changes however is dependent on more than this. It means altering who you are, confronting the way in which early experience has become structured into your character. This implies two things. The first is that this cannot be done without altering things that are deeply unconscious. The second is that your character itself will be operating as a major resistance to the process of change.

In this section we outline some basic methods and techniques for working on these things, along with some more detailed explanations of the processes you can expect to encounter and some of the difficulties you can expect to meet.

Working with unconscious material can of course be difficult and distressing as well as liberating and rewarding, so we'd like to repeat here what we said at the beginning of the book. If you are already feeling anxious and distressed you may find that working with unconscious material increases your anxiety. Don't push yourself to do anything you don't feel sure about. We suggest that you read through the whole of this section before you start on any of the exercises.

KEEPING A NOTEBOOK

By now you will probably find it useful to keep a notebook about your counselling work and self - analysis. Particularly when you start to work with unconscious material you will find that there is a lot that you tend to forget or re-press very quickly. Keep a note of any dreams you have, free associations you do or thoughts about yourself. It is also useful to make brief notes after each session about how it went, how you feel about it and what you discovered. Write something about how you felt in the role of Assistant as well as the role of Worker. You can also agree, either as an alternative, or in addition, to make notes about each other. If you do this you need to be clear about whether your notebooks are private or to be shared. When working on transference (See p. 246) it can be useful to make notes about how you feel about your partner.

MAKING A CONTRACT

It can be useful to make a contract with your partner about how long and how frequently you are going to work for. This can be particularly important when trying to do more advanced work as it not only gives you a certain and secure framework but structures in opportunities for reviewing your progress and deciding whether, and in what way you should continue. The contract can also include any particular demands you agree to make on each other, or limitations you might want to set.

THE UNCONSCIOUS

To start with we suggest that you re-read the earlier parts of the book that deal with the unconcious (p. 77). This is a condensed summary of what we said there:

-the young baby has orgasmic needs for food, comfort and physical contact. These needs continue through life in changed and changing forms.

-consciousness develops out of the unconscious

-the early experiences and impressions of our senses are never forgotten; essentially they become structured into our psyche as characteristic ways of behaving and feeling.

-our earliest experience of the world is by associative, concrete, sensory motor and emotional means. As we develop these become complex bodily, emotional and cognitive processes.

-the 'language' of the unconscious remains throughout life one of feelings, associations and symbols.

-the unconscious contains both compulsive and creative trends.

-material that can easily be recovered is called pre-conscious.

-some material is repressed and not normally available to consciousness.

An additional point to make is that all psychic life, conscious and unconscious is determined and understandable. By this we mean:

-that however strange, irrational or nonsensical our minds, bodies, feelings or behaviour may appear, ultimately these phenomena are understandable and graspable.

-all psychic processes need to be understood as being determined dialectically, that is understood as contradictory.

THE UNCONSCIOUS AND REPRESSION

All material that is repressed is material that we have once known consciously. The original reason for the repression of any thought, wish or feeling is that by doing so you can protect yourself in some way from pain or anxiety. As your character structure develops you will tend to repress anything that doesn't conform to the idealised image you are forming. Often happy memories will be repressed as well as painful or shameful ones because the latter are associated with the former.

The process of repression is itself largely unconscious. People don't for example suddenly think 'Aha! I would be better off if I didn't know that' and forget the disturbing idea. Something is unacceptable for some reason and so you push it away and then forget that you ever knew anything about it. You are probably not even aware of the original pushing away or of feeling that a particular thing is unacceptable. In many cases the most that you might be aware of is that certain experiences or ideas make you anxious, ashamed or guilty.

When something is repressed and becomes unconscious however, it by no means loses its force. The wish, idea or feeling continues to operate, underground as it were, and will push to the surface in a disguised form. This can happen in a number of ways, some of which leave the unconscious material intact and some of which force parts of it into consciousness.

Here are some examples of this

- the unconscious repressed thought or feeling will come out in a circuitous way. For example, consciously I feel that I love and respect my parents. I have repressed all my feelings of anger and hostility towards them. When we meet, however, and I try to express my feeling of love, they somehow come out in a cold detached and unfriendly way. Another example of this is where a feeling becomes displaced from one person to another. For example, if for some reason showing affection to my friends is taboo for me, I may develop attachments to animals or to good causes as a substitute.

- the repressed material may be expressed on the basis of a rationalisation, particularly one that is socially acceptable. So, for example, an unconscious desire to possess someone else may be expressed as love.

-repressed material may come out in inadvertent behaviour or even in the fear of it.

a) where my hostile feelings are close to the surface I may on some occasion come away terrified that I have just thrown the most terrible insults at the person I have been with. I may be quite unsure of what I actually did say.

b) My conscious image of myself is that I am a smart, efficient and punctual person. I genuinely believe this to be so, yet somehow there is a letter I keep forgetting to post...

c) A word or gesture may belie me. Often what appear to be slips of the tongue may express an unconscious thought.

-repressed material may come out in symptoms, like headaches, fatigue, depression, anxiety or a stammer. These can often be both the means of expression of repressed material and the way in which it is re-repressed. In this example the connections between the original repressed material and its expression are accessible.

-dreams are one of the most important clues we have to repressed material. A dream may express in a clear and graphic way the parts of ourselves that are repressed.

-one of the most comprehensive mechanisms by which repression is effected is projection. Projection can also be an effect of repression. We deal with it in more detail later on.

WAYS OF WORKING ON THE UNCONSCIOUS

FREE ASSOCIATION

So far we have approached the unconscious by scanning and talking about it. This really only taps preconscious material as the 'conscious' me is often resistant to going any further. At night, in dreams, the conscious me doesn't predominate and the unconscious reigns supreme. There is a similar waking state which can be a valuable aid for getting in touch with unconscious material. This is usually called free association. It can be rather like the state you experience just between sleeping and waking which is neither the one nor the other. It has a similar quality to dreams in that you may well find yourself using that same language of association, feeling, image and symbol to express something.

In psychoanalysis free association is sometimes referred to as the basic rule. The patient (our Worker) is simply asked to say everything that comes into his thoughts and feelings without censoring anything, however embarrassing, unimportant, indiscreet, irrelevant or stupid it may seem to him. In this way, the ordinary conscious controls are relaxed. External stimuli are at a minimum, thought is not goal-directed and ideas and feelings which are normally warded off or repressed may find their way through to consciousness.

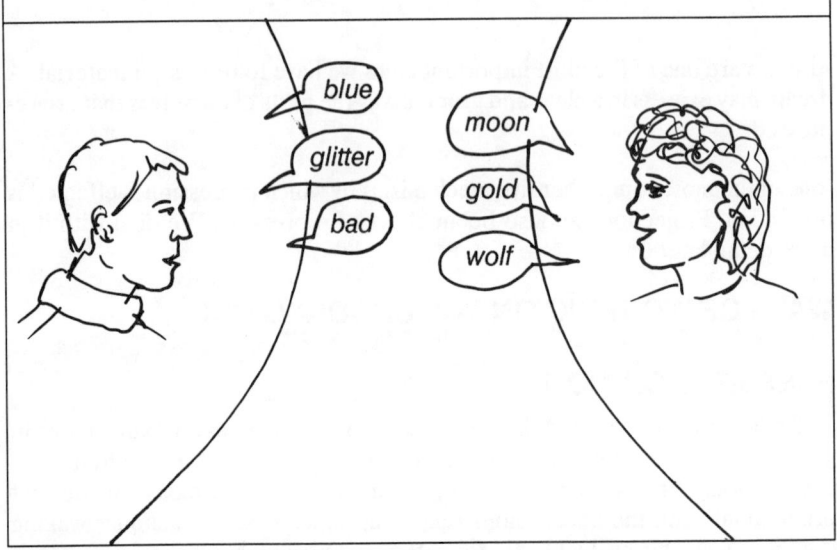

It is not to be confused with simple word association - where you try to spark associations like in a party game -

Of course in practice it is very difficult to obey a basic rule of this kind. Most people leave something out, they quickly shut off a particular line of thought, they fall into silence when an unwelcome feeling arises or they gabble incessantly to keep other emotions at bay. Everyone has their characteristic way of defending against the frightening or unwelcome unconscious feelings. One of the ways in which the analyst (or our Assistant) helps is by observing and understanding the things which are avoided like this. When it feels appropriate he may suggest what it is that is being avoided or suggest that the Worker returns to the feelings connected with the avoidance. He can also assist by following the connections that are sparked in the Worker's associations. He may make interventions based on them, or he may save them for later and share them with the Worker when they discuss the session. At other times he may encourage the expression of unconscious feelings that arise. Free association can quite often encourage the spontaneous discharge of repressed emotions. These can be the 'dramatic' expressions of sadness in crying, anger in shouting, fear in trembling or the much quieter realisation and experiencing of a particular feeling. Simply saying "I feel sad" and letting yourself quietly feel the sadness and aloneness can be just as important and emotionally significant as crying out your frightened distress.

Finally it is important as the Assistant to stay in contact with the Worker and feel what is happening to him. Ideally the process will be one where your unconscious is listening to his. You are listening with the 'third ear'. Your powers of intuition are at their height. You can go with him but also remain in touch with external reality and maintain that contact for him.

Free association can take place at various levels of consciousness. It can be not so very different from an ordinary counselling session or it can be an almost hypnotic state where you are truly at the borderline of the unconscious, moving in a language of symbols and feelings. You can use free association for a very brief period to get at something in particular, or you can use it in a more protracted way for a whole session. We suggest you experiment and discover what is the most useful for you. In the exercises which follow there are various techniques for relaxing and breaking the hold of your conscious control. The more relaxed you are, the more likely you are to reach the hypnotic state of semi-sleep. Don't push yourself. Just let things arise.

Try the following exercise: (the first time for a few minutes only). The worker sits comfortably. Make sure you are relaxed. Clear the top of your head of any trivia of the day

let any image or thought, or feelings arise:

but -

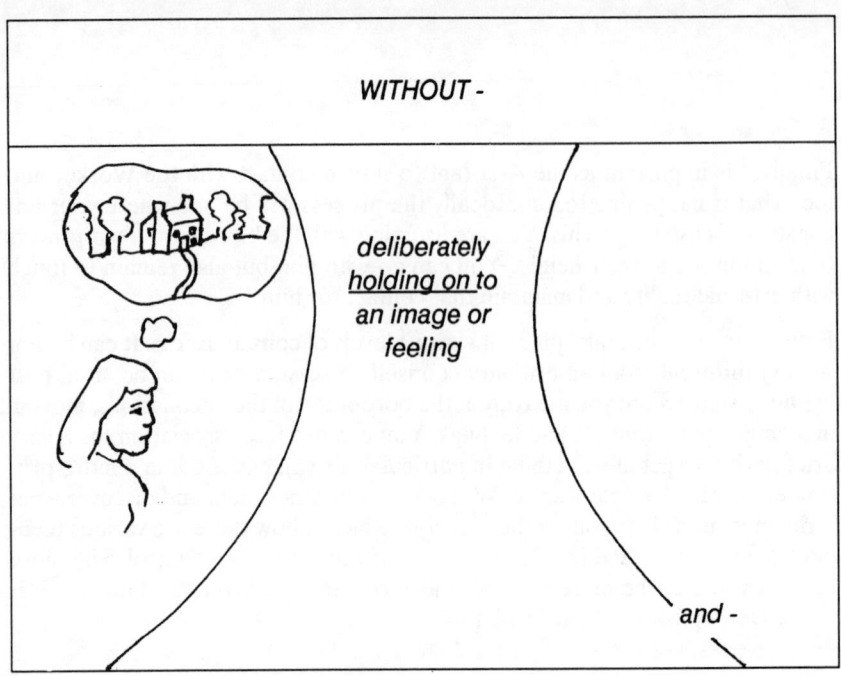
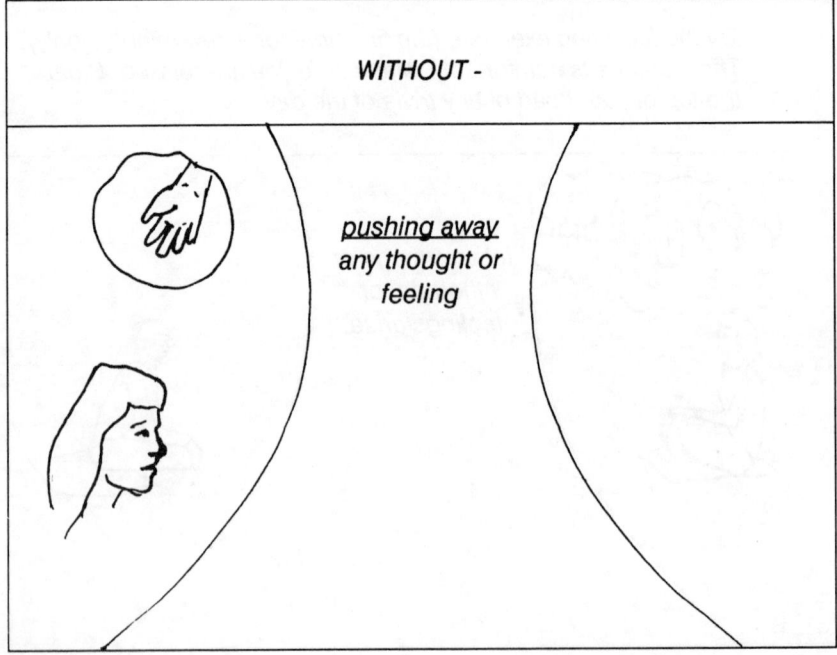

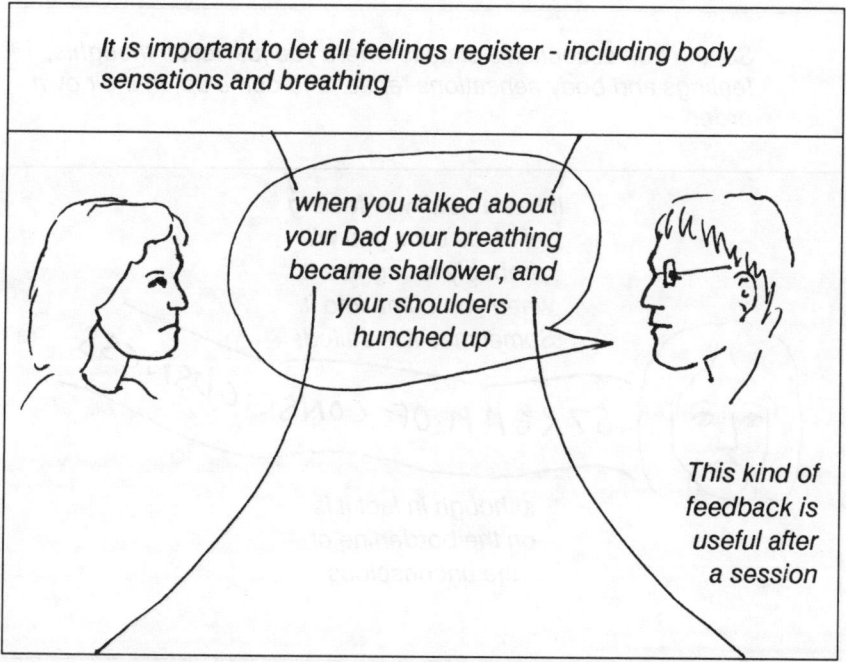

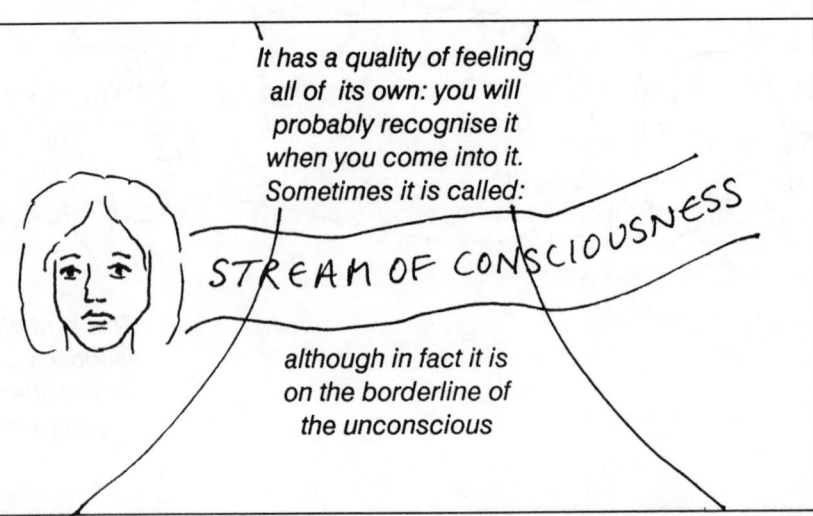

Exercise,-

This is a way of relaxing into the free associative state. Lie on your back with your knees up, feet on the ground and slightly apart. Feel your breath moving through your body.

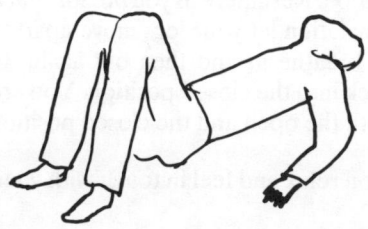

Then, as you breathe out, let your legs move gently apart, as far as you can without tensing up. As you breathe in, let your legs come back together, but don't let the knees actually touch.

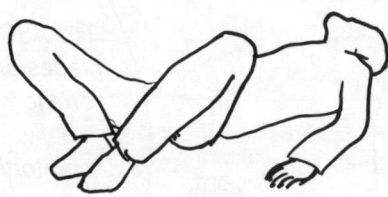

Open and close your legs as you breathe. On the exhalation you open your legs. On the inhalation you close your legs. Find your own rhythm - a movement of *your* breath, that is in tune with *your* body. *Feel* your breathing, feel it going deeper through your body, moving through every part, till you feel there is no longer any effort in either breathing or movement, till you feel it as one synchronised flow.

If you like, you can continue this exercise as follows. When your legs open, let them remain in the open position while you breathe in and out once. Let your legs relax in the open position for a full respiration. Then on the second inhalation you let your legs move back into the closed position as before. In the open state there is a pause. In the closed state there is not. Do this sequence several times before moving on to the next.

In the final sequence you also rest in the closed position. Breathe in, letting your legs move into the open position. Rest there as you breathe out and then breathe in again. On the second exhalation let your legs move apart to the open position. Rest there while you breathe in and then out again. On the following inhalation move the legs back into the closed position. You are now resting for a complete repiration in both the open and the closed positions.

This exercise should help you relax and feel in touch with yourself as a totality.

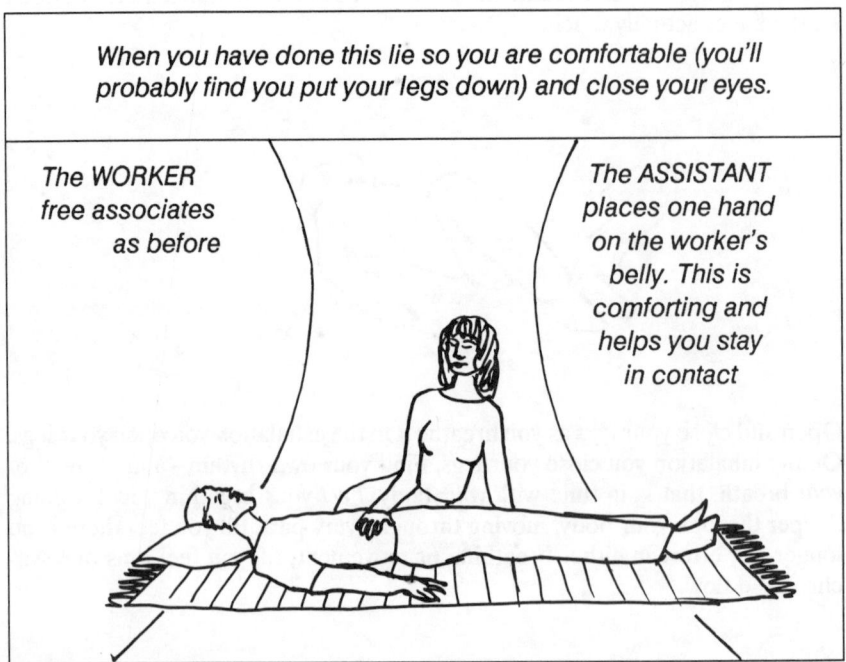

During discussion look at the connections between the associations - what underlying threads run through them, for instance? Can you connect them with other things you have discovered in yourself?

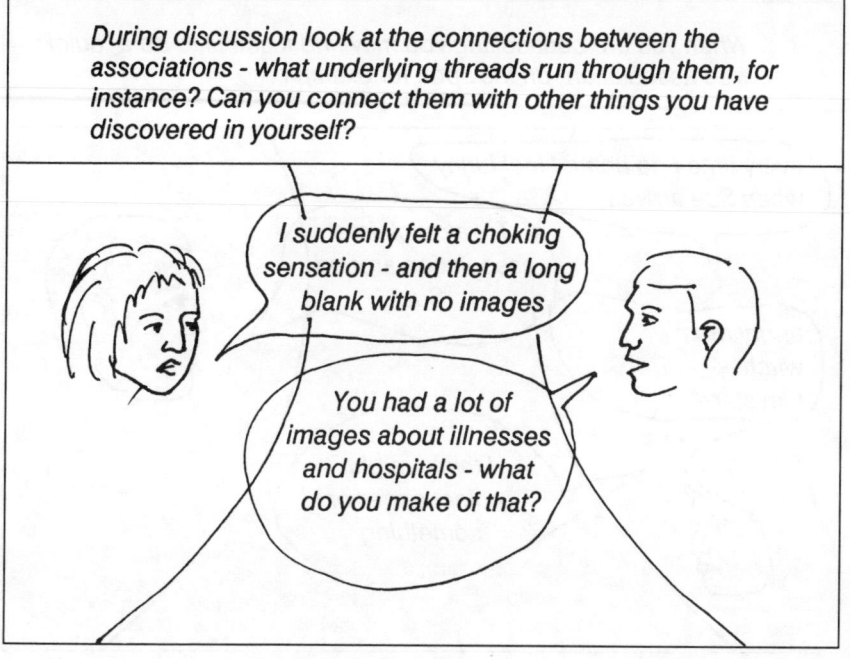

"I suddenly felt a choking sensation - and then a long blank with no images"

"You had a lot of images about illnesses and hospitals - what do you make of that?"

Spometimes you will find a "block" or resistance to free associating - you may be just theorising or "thinking aloud" <u>controlling</u> what happens. The Assistant can try the following intervention:

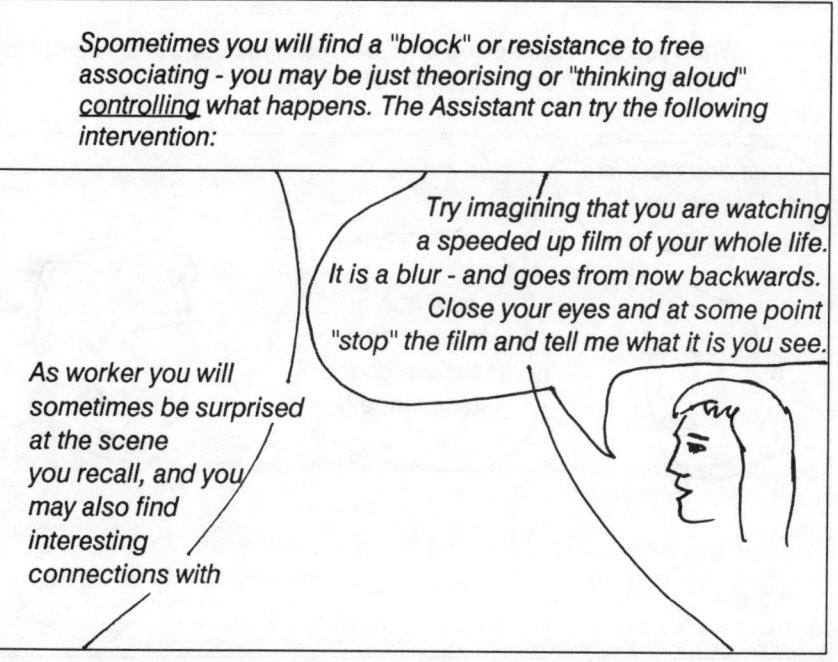

"Try imagining that you are watching a speeded up film of your whole life. It is a blur - and goes from now backwards. Close your eyes and at some point "stop" the film and tell me what it is you see."

As worker you will sometimes be surprised at the scene you recall, and you may also find interesting connections with

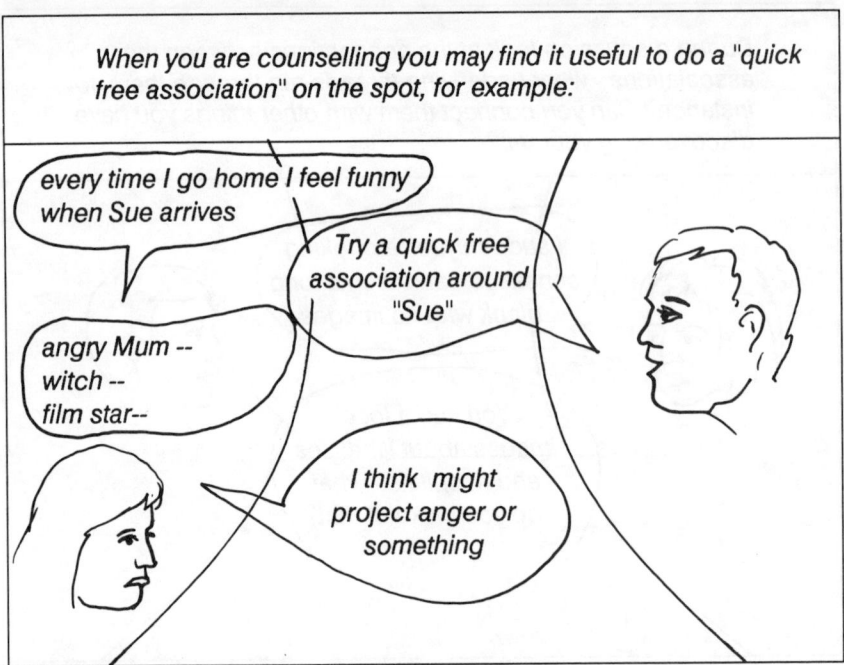
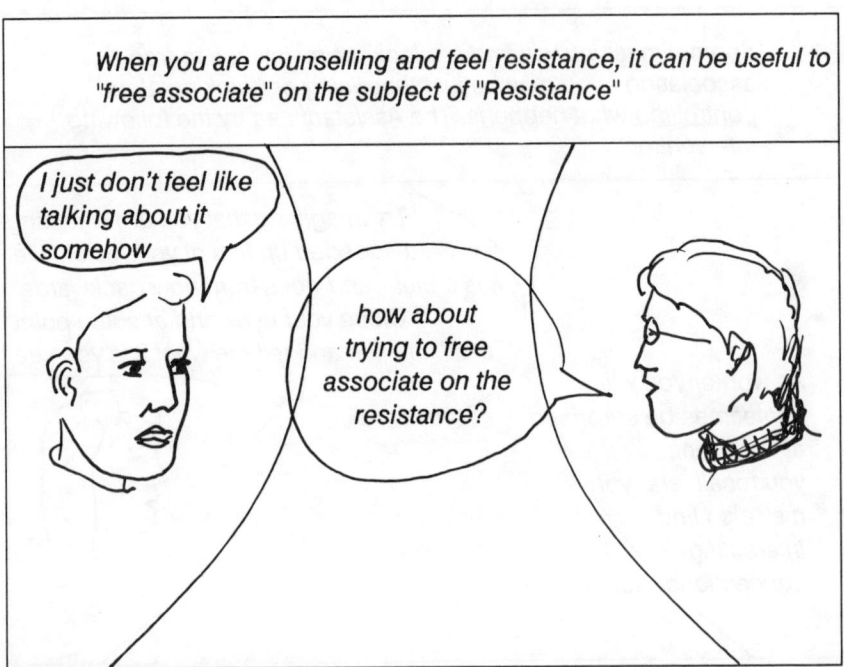

Sometimes the Worker may still feel inhibited or tense. Here are some things you can try as Assistant which may help this. Some of them involve touch and massage and there is an important 'golden rule' here. Any approach to your partner's body should be delicate and responsive to her tensions and resistances. The body doesn't stop at the skin and can easily be invaded, setting up further tensions and unpleasant sensations. Imagine that your partner's body begins three feet away from where you can see it.

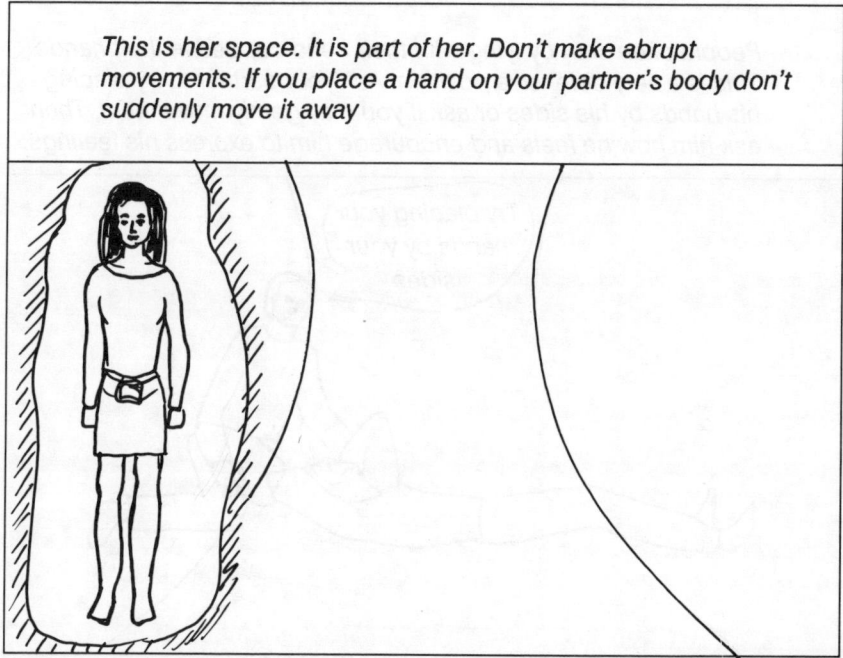

This is her space. It is part of her. Don't make abrupt movements. If you place a hand on your partner's body don't suddenly move it away

If your partner seems tense and worried, you can ask if she would like you to massage her scalp. The movements you use are just like gently washing your hair.

WORKER
Tell her how you feel and if you would like more or less pressure

ASSISTANT
Imagine you are washing a baby's hair

People often start by lying with their head cupped in their hands. This is a very defensive position. Ask your partner to try placing his hands by his sides or ask if you may gently move them. Then ask him how he feels and encourage him to express his feelings.

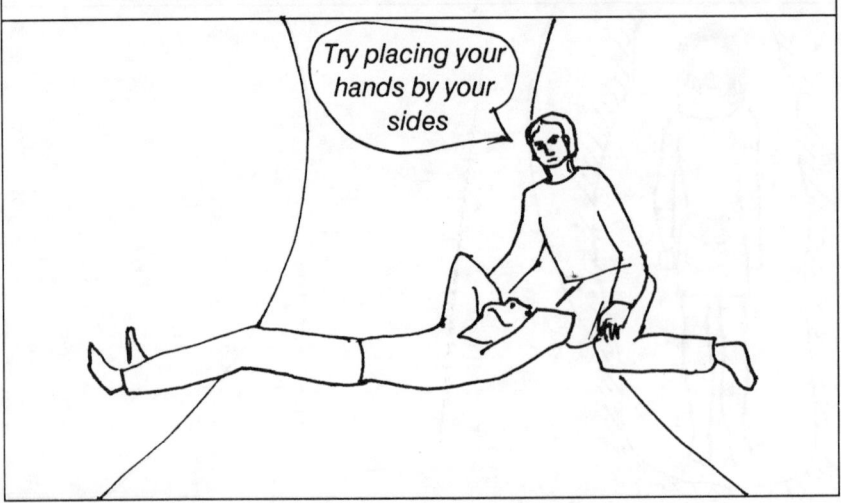

Try placing your hands by your sides

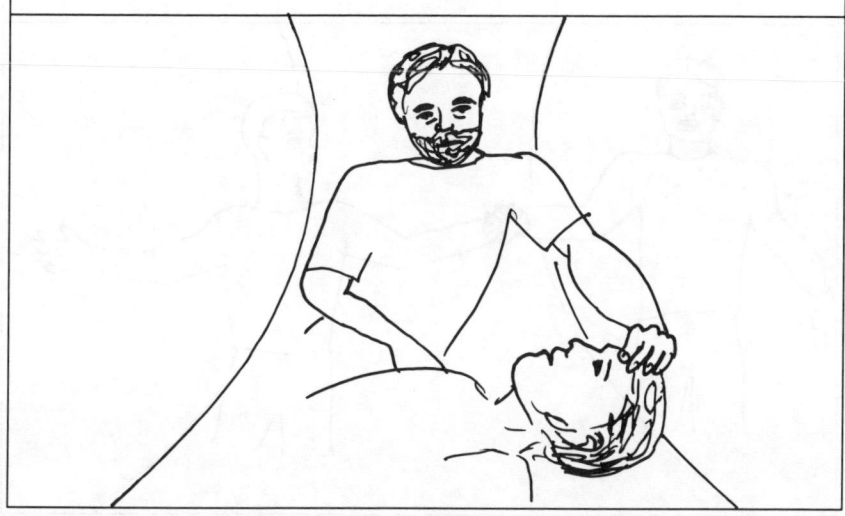

If the worker seems stuck or inhibited try placing your hand gently on his forehead. This is often felt as a permission giving gesture

Sometimes people get quite distressed or spaced out doing a long free association. They may feel disconnected, feel they are miles away from you, frightened and out of contact. If this happens, you need to bring them back into the present and back in touch with you. Stay with what they are feeling and try to understand the space they are in. Be straight about your own feelings and give them any feedback they ask for. Interact. Get into dialogue. You may find it useful to ask them to do things like describing the room, describing you or describing what they are going to do with the rest of the day. Your object is to get the 'conscious me' back in control without denying the validity of the painful or distressing experiences.

Another thing which sometimes happens is that people get overwhelmed emotionally. Emotional discharge becomes accompanied by panic and there is no free attention left which can help to deal with the experience. In this situation you shouldn't encourage the discharge but should help the person come away from it. Bring his attention back to you and the situation of the two of you in the room. Your real support and attention is crucially important here. It can sometimes help to talk about what has happened, discuss it and try to understand it.

Remember the most important thing is to keep in contact. If the worker gets lost in subjective reality you are his only link with the objective world. You are his transitional link.

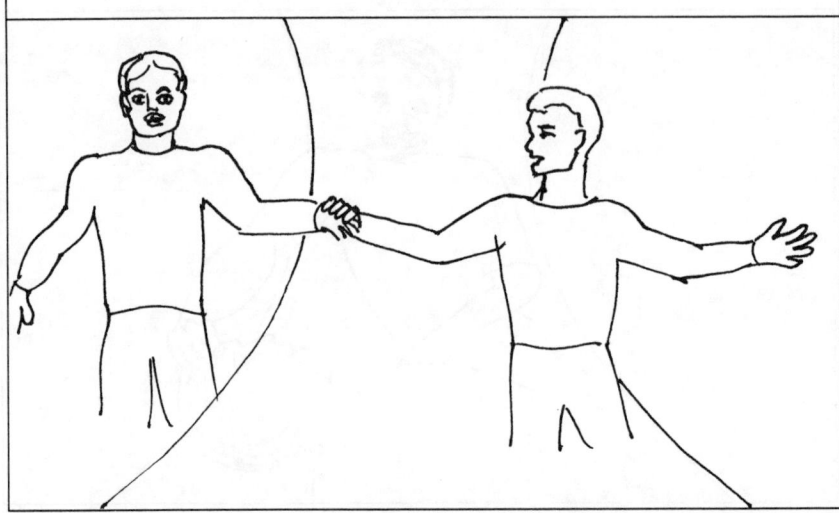

A comforting thing to do is to get the worker to lie on his left side in a comfortable position. Place one hand gently on the back of his neck and the other gently on his belly. Encourage his breathing to become regular through gentle pressure on the belly.

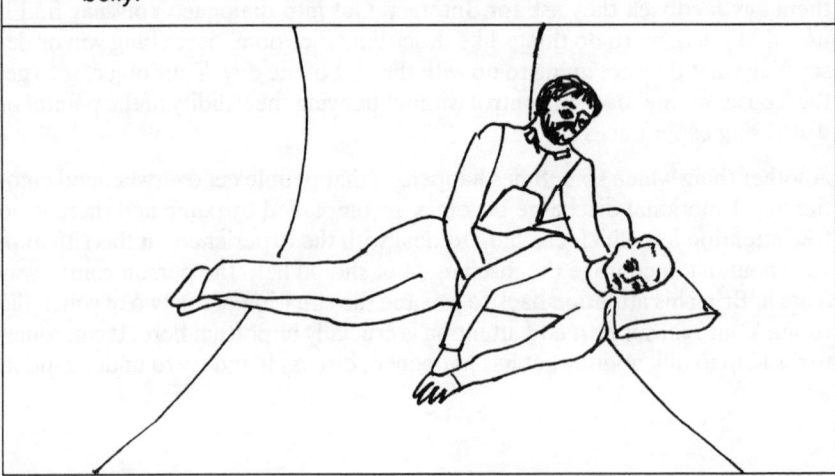

If the worker is still lying down, you can press against the ends of his feet with gentle firm pressure. This often helps restore the feeling of being "here" and "in the world".

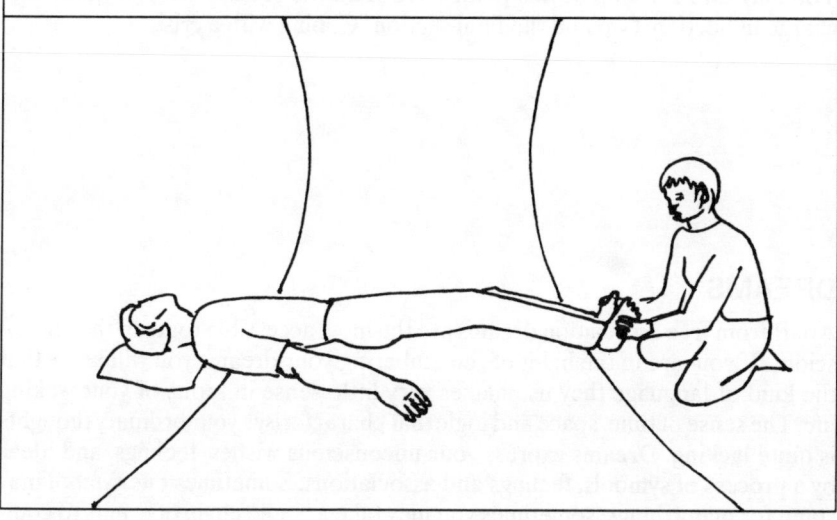

Another exercise which has a similar effect is to raise your partner's knees and then apply pressure downwards on them

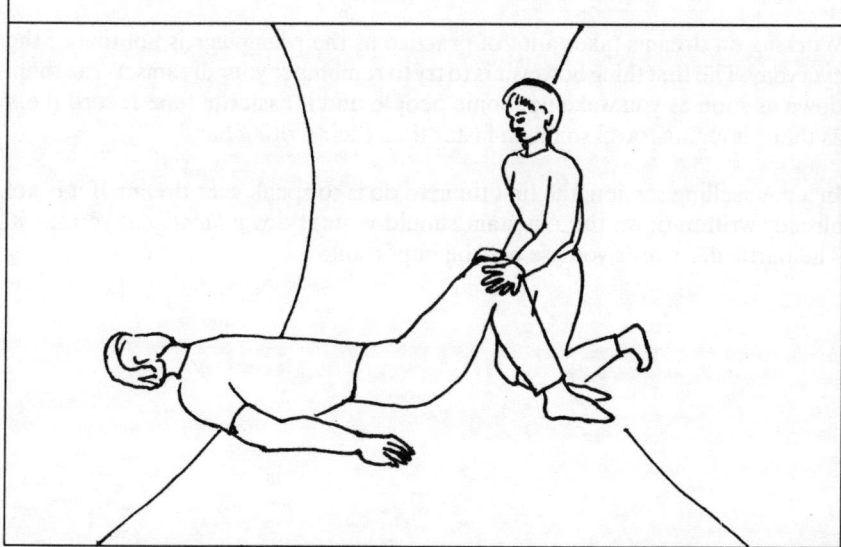

You may find it useful at this point to re-read the section on emotional discharge in Section Two and the final section "Coping with a crisis".

DREAMS

Apart from free association dreams are the most accessible route to the unconscious. If you are in the habit of remembering your dreams you will know that the kind of language they use makes very little sense in terms of your waking life. The sense of time, space and logic that characterises your ordinary thoughts is quite lacking. Dreams express your unconscious wishes, feelings, and ideas by a process of symbols, feelings and associations. Sometimes one symbol may stand for many things, sometimes you may take a whole chain of events to communicate one idea. The most comprehensive work on interpreting dreams is still Freud's *The Interpretation of Dreams*. At some point you may like to read this or his shorter essays in the *Introductory Lectures*. In the meantime we suggest you start to approach this area through looking at and working on your own dreams.

Working on dreams takes a lot of practice as their language is not that of the everyday. The first thing however is to try to remember your dreams. Write them down as soon as you wake up. Some people find it easier to tape-record them as their thoughts travel so much faster than their writing hand.

In a counselling session, the first thing to do is to speak your dream. If it is not already written down the Assistant should write it down *literally* as you say it. The particular words you use may be important.

To illustrate the various methods we will use the following short dream:

"I was walking down a street that looked like a mixture of my childhood town and where I live now. A girl is holding my arm. I'm happy. We pass a shop full of naked old ladies. I panic and rush off down a maze of narrow passages, and into a hall addressed by a Prime Minister. I sit, quiet and anonymous amongst the thousands of delegates."

It often helps to retell the dream as if it were happening here and now - paying attention to how you feel now, and how you felt when you were originally dreaming

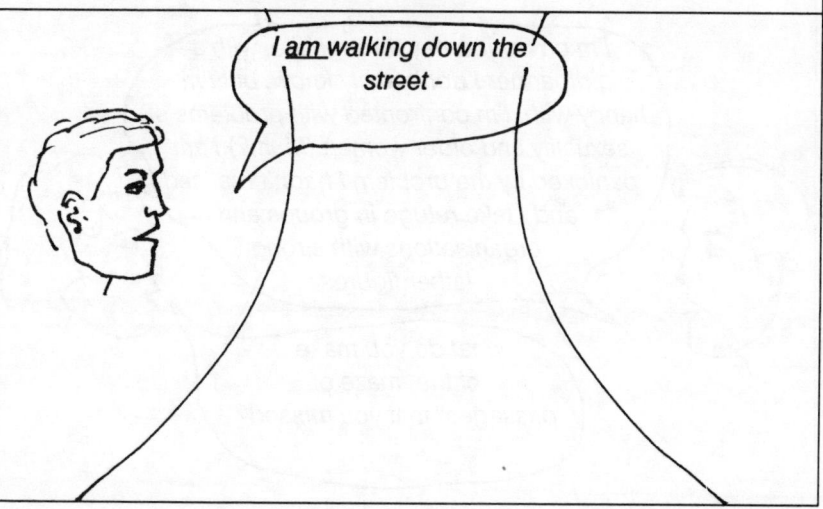

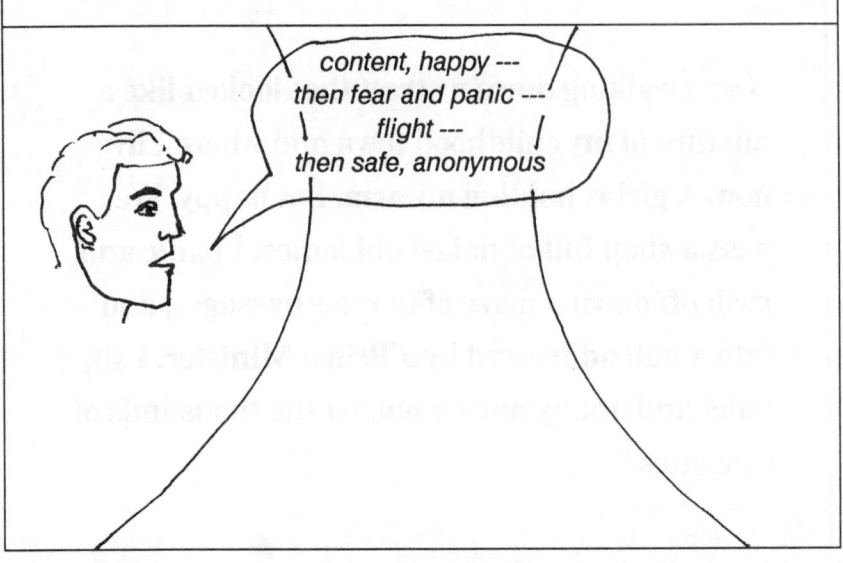

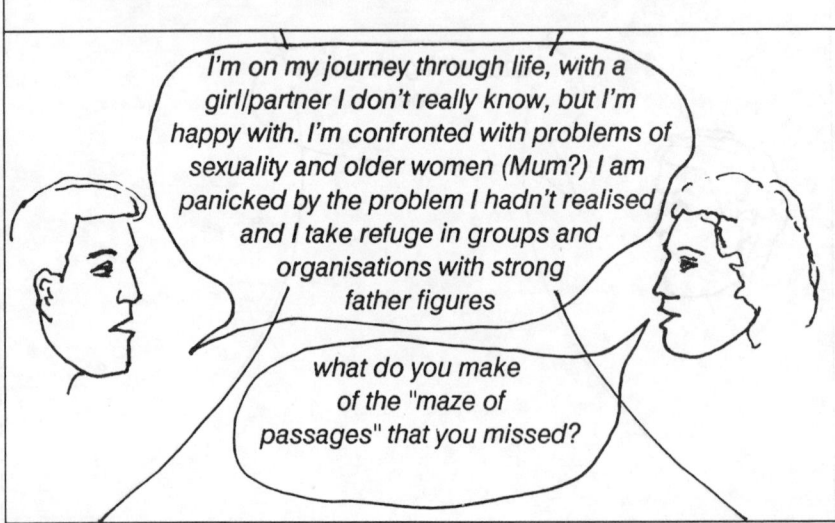

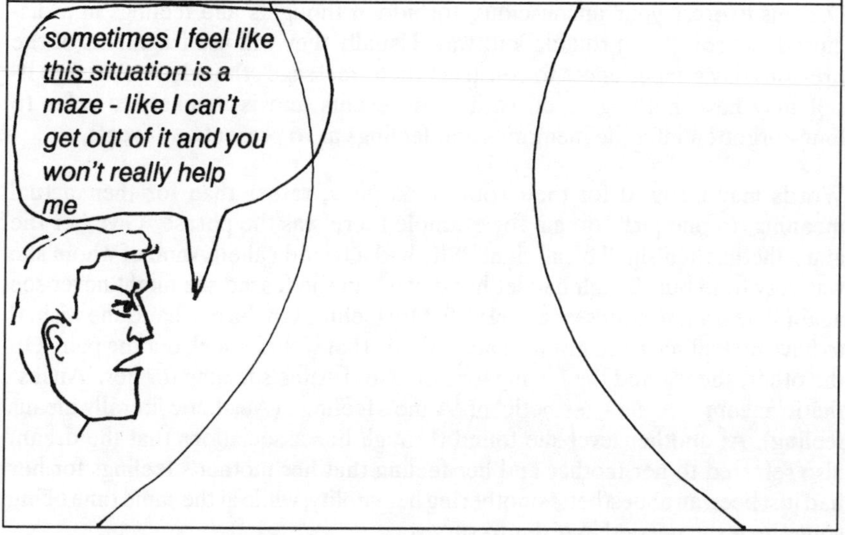

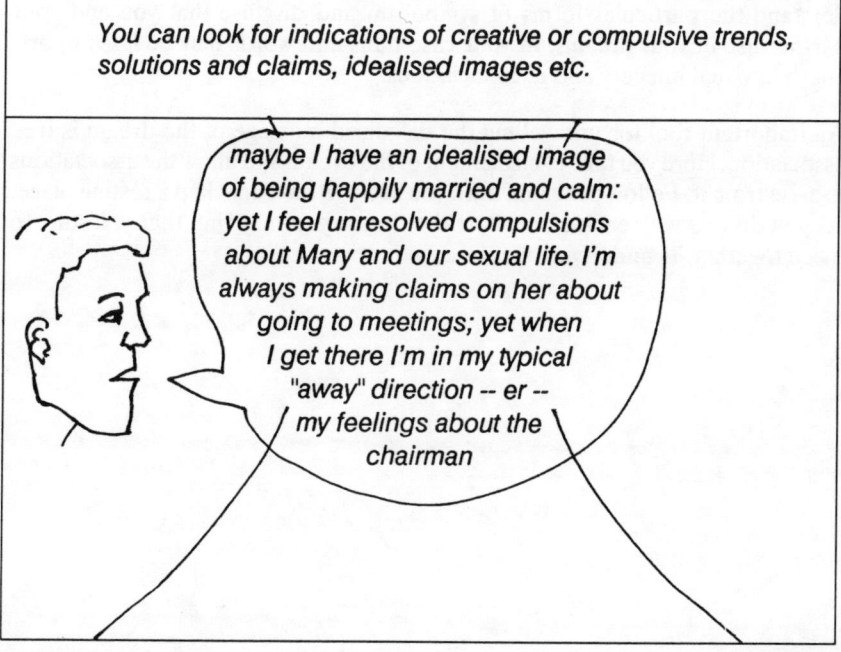

Dreams express your unconscious, forbidden thoughts and feelings in a disguised, censored and roundabout way. Usually they will use fragments of the previous day's experiences to construct their 'message', though the message itself may have nothing to do with those events and is as likely to refer to long-forgotten infantile memories and feelings as to present day events.

Words may be used for their sounds, as puns, rather than for their actual meaning. In one girl's dream for example there was the phrase "Give her the anaesthetic, then she'll be all right". She had a friend called Anne of whom she was very fond but she felt had let her down and she feared she might never see again. The dream expresses a contradictary feeling. On the one hand she wished to have no feeling, to be given an anaesthetic that would knock out the pain. On the other, she wanted the feeling for Anne and Anne's feeling for her. 'Anaesthetic' meant - 'Anne - aesthetic' or 'Anne - feeling'. (Aesthetic literally means feeling). At another level she found through her associations that the dream also referred to her mother and her feeling that her mother's feelings for her had just been an anaesthetic smothering her vitality, while at the same time being something she needed in order to survive.

By remembering and working on your dreams you can gradually come to understand the particular forms of symbolism and disguise that you and your partner use in your dreams. In your case puns and words may be less important than visual imagery and its associations.

An important tool for unravelling the disguised message of the dream is free association. Here you take each element of the dream and allow the associations to arise from it. Follow the chain until you seem to have reached a resting place. As you do this with each element of the dream you may find that you start to piece together its underlying message.

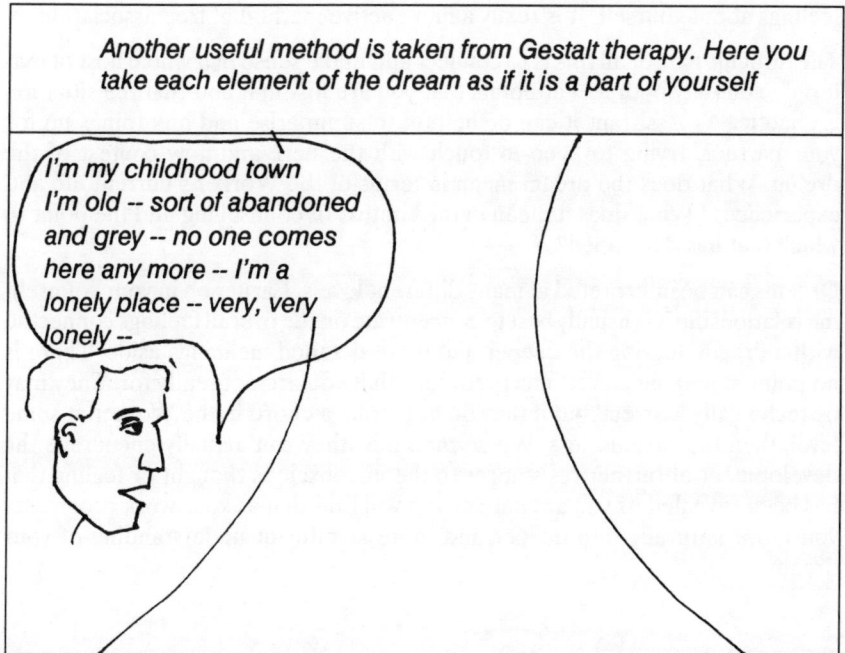

You can if you like "have a conversation" between different parts of the dream, where you act the roles alternately. The assistant can suggest changing roles by saying "try switch".

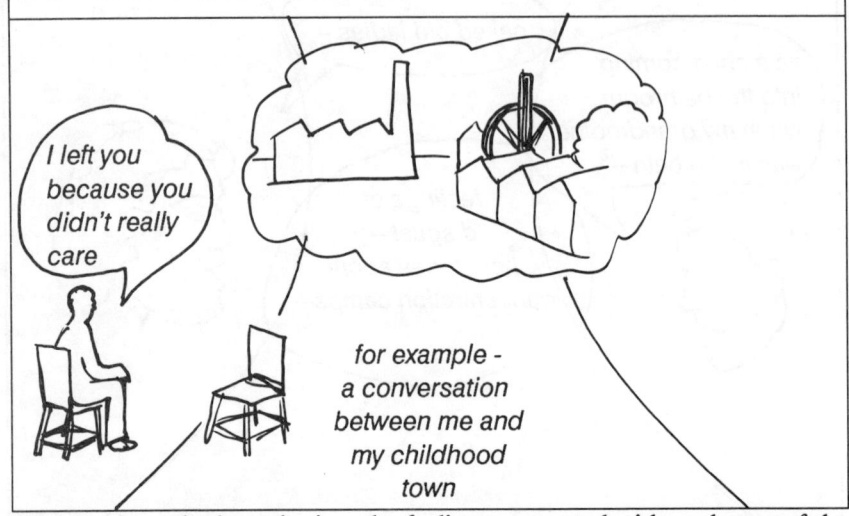

The gestalt method emphasises the feelings connected with each part of the dream and the idea that each part of it represents a part of yourself and your feelings about yourself. It is really a more active method of free association.

The difficult part of all this is to connect and make sense of a whole host of material. You may both feel at points that you are lost in it and that the situation is chaotic. As Assistant it can be helpful to summarise and link things up for your partner, trying to keep in touch with the here-and-now context of the dream. What does the dream mean in terms of the Worker's current life and experiences? What does it mean in the context of counselling and the point to which that has developed?

Dreams can be interpreted at many different levels. Earlier on in your counselling relationship it is usually best to concentrate on the overall feelings connected with a dream, leaving the deeper and more detailed meanings aside. There is no point in making clever interpretations that you are not ready for. They may be technically 'correct' but if they do not strike a chord in the Worker at some level, then they are useless. Worse than this, they can actually encourage the development of further resistances to the unconscious thought or feeling that has been revealed. If you are patient you will find that as your work progresses you move naturally into deeper and more significant understanding of your dreams.

RESISTANCE

In the section of repression we said that there is always a very good reason why something is repressed and that you will have very good reasons for keeping it that way. It protects you from something, it maintains the particular solutions you've been forced into taking, it's your way of defending yourself.

The object of advanced counselling is to make the unconscious conscious however, so what happens when these conscious and unconscious objectives clash? The answer is resistance and this can be expressed in many different ways. It happens in ordinary life as well as in counselling.

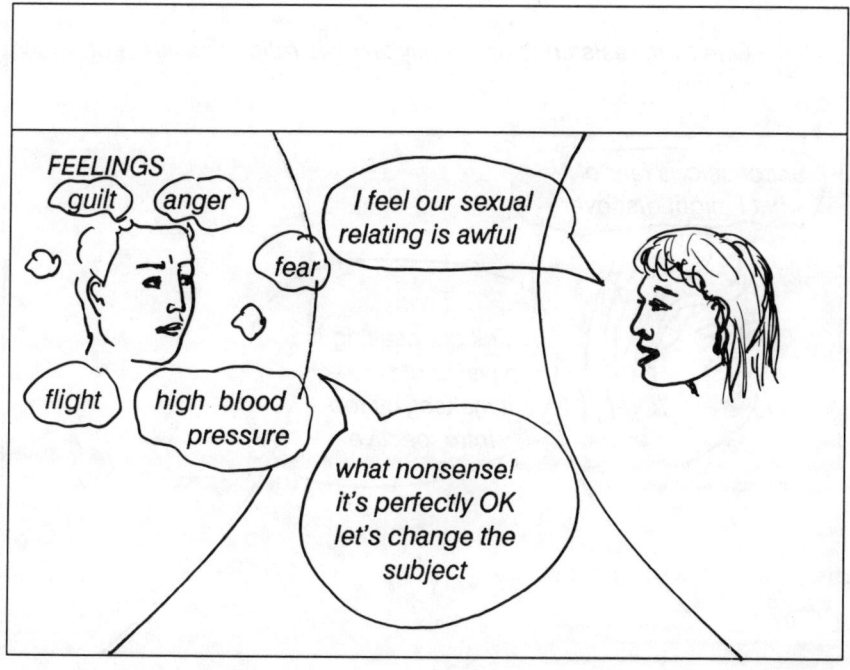

Of course not only sexual relating is subject to resistance. You will probably find that you are resistant to bringing out unconscious material of many kinds. However, it may well be worth looking at sexuality in a counselling session since in our culture it is subject to considerable repression due to social pressures.

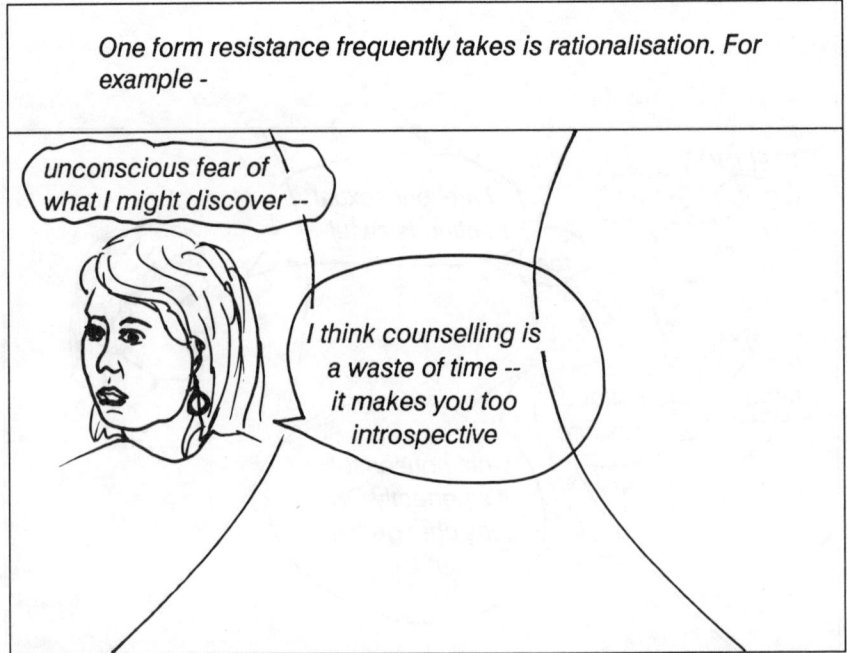

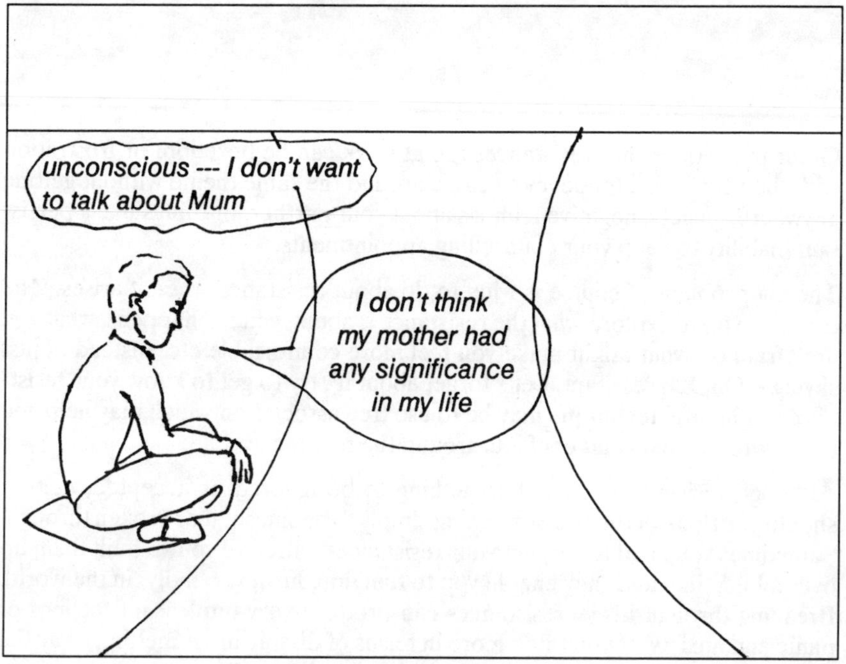

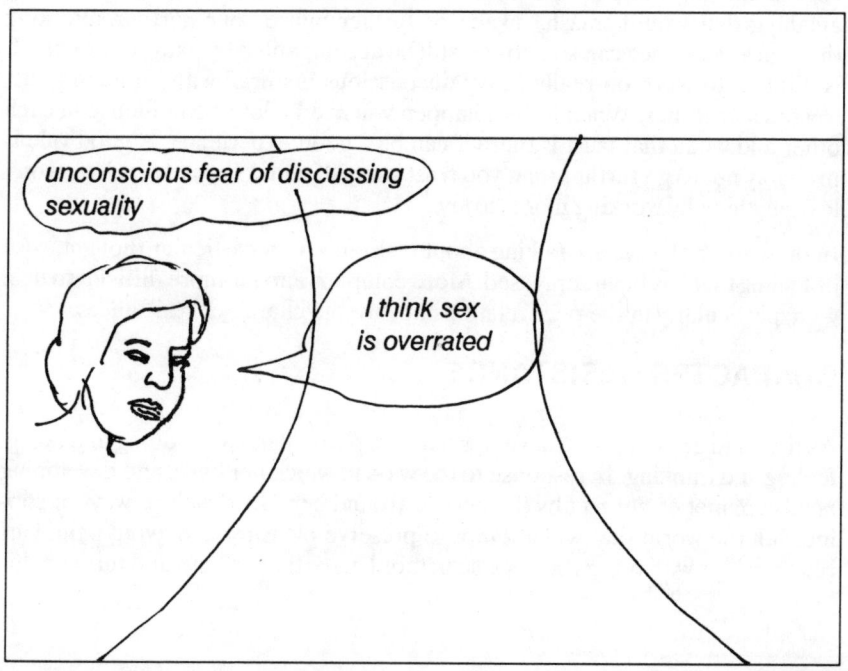

Other indications that resistances are at work can be boredom or frustration with the situation, a tendency to circle around the same theme without getting anywhere, anxiety, negative feelings about your partner, or things like a persistant inability to keep your counselling appointments.

The big problem of course is what to do about resistance when it arises. One thing is to try to explore what the resistance is about, when it happens, what you are afraid of, what might make you feel more comfortable etc. Instead of just saying - 'Oh, I'm resistant. Let's forget about it', try to get to know your resistances. A helpful technique may be to use free association which may help you to explore the fears and conflicts around the resistance.

Although resistances are not something to be ignored or accepted, neither should you think of them as something simply to be smashed or broken through. Sometimes you need to respect your resistances - after all you've built them up over a long time and they enable you to function, however badly, in the world. Breaking through heavy resistances can produce very unpleasant feelings of panic and anxiety. If you think more in terms of dissolving or melting away the resistance you are more likely to be on the right lines. This may sometimes involve being tough and confronting as the Assistant, but shouldn't involve doing anything that would smash, invade or further injure your partner. Working through a resistance can sometimes still be accompanied by panic or anxiety. It is difficult to work on really heavy unconscious material without getting distressed sometimes. When it does happen you need a lot of confidence in each other and when that trust is there it can be a good experience. A good rule is probably not to go further than you trust yourself and your partner. You won't lose anything by working more slowly.

In these examples we are talking about resistance to a particular thought, wish or feeling that has been repressed. More complex, and far more difficult to deal with, particularly in the peer relationship, are the character resistances.

CHARACTER RESISTANCE

As the child grows up, she develops her own particular way of doing and being, feeling and thinking. In response to the ways in which her basic and developing needs are met or not met by the people around her, she develops ways of coping with the world that will attempt to preserve pleasure and avoid pain. Her relationships with others become structured in particular ways and through this the child herself becomes structured. Her total organism - mind, body, feeling, gut, brain, muscular structure, thoughts ideas and action - becomes organised in a particular way which will allow certain experiences to be absorbed while others are defended against. This particular individualised way of being, doing and feeling is what we call character. To the extent that it is rigid, inflexible and compulsive it is a character- armour defending her, though often ineffectually, against the possibilities of pain. It is what I feel as me. It is what Karen Horney calls the actual self, the combination of all the patterns and trends, adopted throughout life.

Character is structured physically in the body

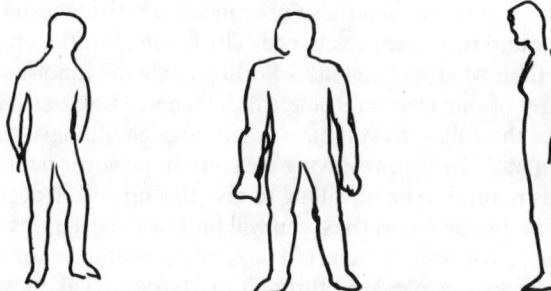

Particular muscles or parts of the body may contain particular memories which can be recalled through working directly with the body. More importantly though the body is the physical, outward expression of the individual's particular history of repression.

Character is structured emotionally and mentally in the psyche.

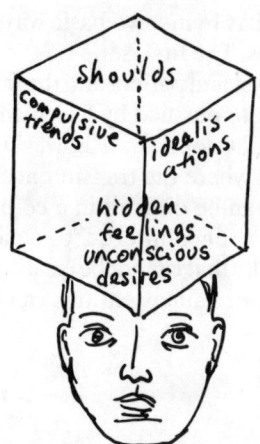

It follows from this that change cannot simply be effected by 'getting out' the repressed material, making the unconscious conscious or discharging the pain, distress or anger. You cannot discharge a psychic structure any more than you can discharge a muscle. What has to occur is an alteration in structure, a shift in the unconscious and the body. You can think of it like the shifts that occur geologically in different periods, throwing up different formations of rock and earth, allowing different vegetations and cultures to flourish. Discharge may be part of the process of change, like a volcanic eruption or the slow melting of a glacier, freeing you in the expression of previously forbidden, unacknowledged or repressed feeling but it cannot be the whole story. Your past is not simply waiting inside you to be let free. It is part of you and what you feel as you.

A consequence of this is that character also operates as a resistance and generally as the most profound resistance to change. The feeling is often one of fear that if 'I' disappear then what will be left? - Perhaps only the inner emptiness that lies behind many of our characterological defences. However miserable you may feel at times the solutions you have taken through life have also been a way of keeping you alive and of preserving pleasure in however neurotic and deformed a way. It is natural to be unwilling to give this up and in accordance with whatever your character - pattern is, you will find rationalisations and justifications for staying as you are. The morbid dependent character for example experiences a strange sort of pleasure through martyrdom. Take away martyrdom argues the unconscious and what is left? In counselling this might emerge in a tendency to *always* want to take the role of the Asssistant, martyring yourself over the misfortunes and miseries of others. More often however the process will be more subtle and less obvious. As you try to counsel at greater depth character resistances will become more important and will emerge particularly in the processes of projection and transference.

Psychoanalysis as it has developed has found two basic ways of working on the problem of the character resistances. The first is the classic solution of emphasising the relationship between analyst and patient and the transference relation that develops. The second is the route pursued by Reich and involves working directly with the body. This latter development is however dependent on the first and cannot be effectively used where the transference relationship is not understood. Working at this level can be difficult in a co-operative peer relationship and it is where we have encountered the most profound and intransigeant problems. One difficulty that cannot be easily overcome is the lack of experience and knowledge. To a certain extent this can be helped by reading, studying and discussing what you are doing with others. There is no substitute for practical learning from experience however and you are bound to make mistakes which although you may learn from them in the long run may also result in your counselling developing to a dead-end or in a counselling relationship breaking up. There is also the contradiction involved in studying that the understanding you gain from books can also be used as an intellectual defence - the more you know, the more you can defend against.

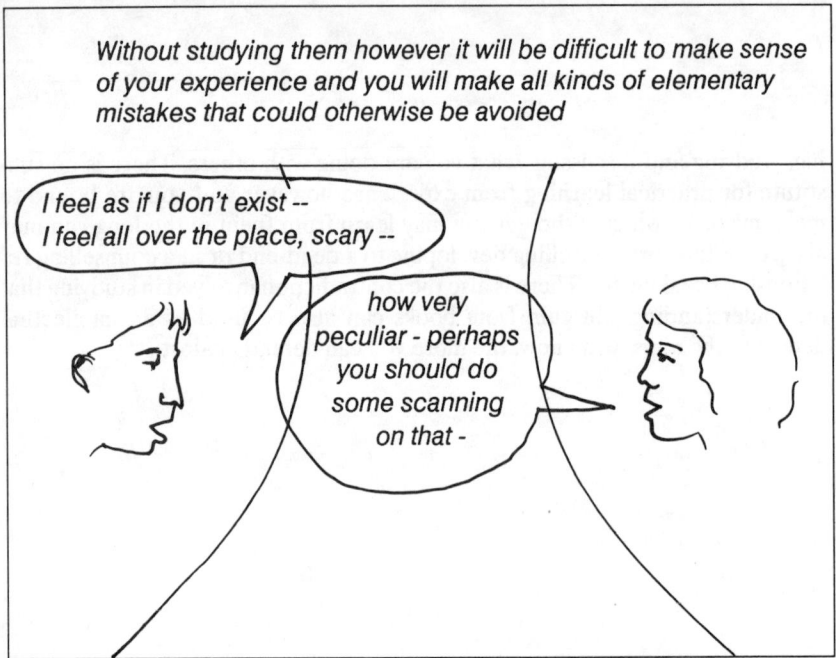

In the following section we discuss the problems of transference and projection, particularly in relation to how they occur in a peer relationship. Working directly with the body other than as a means of relaxation is beyond the scope of this manual and seems anyway, to us, to be even more crucially dependent on the direct learning experience. It is of course possible to use co-counselling in conjunction with other forms of therapeutic help and this may be a direction people might find fruitful.

It's possible to do many things and some would argue that anything that can be done in a one-way therapeutic relationship can also be done in a peer relationship. Peer counselling is in its infancy and experimentation is required.

PROJECTION

In a mild form projection is perhaps not so different from the belief that everyone feels the same as you do - that if this injustice has made me angry, for example, then surely it must make you angry too. As you get to know someone better these sorts of ideas diminish. You progress to the reality of their feelings and yours which you can discover and admit may well be different. When projection is the result of the need to repress certain ideas and feelings this process is much more difficult. For in this case seeing something in someone else is a means of denying its existence in yourself.

Projection basically means putting out onto other people or things, ideas and feelings that come from within you. You can think of it rather literally as yourself as a cinema projector and other people as the screen.

Some examples -
-I hate and despise myself. If these feelings were conscious they would destroy or incapacitate me. As a result I instead feel that it is other people who hate and despise me.

-Unconsciously I feel myself to be the helpless victim of fate. Consciously I need to maintain a picture of myself as vigorous and strong. I project onto the world that it is cruel, vicious and unjust.

-As a result of my need to feel punished over something I have done, I project onto you that you are angry with me.

Projection is a process that goes on to some extent in all human relationships. Where it is a conscious process (a conscious fantasy or a conscious plan for example) you can check out by the ordinary deeds of interaction and giving feedback what the truth is.

A lot of projections will often arise where a situation provokes fear or anxiety in people. This is very common in a large group of people where you will find that you have all sorts of ideas about what people are like whether or not you have interacted with them. Try remembering some situations from the past where you felt anxious or worried and look at what you thought people must be thinking about you. For instance - your first day in a new job, going for an interview, arriving at a party where you didn't know anyone, speaking at a public meeting. Some of your ideas and feelings in these situations may be close to reality. Others may be quite fantastic - phantoms if you like. You will probably find it difficult to distinguish which is which.

Here is an exercise you can try in a counselling session to try to look at the sorts of phantoms you have about others you are close to in your life.

EXAMPLE OF COUNSELLING ON PROJECTIONS

WORKER "It's years ago now... the first boy I slept with... he was an art student... very cool and arrogant... I was so ashamed afterwards... I really wanted to sleep with him... but I felt terrible about it... I thought I was really unattractive... I still don't like my body much... but when I woke up in the morning and we were lying there naked in his bed I looked at myself and I thought how he must hate to have slept with someone as ugly as me. I tried to get up without waking him. I wanted to put my clothes on and go without having to say anything to him but he woke up and said 'Where are you going?' and I said 'I'm going home now because I don't want to cause you any embarrassment' - I felt he'd be really embarrassed and ashamed to have slept with someone as ugly and silly as me. He was still half-asleep really and muttered something about - 'Oh, don't be so silly' and turned over and went back to sleep.

I left. It was really early. I crept down the stairs and outside. It was all misty and quiet. I felt kind of sick. I was sure he hated me. I tried to avoid him after that. I met him one day on the street much later and he tried to ask me what had gone on that night and why I'd rushed off. He was quite nice - concerned almost, but I thought he was just doing it to be nice to me because he felt so sorry for me because I was so ugly. For years I used to think that men only slept with me because they felt sorry for me so I'd hardly ever form a relationship with anyone - I'd just have all these one night stands... and then because of that I got into thinking that men only fancied me because I was an easy lay and no strings attached. (Pause) I think a lot of that was my self-hate. I projected it out onto other people and felt that *they* thought I was ugly and not worth bothering with; *they* thought I was just an easy lay. It took me ages to realise that some men actually *did* like me for reasons other than sex. (Pause)

I remember my mother telling me before I came to London that I would have to be careful with the men - I don't know what the hell she thought was going to happen - I suppose she had all sorts of projections and fantasies too. My father was worse - I think he was convinced that every man that clapped eyes on me would be rushing to rip my clothes off - I suppose that says something about him. The reality was that I was lonely as hell, didn't know a soul, and was incarcerated in a nurses' home where you had to be in before the pubs shut."

Where projection is an unconscious process it often results in feelings of emptiness and futility. You can feel literally emptied and exhausted of all that is somehow you. Your internal world feels insubstantial and shaky and you may feel unsure of who you are. Both 'good' and 'bad' parts of the self can be projected onto the external world, though more often it is the bad parts. The 'against' characters are most likely to direct persecutory and attacking feelings against others rather than against themselves. The arrogant - vindictive character for example may project his own despised, weak and vunerable feelings onto others who he will then attack. A morbid - dependent character on the other hand is more likely to project his own spiteful, aggressive feelings onto others who he then experiences as attacking and victimising him. Take the latter example. My bad, persecutory feelings (self-hate) about myself are intolerable to me, leaving me in a state of perpetual conflict, pulled this way and then the next. As a result I project this badness out onto you. This may bring me temporary respite but I now feel that *you* are attacking and persecuting me. In addition, since I have put all the forceful attacking parts of myself into you, I feel weak, impoverished, victimised and unable to retaliate. Whereas before I felt helpless against the attacks coming from *inside* me, I now feel empty and insubstantial against attacks coming from *outside* me over which I have even less control. These sorts of patterns are usually quite deeply rooted in character structure and may occur so frequently that they seem like 'normal life' to you. In situations of anxiety they are likely to become more acute.

Projections are usually hung on some real characteristic of the other person. This may be a very tangible thing so that for example I project my bad feelings onto someone who tends to criticise me, or it may be less tangible. For example, I tend to associate middle-aged women with criticism so I project onto them that they are angry with me regardless of their actual behaviour towards me. Where there is a 'fit' of the projection with the character of the other person there can be a tendency for him or her to accept it. This is more usual where positive parts of the self are projected. Thus if you project your good parts into me I may feel flattered and pleased and, as it were, take them away from you. Your bad, negative projections I will be more likely to react angrily to, confusing you further.

Projection is often activated as a defence in the face of anxiety and you may find that it occurs frequently in your counselling. Between two people or in a group it can be extremely confusing and disabling process. One example can be that given above where one person becomes the attacker and the other the victim.

Here the relationship may take on the feel of a mutually collusive phantasy. Equally likely is the feeling of utter confusion, of not knowing what is and isn't real and what is and isn't you. The feeling can be one of uncertainty about where you stop and the other person begins. Or you may cling desperately to a particular assertion (for example "It's you that's angry not me" in order to hold onto your own sense of reality.

This is a situation that can arise where the counselling has been going badly or perhaps defences have been broken through before you were ready to give them up. Projection may be being used as a last protection against feelings of disintegration, chaos and unrealness. As Worker the underlying feelings are likely to be of weakness, vunerability and fear, accompanied by mistrust, suspicion and lack of confidence in the Assistant. At the same time you are likely to feel extreme dependence on the Assistant and unable to extricate yourself from the situation. You may experience extreme feelings of rage and anger towards your partner while fearing to express them because of the threat of retaliation. You may also feel that your partner is attacking you and trying to destroy you, or less disastrously, simply not helping you. You are unlikely to have much awareness of where these feelings are coming from or what to do about them.

You are likely to feel locked into the situation with little free attention. As Assistant, you will probably feel confused and that the situation is one of chaos. You may also be experiencing feelings of anger and frustration with the Worker, particularly if she seems to be attributing to you feelings you don't think 'fit'. The situation is of course intensified by the fact that where projection is an unconscious process and while anxiety continues, mutual checking out or reality-testing is unlikely to help very much.

If you have got to this kind of impasse, where further creative work is jeopardised, you will probably need to involve someone else to help you in the situation. Try to hold the situation where it is for the time being and find two other people who are also experienced co-counsellors who you trust. (This is where working in a group is an advantage.) Each of you then does a session as Worker with one of these people. You can use this session to express all your feelings about your original partner. However unjustified, irrational, crazy or angry they may seem, let them come out. If you are the Assistant in this situation it is particularly important not to lay your trip on the Worker. Don't give her your version of reality. Help her to explore her feelings, what they are about and where they come from.

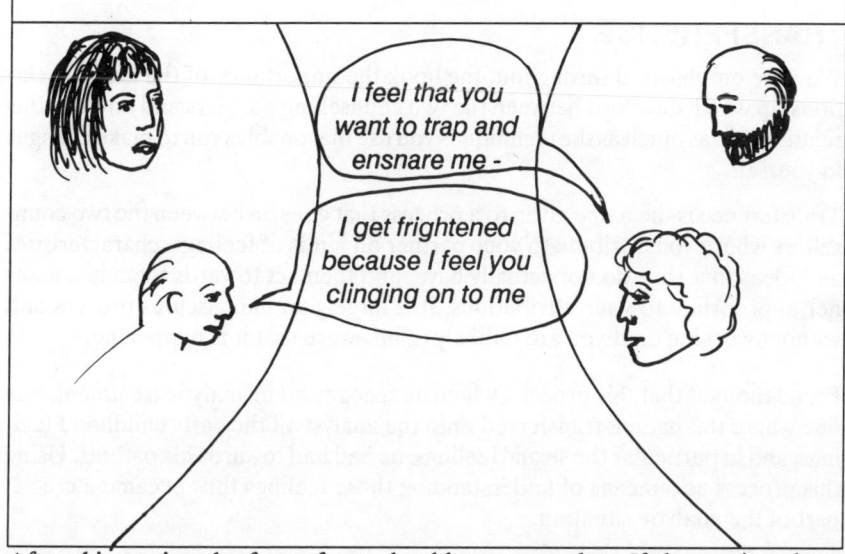

After this session the four of you should meet together. If the sessions have helped to alleviate the situation you may just want to talk and share the feelings you now have. Remember however that every counselling session is confidential and before sharing things you must be clear that you all feel ok about this or about what is to remain private.

These things may help but you may still be left with your original feelings. It isn't always possible to sort everything out, help everyone or work with everyone. Impossible situations do arise sometimes. Don't blame yourselves if you can't work magic.

TRANSFERENCE

We have emphasised throughout the book the importance of the kind of relationship which develops between the two counselling partners and how it is this relationship as much as the techniques you use that enables you to make changes in yourself.

Transference is the name given to a process that goes on between the two counsellors where you attribute to your partner all kinds of feelings, characteristics and ideas that they do not actually have, and then act towards them in a manner appropriate to your attributions. It is largely an unconscious process and without working on it you are unlikely to be aware that it is happening.

Freud thought that this process, which he recognised in analytic treatment, was one where the patient transferred onto the analyst all the early childhood feelings, and in particular the sexual feelings, he had had towards his parents. Using this process as a means of understanding those feelings thus became a crucial part of the analytic situation.

Karen Horney takes a wider view of the process. She argues that you bring into the analytic process the same characteristic ways of behaving that you use elsewhere. The analytic situation is one where these ways of relating to others will be brought into sharp relief. It should theoretically be easier to work on these things as the analyst should be less patterned because of her analytic work and so will be transferring less onto her client. She is also not so intricately involved in the client's life and so can experience his ways of behaving and relating without becoming entangled in them. She argues that the transference experiences will not necessarily be simple repetitions of childhood experience as she thinks that where an early behaviour pattern continues it does so because it is in some way a solution *now* as well as having its origin in history. Like Freud she argues that understanding and working on transference is crucial in the analytic relationship.

In the early stages of a counselling relationship you are likely to experience a lot of very positive feelings about your partner. You may well feel that she is the most marvellous person you have ever met, that the relationship with her is the solution to life's problems, that counselling is a magic and exciting experience. The feeling can be rather that of being in love and indeed you can easily mistake these feelings for a belief that you have found your perfect partner.

After a while however these feelings begin to wear off. You may well start to experience resentment towards your partner because the 'magic' hasn't worked. All sorts of feelings of disappointment, spite and anger may start to emerge towards your partner. You may feel that she's inadequate as a partner and doesn't understand you. You may decide to give up counselling with her and find another partner who offers you more hope of 'magic' solutions. You will quite likely feel jealous and envious of other people's counselling relationships, certain that other people are experiencing goodies that you are missing out on. As you start to experience such feelings you are likely to repress them because they are unacceptable to you and threaten the earlier golden age you experienced. You may also feel that such negative feelings are antithetical to a peer counselling relationship, unworthy of two people who are equals, and rationalise the repression this way.

The first 'golden age' feelings are usually referred to as the initial positive transference; the negative feelings which follow as a negative transference. It is important that both sets of feelings are expressed and worked through in order that a relationship of basic trust can be established and maintained. Depending on your particular character structure the negative and positive feelings are likely to be of varying importance and varying intensity.

One point at which counselling relationships often stagnate is that of the initial positive transference. A collusive process develops which gives the appearance that significant work is being done and indeed much emotion may be generated, early memories may be re-called, dreams may be remembered and interpreted. There will however be certain things that will not be approached. The counselling will in fact be restricted to certain areas that do not threaten the character-structures of the people involved. If you are in the middle of a process like this it is very hard to recognise as you have an unconscious motive in maintaining the collusion. A rough rule-of-thumb guide however is that the honeymoon has to end sometime! If you *never* experience anxiety, *never* feel threatened, *never* feel conflicting feelings about your partner, it is likely that you are into just such a collusive process. Experiencing negative feelings should not mean that all positive feelings disappear. The initial transference is in fact your first bond with your partner and you should not attempt to analyse it away. Expression of all feelings, negative and positive, should gradually establish a positive relationship on a more secure, less magical and illusional basis however. It is generally important to express negative feelings as they arise and as Assistant you should encourage this as far as you feel able to.

EXAMPLE OF COUNSELLING INVOLVING EXPRESSION OF NEGATIVE TRANSFERENCE

The session has been going for about half and hour and the Worker has been talking fitfully, falling into silences, avoiding obvious connections.

ASSISTANT Try saying what you're feeling about me.

WORKER (surprised). About you? I'm not feeling anything about you. I was talking about problems I'm having at work. What makes you think I'm thinking about you?

ASSISTANT You seem irritated.

WORKER Well of course I'm irritated. I was talking about problems I've got at work and you ask me how I feel about you. What's that got to do with anything? I'm the one that's supposed to be the Worker, not you. (Long silence). Anyway, as I was saying before you interrupted it was Phil;s fault because he should have known that I couldn't possibly have got around to seeing four people in one afternoon, but when I came in the next morning and there was this phone call about Mrs Jones and he started going on about how I was basically untrustworthy because I'd said I'd see her and I hadn't and all that... Oh I don't know... what's the point...(Long silence).

ASSISTANT I'm getting the feeling that there's something around that's very difficult for you to say.

WORKER I don't know..

ASSISTANT Try saying what you're feeling now.

WORKER (Pause) I can't... it's as if there's a great weight on my head... (pause).

ASSISTANT Try saying what it is you're afraid of.

WORKER I'm afraid of what you might say. I'm afraid you're going to sit there and judge me with your smart intellectual ideas, that you're going to go off and talk to your friends about this bloody neurotic woman you counsel with that's so useless, or that you'll write me down in some book or some article for a magazine. That's the only reason you're interested in me. I'm just a case to you. You don't really cae about me at all. You think I'm useless. Like when I arrived here this afternoon you were in the middle of writing something and you said, just a minute while I finish this, and I felt like, well that's all she thinks about me, I can sit here like some piece of furniture till she's ready for me... (pause).

ASSISTANT I'm sorry I made you feel like that, because that's not actually the way I feel about you.

WORKER I guess I don't really trust you, you know. Like when you say things like that I'm pleased but at the same time I'm thinking, "Huh. She doesn't really mean that. She's only saying that to be nice.

ASSISTANT Where else do you feel like this?

WORKER Well in one way, I feel it all the time. I feel it with everyone. It's something I've always felt. It's like the thing at work. I mean I feel if Phil thinks I'm untrustworthy then he must be right and so I don't have any right to be angry about what he said, and if you don't think I'm worth counselling with, then that must be right too, so what rights do I have?

ASSISTANT Who says you're not worth counselling with?

WORKER (pause) I do. (pause). Then it all becomes my fault again. I feel as if it's all my fault and you won't take any of the blame. (Pause) When I was a kid my Dad always used to say "Own up, because God can see the silent sinner." I always used to feel I was so full of badness, like I was a really evil person, and I'd own up to things I hadn't done, just because it felt safer. I used to get very confused about whether I'd done them or not. Sometimes I'd own to things I knew I hadn't done, and then I'd be punished and I'd feel angry because it was unjust and that would make me feel even more bad inside and I'd look around for something to be punished for, and so it would go on...

ASSISTANT You're afraid I might judge and punish you like your dad?

WORKER Yes. And the awful thing is I feel you'd be right. I sort of wish you would in a way. It would be easier somehow...

ASSISTANT Easier than trusting me...

WORKER Yes. *etc, etc.*

You will notice that in this example the Assistant is technically breaking the 'golden rules' about interventions in order to get at what is important. Hopefully by this point you too will be able to work according to their spirit rather than to the letter of the law.

Being told that you're a useless Assistant or that you're untrustworthy can of course be a very hurtful experience. Feelings are no less powerful because they are based on transference and this aspect of counselling can be very hard to take. If, as the Assistant, you encourage the Worker to express her negative feelings about you and the counselling process you must be prepared for what comes. It may be that one aspect of your character structure is a tendency to collapse under criticism and accept it all at its face value. If this is the case you clearly need to do some work on this aspect of yourself, before encouraging anyone to express hostility towards you. It can also be important to show the Worker when you've been hurt by what he's said, without (as well may occur) using this to induce guilt in him as a means of revenge. It will also happen of course that you do make mistakes, make crude or insensitive comments or interventions or misunderstand what is happening. Not all feelings are transference and you may really be making a mess of things. Where this is the case try to be straight about it and admit your failures honestly. You're not perfect and there's no reason why you should be expected to be.

It will probably be apparent from the little we've said so far, how difficult but how essential a process transference is. It is in one sense the medium with which you are working all the time, as it is in your relationship with the other person that you express your characteristic conflicts, problems and ways of dealing with life. If you ignore transference you are likely to get caught in its knots and end up in a collusive process that benefits neither of you. On the other hand if you concentrate your sole attention on its problems you are equally likely to end up in a mess as you find yourself utterly confused as to the meaning or roots of any of the feelings you have.

In the classic psychoanalytic relationship the feelings the patient transfers onto the analyst are referred to as transference, those the analyst transfers onto the patient (generally considered to be less) as counter-transference. Awareness of the counter-transference by the analyst is generally considered to be important, both for checking its influence on the relationship and for the intuitive clues it can give about what is going on. In a peer relationship where you are reciprocating directly you obviously have both transference and counter- transference with a vengeance with the disadvantage that probably neither of you have previous experience of what to expect. It is this accompanied by the increased vulnerability of both parties as defences are lowered, that tends to give rise to a lot of the problems of mutual collusion or counselling relationships getting stuck or breaking down.

One partial solution to this problem can be to alter your counselling relationships so that you work in three rather than in pairs. You still *meet* in pairs for the actual sessions but they are now one-way only. By doing this you knock out one of the complications of transference while maintaining a reciprocal relationship in one aspect. You can all three of you meet to discuss how this works.

But doing this you do of course remove one of the reciprocal, egalitarian planks from the relationship as it becomes in one respect one-way, more like the classical analytic relationship. This has both advantages and disadvantages. In a two-way relationship a lot of transference feelings tend to arise that are connected with early feelings about brothers and sisters and peers. Very often people experience quite acute feelings of competitiveness about their partners or in relation to other pairs. These often become repressed because they are felt to be against the spirit of co-operative counselling which is meant to be non-competitive. The contradiction of course is that this is the best place to try and explore such feelings if they come up! Another common feeling, often experienced by people who as children either took or were pushed prematurely into independence and responsibility is to feel resentment towards the partner as again here is a situation where reciprocation and responsibility is required.

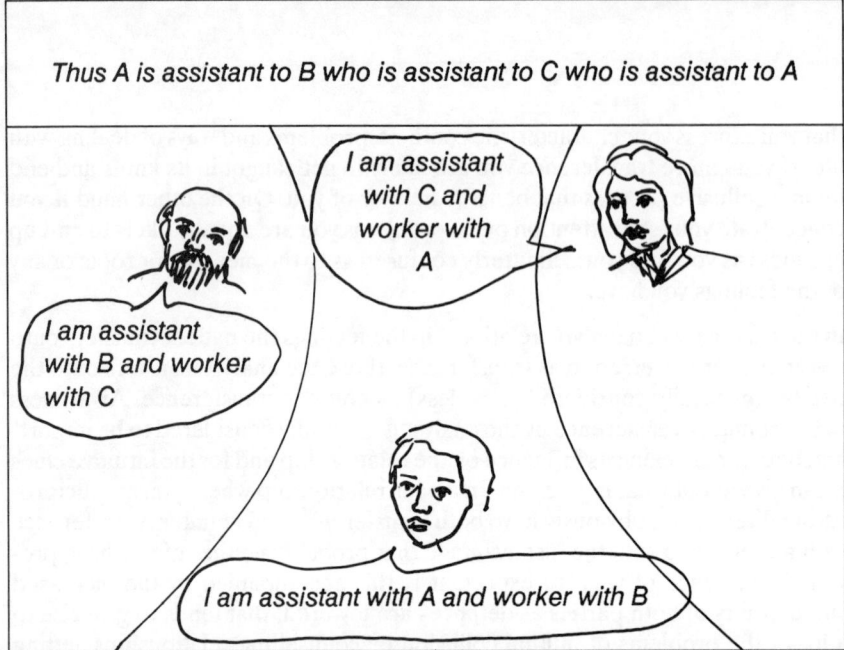

The arguments made against one-way counselling are often that it induces dependence, perpetuates unhealthy, hierarchical power relationships and mirrors the oppressive power structures of society. In our view the situation is far more contradictory than this. We have found that it is very difficult to work on certain areas, particularly those of infantile dependence and weakness for example, in a directly reciprocal relationship. Since these areas are primary in the development of character-structure it seems to us important to create a situation where such things can be worked on in a non-oppressive way. It is important to remember that being dependent is not the same as being oppressed and being independent is not the same as being free. We hope that you will be able to experiment and come up with some creative solutions

CONCLUSIONS

We would not like to underestimate the difficulties of taking co-operative peer relationships to these kinds of levels. You may not want to and may prefer to keep you co-counselling as a method of mutual support that does not aim at quite such radical change. Or you may decide that some other therapeutic method will be more helpful in your particular circumstances. Not everyone can gain something from co-counselling and it can be important to recognise this and direct them to the help they need. We feel that it is more a reflection on the families and society we grew up in that people are not always able to give and receive help from their comrades than a reflection on those individuals.

Whatever the direction you take we hope that you've found this book useful. We'd like any feedback, new ideas or solutions to the problems, so please write to us at the address at the front of the book.

APPENDIX ONE

COPING WITH A CRISIS

We had intended to write our own notes on this but we decided that this reprint from *The Radical Therapist* covered all the points we wanted to make, is in keeping with our roles of Worker and Assistant, and expresses things far more eloquently than we could.

People's Psychiatry Sheet 1

Handling Psychiatric Emergencies   Michael Glenn

You and your friends can handle many psychiatric emergencies. The crucial elements are trying (instead of drawing back), and trusting your own intuition. This sheet is meant as a simple guide, saying no more than common sense but legitimizing people's efforts to help their sisters and brothers in trouble. Experience is, of course, the best teacher of all.

1 The first thing to do is LISTEN. Don't be in a hurry to give advice. LISTEN first; try to understand what's happening, what the person is feeling. Get into the person's frame of reference.

Look for a handle to their situation. Try to figure out what's oppressing them, what's making them feel the way they feel. Once you've done that, you can start looking for options, for a way out of the dilemma.

2 You need to be CALM. If you can't be calm, find soneone else who can be. As you listen, try to be accepting; don't start laying your trip on them. If they feel something they have reason for feeling it; respect their integrity. If you're calm and listening, you can start responding to them, which will help clarify the situation.

3 Understand how people's SELF ESTEEM can be shot to pieces by crassness; inappropriate humour, or a casual air. Most people in emotional distress are feeling empty and helpless. Try not to make them feel worse about themselves. Look for the genuine assets in them, and in their situation. Try to restore their self confidence.

4 Follow your hunches and your feelings; they're almost always right. Get in touch with what you feel, then think about it. If you feel sad, chances are the other person feels sad. If you feel scared, chances are the other person is scared too. If you feel angry, chances are the other person is angry too, or manipulating you. If you feel confused, chances are the other person feels confused too. Go ahead and say things like 'I'm really confused by what you say,' or 'You must feel really horrible about all that.' Use feelings not ideas as your main guide.

5 Don't be ashamed by being ignorant or feeling helpless. The other person probably feels the same way. Therapy is a human act, not some mysterious mumbo-jumbo; ask questions if you're ignorant; admit it if you feel helpless. Don't pretend to know what you don't. (That's mystifying the other person).

6 Let the other person tell you in their own way what's wrong. Don't make them follow your rules. Don't get them to 'act out their feelings' or do things you learned in some groovy encounter group. This isn't fun and games: if you're trying to help a sister or brother through a trying time, you'd better accept the responsibility that goes with that.

7 People become disturbed in different ways. Some are horribly depressed; some in a state of panic; some violent; some confused and irrational; some incomprehensible. Almost everyone in an emotional crisis is terrified of LOSING CONTROL. They want to feel some kind of support, some kind of protection. Try to give them that. Try to talk in as quiet a place as possible. If you can see them again, let them know that, and do it. If you can help them deal with their problem without losing control (and humiliating themselves), you are doing good work. (At some future time they may want to relax their control: but they'll do it some place that is protective.)

8 In the same line of thought, if you feel they are out of control, or they are too much for you to deal with, don't pretend you can do what you can't. Decide on bringing someone with more experience to see them, or think about a hospital.

Many people are terrified of mental hospitals. You and your friends should know which hospitals in your area are good and which are atrocious; which shrinks are sympathetic and which are absolute pigs.

If a friend is too disturbed to handle, get them to someone who can help them calm down or to a hospital. It's foolish to take chances with other people's lives, especially if they are dangerous to themselves or others.

Don't get hung up on the rhetoric of we-should-all-be-able-to- take-care-of-one-another. Sometimes we simply can't. Then it's good to know what your options are.

9 Tell people what you're doing. Don't mystify them. Don't make phone calls behind their backs, or agree with them when you're planning something else. No matter how flipped out someone is, there's always a part of them that's aware of reality: speak to that part, and they'll respond.

10 If you start feeling bored, try to focus in on the problem. That's where you should be anyway. What's going on? How can you help? How can they help themselves? Do they need a hospital? A shrink? medication? (Although medicines are grossly abused, sometimes they're useful: especially if they can keep a sister or brother out of the hospital). What is the real problem and what are their options?

11 A word about DEPRESSIONS... Life in this oppresseve society is filled with insults, painful experiences and real losses. Not only is our SELF ESTEEM smashed time and time again. We also have to endure separations from people close to us - friends who leave, who die, who are killed, who go to jail etc. There's a natural healing-over after such a loss, but it takes time. Don't expect people not to feel these human feelings. Help them integrate their experience and feelings into themselves.

Often DEpression is a cover for OPpression. If there's no 'real' loss going on, look for the oppression that's making the other person feel like shit. Help them understand that it's not 'in their heads' but in the real world that such oppression exists.

Help them get in touch with others who share their oppression. Agree with them that they're not bad or crazy. Help them get angry if they deserve to get angry.

12 A word about PARANOIA...Paranoia, as radical therapist Claude Steiner has said, is a state of 'heightened awareness'. Paranoid feelings are almost always justified, at least in part. Don't argue with them, try to see where they're true and what this means for the person.

This society makes all of us suspicious, mistrustful, manipulated; 'paranoid'. Help the paranoid person recognise the truth of their paranoia, and then help them to stop being immobilised or destroyed by their awareness.

13 A word about VIOLENT people... Violent people are often very frightened, and can be calmed down if you protect them and treat them as people, not monsters. Sometimes, though, people are just out of touch. Don't try to be a hero and endanger yourself and others. Do what you can without being foolhardy. Talk straight to someone who's violent; be reasonable, not threatening.

14 We all need to share experience in handling common psychiatric problems. You and your friends can build a list of half-way houses, decent hospitals, and other therapy resources. If you deal with these problems yourself, you can encourage others to do the same.

15 It's important to remember that the roles of therapist and patient are interchangeable. You may be helping someone today and being helped tomorrow. That's the way it should be. Our common task is developing our skills, so we can help and strengthen one another and the movement for social change.

APPENDIX TWO

USEFUL ADDRESSES

If you need help that your partner or group can't give, these organisations may be some help.

Arbours Association. 6 Church Lane, London, N8. (01) 340 7646.
Crisis centre and low- cost therapy.

Philadelphia Association. 14 Peto Place, London NW1. (0) 486 9012.

Richmond Fellowship. 8 Addison Road, London, W14.
Run short and long-stay hostels for people who've been in mental hospitals.

Women's Therapy Centre. 6 Manor Gardens, London N7 6LA. (01) 263 6200.

The Association for Humanistic Psychology, c/o Tony Merry, 26 Huddlestone road, Forest Gate, London E7 *have an address list of organisations who run therapy groups and classes of various kinds.*

The British Association for Counselling 37a Sheep Street, Rugby, Warwickshire CV21 3BX. (0788) 78328/9 *publish a directory of their members.*

BIBLIOGRAPHY

This bibliography contains books we have either used in writing *The Barefoot Psychoanalyst* or found useful at one time or another in co-counselling. Those marked ** are ones it would be good to start with if you are new to the area. Those marked * are more difficult and theoretical but important to read.

** A & Z. *Lenin for Beginners.* Writers and Readers, 1978.

W.R. Bion. *Experiences In Groups.* Tavistock, 1961

** David Boadella. *Wilhelm Reich, the evolution of his work.* Dell, 1975.

Maurice Brinton. *The Irrational in Politics.* Solidarity, 1974.

Phyllis Chesler. *Women and Madness.*

David Cooper. *The Death of the Family.* Penguin. 1971.

** George Downing. *The Massage Book.* Penguin, 1974.

Frederick Engels. *Origin of the Family,* Private Property and the State. Pathfinder, 1972.

Dialectic of Nature. Progress Publishers, 1974.

Aaron Esterson. *The Leaves of Spring,* Penguin.

W.R.. Fairbairn. *Psychoanalytic Studies of the Personality,* Tavistock, 1952.

Otto Fenichel. *The Psychoanalytic Theory of Neurosis.* Routledge and Kegan Paul, 1955.

Sandor Ferenczi. *Further Contributions to the theory and technique of psychoanalysis.* Hogarth, 1969.

Paulo Freire. *Education: the practice of freedom.* Writers and Readers.

Sigmund Freud. *The Interpretation of Dreams.* Avon, 1965.

** *Introductory Lectures.* Penguin.

New Introductory Letters. Penguin.

Gestalt Therapy Now. ed. Joen Fagan. Penguin, 1972.

Joanne Greenberg. *I never promised you a rose garden.* Signet Books.

George Groddeck. *The Book of the It.* Vintage, 1949.

Harry Guntrip. *Schizoid Phenomena, Object Relations and the Self.* Hogarth, 1977.

Personality Structure and Human Interaction. Hogath, 1961.

** Karen Horney. *Our Inner Conflicts.* W.W. Norton, 1942.

* *Neurosis and Human Growth.* W.W. Norton, 1950.

** *Self-Analysis.* W.W. Norton, 1942.

The Neurotic Personality of our Time. W.W. Norton, 1937.

New Ways of Psychoanalysis. W.W. Norton, 1939.

Feminine Psychology. W.W. Norton, 1932.

Harvey Jackins. *The Human Side of Human Beings.* Rational Island Press.

Arthur Janov. *The Primal Scream.* Abacus, 1973.

Melanie Klein. *Love Guilt and Reparation.* Delta, 1977.

R.D. Laing. *Sanity, madness and the family.* Tavistock, 1965.

The Divided Self. Penguin, 1965.

Self and Others. Penguin, 1969.

V.I. Lenin. *Volume 38, Collected Works.* Progress Publishers.

State and Revolution. Progress Publishers.

Alexander Lowen. *Language of the Body.* Collier, 1971.

Margaret Mahler. *The Psychological Birth of the Human Infant.* Hutchinson, 1975.

Juliet Mitchell. *Psychoanalysis and Feminism.* Pelican, 1974.

Jean Piaget. *Origins of Intelligence in the Child.* Penguin, 1977.

Play, Dreams and Imitation in Childhood. Routledge and Kegan Paul, 1962.

R.T. Collective. *The Radical Therapist.* Penguin, 1974.

Evelyn Reed. *Woman's Evolution.* Pathfinder, 1975.

* Wlihelm Reich. *Character-Analysis.* Farrar Strauss Giroux, 1961.

The Mass Psychology of Fascism. Souvenir, 1972.

The Function of the Orgasm. Farrar Strauss Giroux.

People in Trouble. Farrar Strauss Giroux.

Selected Sex-Pol Essays. Socialist Reproduction, 1972.

What is Class-Consciousness. Socialist Reproduction, 1972.

** *The Sexual Struggle of Youth.*, Socialist Reproduction, 1972.

Theodor Reik. *Listening with the Third Ear.* Farrar Strauss Giroux.

Ruis. *Marx for Beginners.* Writers and Readers, 1977.

John Rowan. *Ordinary Ecstasy.* RKP, 1976.

** Anne Kent Rush. *Getting Clear.* Random House. 1973.

Marguerite Sechehaye. *Autobiography of a schizophrenic girl.* Signet, 1970.

Hanna Segal. *Introduction to the work of Melanie Klein.* Hogarth, 1975.

John Southgate. *Dialectic Peer Counselling,* 1974.

John Southgate and Rosemary Randall. *Work Democracy and Character* Energy and Character, May 1978.

* D.W. Winnicott. *Playing and Reality.* Penguin, 1974.